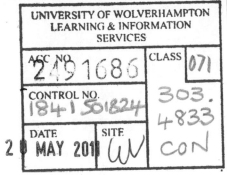
Convergence and Fragmentation
Media Technology and the Information Society

Edited by Peter Ludes

intellect Bristol, UK / Chicago, USA

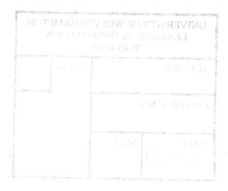

First Published in the UK in 2008 by
Intellect Books, PO Box 862, Bristol BS99 1DE, UK

First published in the USA in 2008 by
Intellect Books, The University of Chicago Press, 1427 E. 60th Street, Chicago,
IL 60637, USA

A catalogue record for this book is available from the British Library.

Cover Design: Gabriel Solomons
Copy Editor: Holly Spradling
Typesetting: Mac Style, Nafferton, E. Yorkshire

ISBN 978-1-84150-182-6

Printed and bound by Gutenberg Press, Malta.

CONTENTS

FOREWORD

This volume is the product of a major programme under the title Changing Media – Changing Europe supported by the European Science Foundation (ESF). The ESF is the European association of national organizations responsible for the support of scientific research. Established in 1974, the Foundation currently has seventy-six Member Organizations (research councils, academies and other national scientific institutions) from twenty-nine countries. This programme is the first to be sponsored by both the Social Sciences and the Humanities Standing Committees of the ESF, and this unique cross-disciplinary organization reflects the very broad and central concerns which have shaped the Programme's work. As co-chairpersons of the Programme it was our great delight to bring together many of the very best scholars from across the continent, but also across the disciplinary divides which so often fragment our work, to enable stimulating, innovative, and profoundly important debates addressed to understanding some of the most fundamental and critical aspects of contemporary social and cultural life.

The study of the media in Europe forces us to try to understand the major institutions which foster understanding and participation in modern societies. At the same time we have to recognize that these societies themselves are undergoing vital changes, as political associations and alliances, demographic structures, the worlds of work, leisure, domestic life, mobility, education, politics and communications themselves are all undergoing important transformations. Part of that understanding, of course, requires us not to be too readily seduced by the magnitude and brilliance of technological changes into assuming that social changes must comprehensively follow. A study of the changing media in Europe, therefore, is indeed a study of changing Europe. Research on media is closely linked to questions of economic and technological growth and expansion, but also to questions of public policy and the state, and more broadly to social, economic and cultural issues.

To investigate these very large debates the Programme was organised around four key questions. The first deals with the tension between citizenship and consumerism, that is the relation between media, the public sphere and the market; the challenges facing the media, cultural policy and the public service media in Europe. The second area of work focuses on the dichotomy and relation between culture and commerce, and the conflict in media policy caught between cultural aspirations and commercial imperatives. The third question deals with the problems of convergence and fragmentation in relation to the development of media technology on a global and European level. This leads to questions about the concepts of the information society, the network society etc., and to a focus on new media such as the internet and multimedia, and the impact of these new media on society, culture, and our work, education and everyday life. The fourth field of inquiry is concerned with media and cultural identities and the relationship between processes of homogenization and diversity. This explores the role of media in everyday life, questions of gender, ethnicity, lifestyle, social differences, and cultural identities in relation to both media audiences and media content.

In each of the books arising from this exciting Programme we expect readers to learn something new, but above all to be provoked into fresh thinking, understanding and inquiry, about how the media and Europe are both changing in novel, profound, and far reaching ways that bring us to the heart of research and discussion about society and culture in the twenty-first century.

Ib Bondebjerg
Peter Golding

Introduction: Unity in Diversity

Peter Ludes

In this book, media specialists from the humanities and social sciences have integrated empirical evidence on technological, economic, social, political and cultural trends with models of explaining changing media as a prime interpreter of changing Europe. The contradictory tendencies of convergence and fragmentation are tied to the question of whether we are really moving into a new European Information Society. The EU defined 'convergence' in general as the ability of different platforms to carry similar kinds of services, or the coming together of consumer devices such as telephone, television and personal computer. This technological convergence can be supported by converging markets and user habits – yet also be questioned and suspended in terms of a fragmentation of economic chances and media preferences (cf. Schorr 2003).

Denationalization, media entertainment and e-pleasure

Seen from outside, Europe appears as relatively homogeneous. Yet, the major mass media still refer mainly to national events, actors and developments, even when in trans-national media formats. Illegal immigration from the neighbouring African and Asian countries, terrorism within Europe and from other parts of the world, unemployment, global competition and shifting military, economic and cultural identification alliances are often the topics of nationally framed information, education and entertainment in the media; in these terms, they also constitute issues of expert and decision-maker circles. Denationalization grows, partially veiled by media entertainment and e-pleasure. Beyond (or behind) the pleasure principle, economic, military, political powers prepare decisions, re-confirm alliances, re-shape the agenda and frameworks for dealing with the major issues.

Convergence under pressure leads to fragmentation. Therefore, the role of the newest information and communication technologies (ICT) and formats in a changing Europe must be analysed not only in terms of optimistic market projections but also in terms of realistic trends toward complementary fragmentations.

From 2000 to 2004 eighteen senior and three junior scholars from twelve countries in Europe formed Team 3 of the ESF's programme *Changing Media – Changing Europe: 'Convergence and Fragmentation: Media Technology and the Information Society'*. Some of the foci of our discussions are summarized below.

Shifting balances and conflicts

The exclusion of majorities of the populations of most European countries from technologically advanced and expensive consumer devices means that we should take into account the shifting balances and conflicts of inclusion and exclusion. Continuity and discontinuity in the development of media technology and the Information Society requires us to leave behind a number of traditional notions, methods and data used for national developments and international comparisons.

The contradictory tendencies of convergence (implying a similarity and increasing unity of experience) and fragmentation (implying a growing differentiation of experience) are tied to general aspects of this development and to the question of whether we are really moving into a new European Information Society.

Maria Heller (Hungary) and Ursula Maier-Rabler (Austria) discuss whether global development and the modifications it enhances follow more a pattern of convergence or fragmentation. Actually, both patterns can be observed in different domains including communications. The overall trend of globalization affects the sphere of communications: ICT use, regulations and the functioning of the public sphere seem to converge among different societies.

However, the appearance of new information and communication technologies also reinforces trends of fragmentation and divergence. Different societies or different layers of a society may diverge in their use of the ever-changing ICT devices. Different information cultures co-evolve with different institutional structures, regulations and patterns of use of ICTs. Institutional structures and policies are in close connection with patterns of usage and both are affected by a society's information culture, communicational traditions, strategies and cultural heritage.

This interconnection also governs communicational behaviour and strategies inside individual societies, making up for social differences in communicational patterns. Heller and Maier-Rabler focus on how new ICTs are implemented in different European societies according to their information cultures and focus on institutional structures and policies as well as social practices. Different EU and Accession Countries will be compared (see also Tsaliki 2003).

World of games and museums

Rune Klevjer (Norway) and Ed Tan and his co-authors (Netherlands) inquire into the role of computer technology in two distinct forms of pleasurable experience: the computer game and the museum. As cultural genres, they represent different ways of designing technologically mediated experience, both with unique opportunities and challenges. Museums and games are both arenas around which the two social spheres of work and leisure converge. Museums make learning more personal, intimate and even fun, if not fun for its own sake. In contrast, the attractiveness of popular entertainment, also of computer games, implies lack of sanctioned meaning. Converging, however, are expectations that fun and/or knowledge should be just one click away.

This is part of a more general trend in modernity. In the daily lives of increasing numbers of citizens in the developed parts of the world, leisure activities are becoming more similar to typical work-related procedures in significant respects. This development is fuelled by the use of computer-based and networked technology. In games, hard work, patient learning and tedious management are part of the fun. In museums, problem solving and information processing are becoming part of cultural enrichment.

A common aim is to capture some of the range and diversity of technologically mediated pleasure, implying a critical focus on policy-making as a way of managing this diversity. Particularly relevant issues are the common concerns for 'healthy' versus dangerous technological play, and the dreams of perfectly personalized technological environments.

Because technological pleasures are intrinsically part of global commercial culture, the European context is problematic. Obviously, where culture and technology interact, there are always cultural boundaries. However, it is still an open question whether significant boundaries can be identified on the level of 'Europeanness'.

E-learning allows mobility and flexibility

Bernard Miège (France), Lars Qvortrup (Denmark), Knut Lundby (Norway) and Päivi Hovi-Wasastjerna (Finland) interpret ICT in learning and education as a key aspect of the convergence-fragmentation problem of today's Europe. 'E-learning' is given much attention in European convergence policies. ICT is part of the institutional changes in universities in Europe. The use of ICT as a tool or medium implies new forms of education and knowledge. In Europe, universities are being transformed with reference to the Bologna Declaration, aiming at mobility and flexibility. Virtual learning is highly interdependent with a transformation of academic learning towards instrumental rationality, a delimitation of scientific frameworks, new academic surveillance and comodification procedures as well as a shift towards quantifiable academic achievements in contrast to a better understanding of its qualitative dimensions (Baert & Shipman 2005, p.157–177).

The 'virtual university' and 'flexible learning' are explored as alternative strategies and communication practices of learning in universities. For this purpose, two universities in countries with different strategies of Europeanness, Finland and Norway, are compared.

Who can access the 'marketplace of ideas'?

Werner Meier (Switzerland), Tanja Storsul (Norway) and Marcel Machill (Germany) focus on the power structures of the media and telecommunications industries as problems with political, economic and social implications. They give special attention to these structures and networks of power in Europe through discussing three major issues. These relate to questions about convergence and diversification in terms of media conglomeration, political convergence and developments within broadcasting.

The globalization of the media industries is first observed through the lens of media ownership, detecting how the industrial structure of the media affects who may access the 'marketplace of ideas'. Concentration of ownership continues to matter and requires scrutiny. 'Media Governance' is then seen as a model of co- and self-regulation on a national as well as on a European Union level.

Further topics include the policies and prospects for universal provision of telecom services in liberalized markets. This is a key challenge to make the Information Society an inclusive society. However, strong networks of industrial interests contest interference in the market for distributive purposes. It is specified how this is handled in three small European countries.

Finally, in Machill's contribution, the role of public service in broadcasting policy is scrutinized. Many critiques doubt in general the 'raison d'être' of publicly financed television in the era of multiple channels and digitalization. In this regard, France is an interesting case study because French media policy has taken some unexpected measures that can add fruitful discussions for media policy decision processes in other European countries. In order to detect new borders and boundaries (cp. Chan and McIntyre 2002, esp. chaps. 4 and 7) as well as networks in Europe and the modes of their changes and shifts, each of the contributions to this book focuses on a few selected media trends in a few countries in Europe. Despite the analytical concerns, some visions for 'changing media – changing Europe' emerge as well.

EuroVisions in a global context

Gerd Kopper (Germany), who regularly participated in our meetings but could not contribute to this book, has questioned the established focus on national statistics. Generation-specific media usage patterns or the divide between metropolitan areas and rural ones may well constitute a new geography not only of the Internet but also of satellite television or pay TV, of media habits and cultural traits in general. In this book, Ursula Maier-Rabler and Maria Heller show how information cultures shape the introduction and usage as well as the cultural meaning of new information and communication technologies. More specifically, Rune Klevjer and Ed Tan and his co-authors review techno-pleasure in usually sharply distinguished areas, namely computer games and museum experiences. In relation to changing media, 'Europe has a unique tradition of defining expressive culture as a public concern'. For museums, a central question is whether they can 'combine learning with entertainment', especially 'the kind of superior entertainment that is inherent to savouring novelties and break-throughs in art'.

Knut Lundby and Päivi Hovi-Wasastjerna resume fundamental characteristics of virtual and flexible learning strategies and communication practices: they are 'related to the converging media technologies and the converging institutional practices employed'. Yet, 'today's universities have no chance to respond to the costs of the worldwide education business'.

Tanja Storsul concludes her contribution on telecom liberalization with her diagnosis that 'the EU should not delimit, but encourage multiple responses to the challenges of ensuring inclusive network development'. And Marcel Machill makes clear how various European countries might learn something from public service television's mission in France: The dangers of disinformation and commercialization are met by calling for context-related examination of the relevance of information.

The individual contributions taken together provide us with a timely orientation, which can be visualized in the following way:

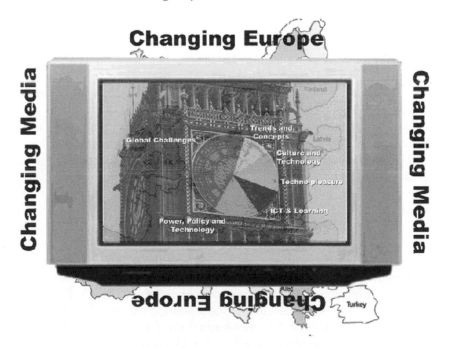

This figure illustrates that media presentations and extra-media developments are highly interconnected. It also shows that global challenges will make up a considerable part of any time schedule on changing media and changing Europe.

Our intellectual challenge has been to look at different types and modes of change across Europe. How media have changed work, education, the civil service, leisure etc. is still to be explored in more detail. There is certainly some technological convergence and some shifting of boundaries between work and home, so 'boundary shifting' should be a more useful term. Institutional changes included changes in technological communication, but the issue still is how far this has changed societal relations.

Instead of an expanding information and/or knowledge society, the emergence of a network society appears as a more plausible concept: Rather than only throwing away old concepts we are looking at them as trends, as part of everyday life. The technological spread in Eastern Europe, for example, has been co-determined by a genuine desire to catch up with the EU 15- 'Europe'. In Hungary some were against the idea of convergence if it threatened nationalism while others were for anything that built a strong Europe that could oppose US dominance. Many western European companies have already moved into eastern European markets. In the east there is the paradox that governments want this because of the resulting financial investment and it also fits in with the public's aspirations for pluralism of the new media market, while PSB is rejected as the tool of the government and is thus in rapid decline.

Beyond the immediate frame of this book's individual chapters, more general conclusions can be offered.

An ignorant Knowledge Society

In the long and often misleading tradition of labelling societies in terms of a dominant or key principle, there have been, for example, the following examples: industrial and post-industrial, capitalist and socialist societies, dictatorships or (parliamentary) democracies etc. Only since the 1970s has there emerged a strand to understand societies mainly in terms of major means of orientation and communication, namely information and knowledge. This implies that organized statements of facts or ideas, reasoned judgments or experimental results dominate communication in the economy, society and culture (cf. Bell 1999). The technologies of knowledge generation, information processing and symbol communication have become major sources of economic productivity. They do not only re-/present matters of fact and/or fiction in selective ways, but also provide potential for coordinating goals, horizons, reference systems, evaluations and concrete interactions. However, the criteria for, and the forms and meanings of, knowledge vary tremendously: from the sciences, the humanities and the arts to economics, politics, the military, religion or mass communication. They also differ significantly between the various world cultural zones. Therefore, we must try to understand scientific and everyday knowledge (common sense), mass and target media information in their respective communication contexts. Only particular types of knowledge are re-/presented in the major media formats.

The concepts of information and knowledge, of the information and knowledge society should always be used as referring to distinctly structured social processes and configurations: Specific types of information and knowledge are bound to become historically obsolete, they are usually means for struggle and competition and are highly interconnected with disinformation and secrecies, ignorance, arrogance or belief systems. Therefore, the concept of a Disinformation and Ignorance Society is as important as that of an Information and Knowledge Society.

The fragility of modern societies is probably not due mainly to their 'highly self-reflexive and self-transformative' character (Stehr 2001: 236, cf. Stehr 2004), but to fundamental conflicts concerning old scarcities of the means for survival or established living conditions and expectations – more than due to often fundamentally different understandings of what can be considered as information or knowledge. The shifting balances of ignorance and knowledge and their contradictory definitions and interpretations leave little space for common knowledge and true common sense: In global terms, the latter is a very scarce resource.

More global than many types and interpretations of knowledge are the formats in which mass media present information, entertainment, commercials or the various mixtures of these major genres. In contrast to, for example, culture-specific prayers or religious feasts, widely distributed mass media re-produce similarly standardized formats, from book chapters or newspaper articles to radio or television broadcasts and the design of websites – almost on a gobal scale. But these common formats are often put into national contexts, based on and framed by national education institutions, languages and hierarchies of relevance. Even websites usually refer mainly to others from the same country and language community.

In media and communication studies, we still detect splits between a focus on (static) media structures and media history, written in terms of unique examples and structured sequences (within national borders). Media history is still often written by non-historians, media change is often focused upon in a short-term, practical policy or professional education-oriented perspective. The specification of time frames to be taken into account, both into the past and into the future, usually does not meet with easy consensus across disciplinary or national borders. From a social science perspective, the dissemination of media cultures across generations requires the study of decades; even the historically new acceleration rates of WWW and mobile phone usage imply more than ten years of study to include the majority of various (western) populations. If we focus on world cultural zones beyond the western and Japanese ones, Internet or mobile phone access for the majorities of the other cultural zones may well need more than a generation.

The co-existence of several generations with distinct media biographies in any society already requires a time horizon of almost a century. Anticipating the life expectancies of those recently born may necessitate another hundred years of study. In technological and institutional terms, for example, the growth of the telegraph and the emergence of news agencies at the end of the nineteenth century have laid foundations still relevant at the beginning of the twenty-first century. In terms of the habitualization of perception modes, the interpretation and usage of media formats, tacit assumptions, communication contexts, cultural meanings, the interplay of traditional media such as face to face communication, the theatre, print, movies, broadcast and Web media must be checked in relation to particular media generations and phases of economic, cultural, political and general societal developments.

Media continuities usually predominate within national media systems: The introduction and spread of information and entertainment technologies (hardware, software, formats, contents) follows patterns which can be characterized by higher levels of inclusion, faster rates of change, more importance in terms of money, time and attention spent on media.

Media discontinuities/shifts/upheavals can be specified in terms of the research programme established in 2002 at the University of Siegen (http: //www.fk615.uni-siegen.de/Mainsites/ProfilENG.html, downloaded July 2004):

> A guiding premise of the investigation is the observation that media upheavals suppose comprehensive, discontinuous, structural changes within media history...In fact, different factual, temporal, social, medial and spatial consequences result from the media upheavals in different cultures. Therefore, the scientific studies are not only limited to the analysis of media-related theoretical discourse, but also requires a trans-disciplinary and intercultural approach to research.

Changing media are a partial process of more encompassing social processes. As means of communication and orientation they have always played a role in human societies. Yet, as symbolically generalized means of communication like power, money, or truth, and as technically distributed (mass) media, like books, journals, movies, radio, television, the Web, they have gained ever more importance. Since the end of the twentieth century, ICTs have been interpreted as the major driving forces of social change, even as revolutionary. Only if we take into account the interdependencies of various types of media over a longer period of time, will we be able to specify the particular role media technologies/formats/contents play for economic/political/cultural developments.

These interdependencies can be patterned as pre-adaptive advances on the side of certain media (technologies etc.); they can be interpreted as co-evolution or as media lacking behind social developments. The current focus on media upheavals in Europe may be limited to a particular phase. For, inevitably, humans are socialized into the usage of the major symbol systems of the families, groups, cultures into which they are born: body movements and sentiments, spoken and written words, numbers and figures, music and visuals configure elements and interdependencies of references and interpretations, relevancies and exclusion, which pre- and re-configure the acceptance and use of media knowledge. Increasing transnational diffusions of technologies, values, information and knowledge shape all societies in the twenty-first century. Therefore we must avoid two fallacies:

The development, distribution and use of mass media technologies, formats and contents cannot be adequately understood without taking into account more general socio-economic, technological and political developments as well as citizens' major symbols and values reference systems (cf. Ludes 2001, 2002 and 2004b). Otherwise, media technological overgeneralizations, implying the dominance of a media society, abound.

The development, distribution and use of contemporary general technologies, formats of discourse and interaction as well as narratives and (types of) explanations can no longer be adequately understood without taking into account the specific formats and contents of widely used mass media. Since the technologically distributed mass media speed up the access to alternate value standards and the global mass media enhance the dissemination of cultures, it would be astonishing if culture shifts in the twenty-first century would occur along the same (territorial) cultural borders and in the same rhythm, speed and mode (as, for example, 'clash' or 'Union') as before.

From media in Europe to European media
In 2004 Denis McQuail emphasized:

> the paradox of unity and dissimilarity of...national 'stories'...European media have much in common with each other and are quite distinct from those of the United States, Japan, Latin America, China, etc...Some of the more common features of the different systems include the: shared basic principles of law, human rights and democracy that have gradually been established since World War II; the existence of a mixed public and private broadcasting system in all countries; a tradition that permits (even if it discourages) some intervention in the media on grounds of public interest; competitive party political systems that still give shape to the outlook of the media and to their opinion-forming role; the role played by institutions of the European Union and the Council of Europe in regulating for access, diversity, harmonization of regulation and the pursuit of some cultural goals; the similar forces that everywhere make for linguistic and cultural identification, even if they then make for differentiation.

In this sense, converging trends have characterized major institutions in European countries and media and enforced increasing trans-European regulations. Yet, as McQuail (2004: 2) continues to argue:

> There are some evident dimensions of difference, with varying origins. One such is the variable grip of the mass newspaper reading in general, some countries being avid readers, others not. A similar but not clearly related variable is the relative appeal of television and other audio-visual media, as measured by time spent.

These particularities in Europe need not be interpreted as fragmentation. They show rather 'unity in diversity' – as the European motto says, a necessary prerequisite for both transcending cultural heritages and combining them in global competition.

Romano Prodi (2004: xiii) identified a European culture on the basis of interpretations of recent world values surveys:

> These surveys were carried out in 36 European countries, including all 25 members of the European Union. They also cover 45 additional countries, making it possible to interpret the beliefs and values of any given society in a genuinely global context. In this broader global context, we find evidence of a 'European culture,' reflecting relatively similar beliefs shared by European publics – but we also find that certain basic values are widely shared by publics throughout the world.

Values, however, differ significantly from experiences and institutionalized ties and options. National and regional communities of destinies and interests, first-hand experiences and liabilities, the same spoken languages and similar codes of conduct therefore will be handed on from generation to generation and (in empirical contrast to Beck 2004, ch. VI) only partially be transformed by trans-national media of communication. Multiple identifications, incoherent understandings of dis-/information, shifting and contradictory balances between tacit knowledge and explicitly codified knowledge systems will continue to prevail. Taking into account more long-term developments, Juan Diez Medrano (2003: 247) summarized his empirical results on 'framing Europe' in Germany, Spain and the United Kingdom as follows:

> [The] fear of losing one's national identity as part of the European Union and the closeness one feels to Europe matter in explaining the degree to which one supports membership in the European Union. ... British scepticism is rooted in a comparatively low degree of identification with Europe and a fear of losing national identity. ...a desire to modernize and to break with isolation in the case of Spain and a desire to regain the trust of other countries after World War II in the case of West Germany are factors behind their support for European integration.

A 'reality check' on the European Information Society (Servaes 2003: 27), therefore, 'has concluded that the so-called information society is "a society in formation" and certainly not immanently emerging. ... There is no single road to the information society. Every country has its own particularities and these are very heavily determined by national political objectives.' In contrast, the 'European Communication Council Report' from 2004 diagnosed 'E-Merging Media'. New types of 'meso-media' (Feldmann & Zerdick 2004) emerge, which target groups between a hundred and a hundred thousand users/consumers: narrowcasting, local TV, on-demand publishing, DVDs, Intranets, SMS or e-mails. Ambient Intelligence regulates ever more of our everyday activities (Ducatel et al. 2004). It is a product of three converging key technologies: ubiquitous computing, communication systems, which are easily accessible in all areas of everyday life, and intelligent, user-friendly interfaces. Thereby, wearable computers or self-steering cognitive systems regulate information-gathering and usage just as traffic signs have regulated cars and pedestrians. The new flexibility and mobility calls for such devices and their interoperability in technological and interpersonal networks.

Yet, such a focus on technological innovations may underestimate the increasing cultural and economic differences between the old EU15-member states, the recent ten accession countries, Bulgaria and Romania, and Turkey, with which talks on a potential membership have a long tradition (cf. Gerhards 2005).

Introductory conclusions

The emergence of a so-called European Information and Knowledge Society is a multidimensional, non-linear, long-term process of shifting balances of disinformation and information, ignorance and knowledge as well as media and culture specific frameworks of evaluation and interpretation. The concepts of 'convergence and fragmentation' appear as too static for an adequate understanding of this process. Therefore, they should be replaced by converging and diverging trends, implying media and social changes and allowing for 'unity in diversity'.

Major deficiencies of the current state of research into media in Europe include:

■ Access to print, broadcast, and web offerings from the media systems in Europe for a common, continuously working media sample server
■ European categories for comparison and a combination of culture-specific with trans-cultural perspectives
■ Data on metropolitan vs. rural or generation-specific usage patterns
■ Studies on transforming networks of orientation, communication, identification in a global context
■ Trans-disciplinary research on the same databases by mixed teams of representatives from the humanities, social sciences, and information management.

'Unity in diversity' requires better access to the diverse and divergent group, target and mass media in Europe. Only when we become ever more aware of their singularities and commonalities, will media in Europe successfully compete with media from outside Europe. European unity will continue to be fragile and should be covered as such, but the trans-national European media institutions have barely tackled this challenge. Citizens in Europe have concrete experiences of improving human development.

The analysis of living conditions in the European Union can be based on European statistics (cf. Ludes 2001, chapter 7) or on the human development data for the EU member, accession and candidate countries and beyond. The HDI (Human Development Index) values for each country are annually determined by the UN HDR office and are calculated on the basis of life expectancy, adult literacy rate, combined primary, secondary and tertiary gross enrolment rate, GDP per capita. (Cf. for the most recent data, usually published in mid-July http://hdr.undp.org/reports/view_reports.cfm?type=1.) It is evident that there is consistent (yet not always continuously increasing) improvement for all these countries (and non-EU countries such as Norway, Iceland or Switzerland as well). This is a rare instance in global comparison, which makes Europe attractive for many non-Europeans.

Yet, old cultural identities are ever more brought into question by collapsing socio-economic and political securities. New anxieties call for re-specifications of safeties and options available for a considerable part of one's lifetime. The worldwide competitive economic, political, cultural struggle has sharpened and Europe has become ever more dependent on trans-cultural interdependencies. But reflections on 'Europe' as a global player and victim remain limited due to persistent regional and national frameworks of living conditions and work experiences, schoolbooks and media. Trans-cultural identifications are no easy voluntary options yet are forcefully shaped and delimited by these frameworks. Contradictory images and experiences confront each and every citizen in Europe throughout his or her more than 70 to 80 years of average life expectancy. The media show young, beautiful and healthy people in their entertainment programmes. The youth and those beyond 50, however, are especially threatened by unemployment. Public authorities lack the money to invest in the renovation of the infrastructure of kindergartens, schools, universities, highways, hospitals, etc. These obvious signs of decline of public and personal fragility are often veiled by more optimistic infotainment. New information and communication technologies and content function not only as driving forces towards a European information and knowledge society; they also provide means of disorientation and ignorance. Therefore, we must take account of the Janus-head of convergence and fragmentation, which may show encouraging and frightening faces, of lacking coherence or cultural diversity, economic profitability or lack of technological safety and personality rights. The already problematic convergence of the old member and new accession countries of the European Union and beyond will be put under pressures from outside Europe. Intra-European processes thereby will continuously face fragmentary convergence and diverting fragments. But such developments often appear too complicated to be covered by mass-attractive media.

During the twentieth century, school education, cheaper books, a relatively inexpensive press, radio and television service have to some extent broken down barriers to the diffusion of knowledge, which can be interpreted as a process of functional democratization, a growing power potential of the masses. Compulsory education and the attendant higher educational level of the masses compared to the past were an indispensable adjunct of advancing industrialization and the mechanization of warfare. State societies where the educational level was comparatively low and oriented toward pre-scientific models were at a disadvantage in their competitive struggles compared to those societies where most people were educated and knowledgeable.

These types of arguments (Elias 1984) may have also led official EU policies to enhance a European information and knowledge society, mainly as a device to improve its competitive power in relation to the other major 'players' in world trade. (See, e.g., 'Facing the challenge' 2004: esp. 6, 9–11, 15, 19–20.) Scientific discovery has long become a planned social process. Discoveries and innovations fuel the development of societies and are fuelled in turn by their national, social rivalries and conflicts. As societies become wealthier and more differentiated, the occupation with symbols is organised as a social specialty. Symbols with the social function of knowledge are only one class of symbols among others. Sculptors, composers, film-makers, playwrights and the mimetic intellectuals are producers of symbols too. Schoolteachers are transmitting symbols from one generation to another. Taking into account all of the reservations concerning the concept of a European Information and Knowledge Society specified so far – and throughout this book – it may be helpful to outline some prerequisites for and characteristics of a society in which reasonable scientific knowledge indeed shapes most decision-making processes.

Therefore I summarize the major points from Elias' utopian tale 'The Great Struggle of the Intellectuals' (Elias 1984: 280–291). In this 'thought experiment', public debates are institutionalized in which 60–90% of the population participate at least as active audiences. Only those who participate are allowed to vote. Two major prerequisites are

1. The educational level of the population is much higher than nowadays, all should have knowledge, competence, and sensitivity of judgment far beyond occupational specialisation;
2. Fossilised and corrupted knowledge has been weeded out from schools, universities, and educational institutions. All have access to 'a clearer, wider, more certain and factual orientation about the internal and external affairs of their country and indeed of humanity' (Elias 1984: 284).

It will require generations of better school education, more informative mass media and new types of scientific and intermediary institutions to allow the majorities of the populations to participate actively and reasonably in information generating and usage. Such long-term perspectives clarify current European speed limits for quite different paces of technological, political, economic, or cultural processes of Europeanisation. They also show how limited and unclear contemporary media signs and contents are in contrast to traffic regulations. From this perspective, any talk of 'information highways' is misleading.

Endnote

I gratefully acknowledge the importance of discussions in our changing team 3 (itself an expression of fragmentation in coherence), especially with Jean-Claude Burgelman (our first team leader), Torben Grodal, Gerd Kopper, Knut Lundby and Frank Webster as well as in the programme's core group, with Peter Golding, Ib Bondebjerg, Els de Bens, Jostein Gripsrud and William Uricchio. Sonja Lijff and Robin Mansell were our team's external advisors whom we owe cordial thanks. Heather Owen performed an excellent task in editing all the various European strands of English of our book contributions. Last, not least, I am indebted to my research assistant, Tobias Kohler, Siegen and Växjö, who prepared first reviews of the literature and of statistical data, which, however, have not been included in this short introduction. A preview of this book was published in Ludes (2004a).

References

Beck, Ulrich (2004), Der kosmopolitische Blick oder: Krieg ist Frieden. Frankfurt/Main: Suhrkamp.

Bell, D. (1999), The axial age of technology: foreword 1999. In: Bell, Daniel. The Coming of Post-Industrial Society. New York: Basic Books, pp. ix–lxxv, Second Edition.

Chan, Joseph M. and Bryce McIntyre (eds.) (2002), In Search of Boundaries. Communication, Nation-States and Cultural Identities. Westport, Connecticut and London: Ablex Publishing.

Diez Medrano, Juan (2003), Framing Europe. Attitudes to European Integration in Germany, Spain, and the United Kingdom. Princeton and Oxford: Princeton University Press.

Ducatel, K., M. Bogdanowicz, F. Scapolo, J. Leitjen and J.-C. Burgelman (2004), Dafür sind Freunde da – Ambient Intelligence (AmI) und die Informationsgesellschaft im Jahre 2010. In: European Communication Council Report: E-Merging Media. Kommunikation und Medienwirtschaft der Zukunft. Edited by Axel Zerdick, Arnold Picot, Klaus Schrape, Jean-Claude Burgelman and Roger Silverstone, Berlin etc.: Springer, pp. 195–218.

Elias, Norbert (1984), Knowledge and Power. An Interview by Peter Ludes. In Nico Stehr and Volker Meja (eds.), Society and Knowledge. Contemporary Perspectives on the Sociology of Knowledge, New Brunswick, Transaction Publishers, pp. 251–291.

Feldmann, Valerie and Axel Zerdick (2004), E-Merging Media : Die Zukunft der Kommunikation. In: European Communication Council Report: E-Merging Media. Kommunikation und Medienwirtschaft der Zukunft. Edited by Axel Zerdick, Arnold Picot, Klaus Schrape, Jean-Claude Burgelman and Roger Silverstone, Berlin etc.: Springer, pp. 19–30.

Ludes, Peter (2001), Multimedia und Multi-Moderne: Schlüsselbilder. (Multi-Media and Multiple Modernities: Key Visuals), Book with CD-ROM, Wiesbaden: Westdeutscher Verlag.

Ludes, Peter (2002), DVD-ROM Medien und Symbole: €uropäische MedienBILDung. Mit zwei Beiträgen zur Medienzivilisierung von Jürgen Zinnecker. (Media and Symbols: European Media Education. With Two Contributions on Civilizing Media by Jurgen Zinnecker), Technik, Gestaltung, Realisation (Design and Realisation): Medienzentrum der Universität Siegen, Siegen: UniVerSi.

Ludes, Peter (2004a), Changing Media as a Prime Interpreter of Changing Europe, in economic trends 1, pp. 30–33.

Ludes, Peter (2004b), 'EUROvisions? Monetary Union and Communication Puzzles', in Ib Bondebjerg and Peter Golding (eds.): European Culture and the Media = Changing Media – Changing Europe Series, vol. 1, Bristol and Portland: Intellect publishing, pp. 215–231.

McQuail, Denis (2004), 'Introduction' in Mary Kelly, Gianpietro Mazzoleni and Denis McQuail (eds.): The Media in Europe: The Euromedia Handbook. London, Thousand Oaks and New Delhi: Sage, pp. 1–3.

Prodi, Romano (2004), 'Foreword' in Ronald Inglehart, Miguel Basanez, Jaime Diez-Medrano and Ruud Luijkx (eds.): Human Beliefs and Values. A cross-cultural sourcebook based on the 1999–2002 values surveys, Mexico, D. F. and Buenos Aires: siglo, pp. xiii-xiv.

Schorr, Angela (2003), 'Communication Research and Media Science in Europe: Research and Academic Training at a Turning Point', in: Angela Schorr, William Campbell and Michael Schenk (eds.): Communication Research and Media Science in Europe. Berlin and New York: Mouton de Gruyter, pp. 3–55.

Servaes, Jan (ed.) (2003), The European Information Society. A reality check, Bristol: Intellect.

Stehr, Nico (2001), Knowledge and Economic Conduct. The Social Foundations of Modern Economy. Toronto, Buffalo, London: University of Toronto Press.

Stehr, Nico (ed.) (2004), The Governance of Knowledge. New Brunswick and London: Transaction Publishers.

SECTION 1: CULTURE AND TECHNOLOGY

Policy papers of the European Union, as well as its member states, celebrate recent developments on the road to the 'information or knowledge society' and define new perspectives in order to reach ever-newer objectives. Maria Heller re-asserts: Information is a basic resource for the most developed societies: safe circulation, access, handling and retrieval of information already constitute a basic need for individual citizens as well as for institutions, political and economic actors. Recent research and resulting technological development, both largely backed by economic interests, have lead to the introduction of new devices of information and communication technology and they have greatly modified the possibilities and the everyday reality of communication for individual citizens, institutions, as well as for the state and the whole civil society. Nevertheless, while it has to be borne in mind that communication and information have always been crucial for societies in every period of history as they constitute the base for social bonds and social activity, one can legitimately ask how and to what extent communication and information in today's societies play a central role or have acquired high relevance.

Like all spheres of social life, the sphere of communications is governed by norms and strategies (Habermas 1962; Heller, Némedi & Rényi 1990). These norms and strategies are not static; they are constantly modified by the communicative actors in their struggle for the distribution and redistribution of forces and resources. Historical and societal changes, as well as technological developments, also modify the underlying rules, norms, strategies and behaviours. In the last years, new ICTs have caused important changes in people's representation of communications, as well as in their communicative behaviours. The use of more and more sophisticated new ICT devices made it possible to extend the space and time limitations of formerly existing situations of communications, thus restructuring these situations and radically modifying the communicative relationships among the users. This development raised a number of questions as to the repercussions of these changes in the sphere of local and global power distribution, in the sphere of work, culture, language, education and leisure and in the sphere of social relationships, social groups, political and civil activity.

It can reasonably be argued that the rapidly changing ICT technologies and the quickly growing ICT sector profoundly modify today's societies, including their economic, political and social structure, as well as people's attitudes, needs and behaviours concerning information and communication. It has largely been debated in the scientific community, as well as in the larger public, whether the use of new ICTs result in more democracy or more leisure in everyday life; whether it is global or local participation that gets enhancement through the new technologies and how these developments concern different societies or different layers of the same society; how power relations are reorganized and who profits from the development.

Social scientists and media scholars nurture different views about whether the use of new ICTs results in convergence among different societies and different social groups or if it contributes to fragmented communication systems and diverging developmental patterns of different societies. Certain researchers fear that problems of access to new ICTs reinforce political, economic and cultural cleavages, condemn large publics to passive consumption of more and more entertainment and hamper the functioning of the public sphere by introducing divergent developments, causing strong fragmentation of publics and the deepening of the digital gap. They point to the danger of loosening social cohesion and weakening intensity of social organization and solidarity. More optimistic social scientists, on the contrary, believe that new ICTs contribute to the construction of more conscious societies, where active and interactive citizens can easily participate in the public sphere, in public decision-making because the new technological development provides them with new devices, new forms and spaces for communication and debate. In this view, new ICTs foster democratic development and the construction of a global world-society, with common universal values.

Although both views have strong arguments in their favour, it is difficult to totally adhere to one or the other opposing standpoints. In the following text, Maria Heller will consider the pros and cons discernable in some of the main trends of ICT development: first, she will examine some general considerations about convergence, divergence and fragmentation before scrutinizing the most important modifications related to the new ICTs in the global political, economic, cultural and social fields. In the final part, convergence and divergence will be tackled from the point of view of the enlarged European Union, taking into consideration the similarities and differences between the fifteen 'old European' and the ten 'new European' countries' economic force and communication culture.

The purpose of Ursula Maier-Rabler's chapter is to analyse the prevailing methods and approaches for developing ePolicies in Europe. This analysis will help determine which priorities are taken into consideration by governmental policy-makers to assist in the development of policies that encourage the transformation of European countries into

Information Societies at both the national and regional levels. Furthermore, this chapter will make a unique contribution to the critical work concerning current ePolicies, which characterizes most of the approaches taken toward the development of ePolicies as technological deterministic (e.g. Webster 2002; Castells 2000; Mansell 2001) and follow marketplace logic (Gandy 2002). Referring to studies of Robin Mansell and subsequently Armartya Sen this chapter will present a human-centred approach, with its emphasis on the human being posessing the right to acquire the appropriate capabilities to choose the manner in which they participate in society. Additionally, this chapter will provide insight into culturally biased concepts of information and communication, which influence the fundamentals characteristics of current ePolicies, insofar as they explain why certain actions are or are not being taken by policy-makers.

Global and European Information Society

Maria Heller

Convergence, divergence, diversity and fragmentation

The general tendency of globalization has created considerable convergence in the domain of European, as well as global economic and social development, information and communication structures, media and cultural consumption. It has also caused growing public concern about the economic, social and ecological drawbacks of globalization. The rapidly developing ICT and media industries have largely contributed to the development of globalization. In the spread of new ICTs there are overall tendencies of convergence: similar ICT devices are used everywhere, with converging functions. Similar information and entertainment tendencies characterize global media, similar contents are available and access to them is facilitated through various devices, ICT networks are globally interconnected and foster all kinds of communication and information-transfer whether public or private, short or long distance. ICTs also make it possible to reach the same entertainment or information contents through different devices and, in the same way, they make it possible to reach interlocutors of all types through various communication channels provided by various ICTs. In this sense, we can witness that ICT developments create a great deal of convergence on the global scale and contribute easy access to communicational and cultural diversity.

But ICT developments do not only back convergence on the global scale: diverging tendencies are also numerous. One should differentiate between divergence and diversity in this respect: divergence meaning development in different or opposing directions or at different paces, and diversity involving variety, a scale of different uses, more choice among possibilities, devices and activities.

The term divergence covers several phenomena: One of the most often cited problems is the deepening digital divide, the info-communicational gap between layers of the same society with different economic and cultural backgrounds, between age groups and sexes, etc. The digital divide, however, can also be defined on a global scale: between different societies and regions of the world having different economic status and different cultural and communicational characteristics. Both types of digital divide constitute a threat to global communication and world integrity.

Another phenomenon of divergence is the so-called fragmentation of the public. Today, there are strong signs showing that the formerly unified public sphere (Keane 1995) has been split up: differently sized public spheres have made their appearance beside former national public sphere(s), which used to be represented or thought of as being uniform and unique (the very place where public affairs, public concerns are discussed by unrestricted publics). Different publics use different ICTs and different media and the former unified (national) publics have been fragmented into social groups having different ICT activities, different centres of interest, and having no common space for the elaboration of common causes and meanings.

Observing what is going on in the differently sized fora created by the new ICTs, we can conclude that, instead of doing away with the public sphere, various new public spheres have appeared and topics of public concern are widely discussed by diverse publics in various new public spaces (Internet fora, discussion groups, chat rooms, even e-mail and SMS). The problem of this new diversity of the public spheres is whether all layers of society have access to them and are willing and capable of participating. The question can reasonably be raised whether new ICTs predominantly facilitate the entertainment function or the information-seeking and democratic function of the new media based on new possibilities of interactivity. Do users/citizens/individuals become more dominated and passive by the entertaining function of the new devices or do they become more active and partaking in growing democratic participatory discussions?

Main modifications in the different domains of social life in societies of different levels of development

The rapid development of ICTs, the restructuring of the public sphere, and the introduction of the Information Society or knowledge society inevitably entail radical modifications in different domains of life.

The power structure of individual societies is undergoing important changes. In fact, political, economic and symbolic powers depend more and more on control over knowledge, and the access to and use of new ICTs strongly influence the new knowledge hierarchy in society. This can hasten major macro-structural changes in different societies. The gap between information-haves and information-have-nots or users and non-users is gradually widening, the often-mentioned digital divide does not seem to disappear, and it reinforces the inequality relations inside individual societies.[1]

Similar modifications in the inequality relations are under way on the global scale, i.e. among different societies: thus recreating and reinforcing asymmetrical relations according to centre and periphery, innovative and traditional societies. The digital divide is deepening between societies participating in or left out of the digital revolution. Whole regions are cut off from the mainstream development or, in other places, certain deprived (or information-deprived) social layers are left out while local bourgeoisie or the national elite manage to strengthen their position and cope with the global development. The dichotomy between democratization of communications and digital divide on the global scale is stronger than ever.

New ICTs and the changes they introduce in the structure of the economy and of the workforce are about to cause radical changes in the relationship between work and leisure, and will also modify the relationship between workplace and home. A great number of activities can be done from anywhere because of online or mobile accessibility. These changes, in turn, will continue to alter the structure of towns, creating new patterns of urbanism, new types of settlements with broadband facilities and dense nets of 'communications' of all sorts, like telecommunication nets and highway nets.

Telework and mobile communication devices contribute to the appearance of different forms of work and radically modify people's timetables and schedules. It is clear that these changes will and already do affect people's lifestyles in the sense that the role of 'place' decreases as the communicative situations are stretched out beyond time and space constraints. This at the same time increases the need for prompt but quickly perishable information in particular situations, in particular places.[2]

Digitalization and, hence, easy accessibility of all kinds of communication contents and cultural products through diverse new ICTs with quickly decreasing technological constraints,[3] introduce radical changes in the access and acquisition of cultural products. All cultural productions become accessible through the same media[4] and digital handling makes it possible to create an infinite variety of relationships among different cultural products (Hypertext). This qualitative change brings about the intertextuality of culture, changing at the same time not only accessibility but also the patterns of acquisition of cultural products. Linearity of most cultural products is replaced by a new complex structure, where acquisition is not directed by the same strict rules as before. Meanwhile we can observe that the earlier 'road' metaphor in cultural reception is by now replaced by the metaphor of 'maze', or 'labyrinth', where the user progresses in his/her own pace and directions according to his/her individual decisions and needs.

With digital accessibility, cultural products also become more vulnerable, more open to alteration or misappropriation. Texts, films, pictures, music, etc. are no longer finished products, their rewriting has become technologically affordable and facilitated: they can best be characterized by time co-ordinates. Thus, the notion of 'document' also has to be redefined because all documents can easily be modified without noticeable traces. While this development involves considerable danger for copyright and autonomy of creative action, it also has socially positive outcomes. Digital technology not only increases the quality of cultural production but also enormously enhances productivity and interactivity and thus may lead to a renaissance of individual productive activity in contrast to the 'age of consumption'.[5]

New forms of cultural acquisition should enhance important modifications in the education system. It is already clear that the meaning and content of 'literacy' is about to change to incorporate 'digital literacy'. Although most countries' school system has difficulties in coping with the radical changes, the necessary knowledge and the skills to get along in the digitalized world has already greatly increased. Research, as well as everyday experience, shows that young generations quickly get used to new technologies and this emphasizes the need for new forms of learning[6] for all generations and the importance of lifelong learning in a quickly changing world.

Scientific communication has also been modified by the new ICTs. Interaction among scientists has become much more frequent, to such an extent that in the case of some innovations even the origin of the scientific thought is untraceable.

The obsolescence factor of the new devices is very rapid, since the continuous innovation process has made people's needs change very quickly. The appearance of the ever-newer appliances recreates consumers' needs, while consumers trapped in the innovation competition feel the former devices to be trashy. New devices go through quick downwards infiltration in society, spreading from the upper classes to different forms of mass uses (either as status symbols or quickly spreading leisure devices[7]).

It is no wonder that all these social changes greatly influence and modify people's behaviours towards communications. The new devices make it possible for people to cope with increasing life speed. This involves changing lifestyles, new relations to space and time, redefinition of public and private affairs, spaces and times. Mobile devices procure more personal or individual freedom, where the individual is less confined by place. Easy accessibility through new ICTs makes modification of previous agreements easily readjustable: indeed, the use of e-mail, mobile communication and SMS has been reported to deal frequently with quick modifications in predefined work or leisure programmes. It follows from this phenomenon that many communications events become situation-dependent: their relevance is restricted to a particular space and time constellation, to a particular communication situation.

With the accelerated lifestyle, news consumption has greatly increased. This is clearly proven by statistics, which show that important layers of the society follow news through diverse media: newspapers, radio, TV,[8] WAP, Internet, etc.

Because ICTs bring about changes in the structure of work-type with the spreading of telework or distance work and learning, it is clear that households and family relationships also change. Not only does child control become easy and frequent through ICTs[9] but public and private places and times, as well as relationships, get modified through continuous accessibility. People try to delimit private or public space or time for communication with subtle methods (e.g. different musical rings, etc.); they also often feel the need to define the space and time co-ordinates of a particular communication on a mobile phone.

The new lifestyle does not modify people's predilections for travel as it was thought, especially because conditions for travelling have become far easier than before[10] while the need for face-to-face communication seems to have been preserved.

Researchers even discuss the use of ICTs as a social problem of addiction, where the very possession of the digital devices decreases the individual's feeling of insecurity and reinforces his/her impression of being part of a community and constitutes a factor for identity construction. The possession and use of ICTs also gives way to specific forms of self-expression.[11]

All the aforementioned modifications of social and work structure, of time and space relations, of people's needs and behaviours lead to new communicative relationships among people. If we consider that human relationships constitute a specific form of social capital (Bourdieu 1970, 1979), it is no wonder that ICTs play an important role in the accumulation and the management of this capital. The more ICTs are available for the individual the more he/she is free to choose the most adequate form to reach a partner according to their relationship, the topic of communication, the situation, etc. (In the choice of ICTs there might be considerations about the accessibility of the person, of the public or private character of the topic and the relationship, the degree of intimacy, the urgency of reply, the degree of facility of immediate or remote communication, etc.)

It can be observed as a consequence of the growing needs of communications that, both in strong ties and in weak ties, communications have become more frequent and higher in density. People find it easier to maintain communicative ties with remote persons: dying relationships have revived via the Internet, and many new relationships have been established between people who would not have met or started discussions had it not been through new ICTs.[12] The growing communication activity through ICTs has changed both horizontal and vertical relations inside individual societies but has also opened up the borderlines among different societies. People engage in a great number of different communicative acts through various channels made available by

ICTs. In this manner, individuals have built up large international networks of relations of both strong and weak ties and these large networks are often combined together into meta-networks through worldwide e-mail chains.

The exponentially growing number of communicative acts testifies to the increased needs for communication and human relations of contemporary humans.[13] The former tendency of passivization of the public (period of the mass media) (Noam 1996) has been overturned. Although important social groups are still passive consumers of mass cultural products, an increasing tendency of interactivity and a certain return to public discussion, to participation in social discourse can be observed due to ICT facilities.

The ever-innovative developments of ICTs generate, however, some global problems. People are more and more concerned by the increased capacity of registration of the new technologies. Individual user's activities, likes and dislikes can easily be traced back and people feel their privacy is put in danger. Although the registration capacity can be useful, when it facilitates e-commerce and m-commerce, creating forms of easy purchase of products and services, the liability of the identifiable registered user[14] seems to create an urgent need for new regulations defending user privacy, data protection or copyrights.

New ICTs also raise some technological problems. There is a constant competition among different industrial fields about how to incorporate more and more functions in the same devices. This creates a peculiar convergence among multifunctional objects that used to be clearly separate.[15] The outcome of the competition will be defined by biological constraints: buttons cannot be too small compared to our fingertips, etc. This problem has, however, been partially overcome in the use of new PDAs or handwritten digital tablets. In a certain sense, biological evolution has been replaced by technological evolution: new ICTs improve our senses. Fortunately, the user might still choose the tendency of divergence and use the most convenient device for his/her goals and situation.

Certain analysts of the developing Information Society fear that the increasing use of new ICTs weakens social cohesion and loosens ties in self-organizing civil groups. They claim that the amount of time spent watching television or surfing alone on the Internet prevents people from pursuing former social activities and from fostering traditional societal relationships (Putnam 2000). They foresee that people using the new devices become more and more isolated and they fear the weakening of trust in social institutions. Certain scholars regard the increasing participation in online communities as a false escape into non-existent communities, where only anonymous, faceless and nicknamed individuals take part in fake interactions. They do not believe this kind of participation can lead to the development of community identity or public consciousness.

It is not yet clear whether the increased communicative activity of online individuals can lead to the elaboration of common meanings and commonly shared cognitive goods or if it will end in cultural and communicational segregation. Do the new means of communications augment the critical potential of the public sphere enhancing more concern in public decision making or do they only facilitate more leisure and entertainment, making the public even more fragmented, scattered and isolated?

More optimistic social scientists see the chances for the elaboration of more democratic societies through enlarged information and communication possibilities and renewed user interactivity. ICT-facilitated processes of communications have been reported to increase citizen activity and this in turn increases users' social capital. While some 20% of Net users reported having subsequently met online discussion-mates offline, they do not spend any less time cultivating their offline relationships with family and friends. Communicative advantages offered by ICTs can foster the rebirth of citizen consciousness and participation. Continuous online presence in differently sized communicative domains of different kinds (public and private spheres), interactivity, the possibility of quick reaction, easy reach of local or global networks of large groups[16] have already turned the Internet and other ICTs into efficient channels for social movements,[17] citizens' debates, political protest and mobilization.[18] These devices also promote easy and quick communications among citizens[19] and state or municipal institutions and make it possible to consult citizens' opinion by easy polling facilities.

Several international research projects have found evidence that participation in various communications communities through ICTs increase communication competence and skills and promotes the accumulation of social capital. It also reinforces the feeling of responsibility towards the community. The fact that many ICT users search for reliable information filtered by the online community shows that ICT use increases social trust.[20] Participation in online communities does not hinder participation in traditional communities; on the contrary, online activity is often concomitant with offline participation (Parks 1996). Increased communicative activity often reinforces strong feelings of belonging to diverse (work, leisure, political, local, religious, ethnic, etc.) communities, both online and offline, whether remote or close. Cyber participation seems to reinforce glocal activities (Wellman 2001) and 40% of people active in cyber-communities report having more intensive participation in local communities as well, even if this does not always mean face-to-face presence.

Indeed, ICTs constitute a horizontal net that reinforces co-operation, information exchange and knowledge generation, the elaboration of common meanings and norms, the production and spreading of values, the co-ordination of activities and the organization of communities as well as social functions like grooming and gossiping (Dunbar 1996; Fox 2001). Participation in such communities answers needs for information, belonging and identity formation. The main problem remains the fact that the distribution of physical and financial access, needs, skills and abilities are unequally distributed in the individual societies as well as on the global level.

European information societies, EU-15, EU-25

European history in the last centuries has known strong tendencies of common development of communication culture. The emergence of the public sphere has established the same norms and functions in most European societies. The development of a normative idea about the public sphere (in the Habermasian sense) is commonly shared in most European societies, even if the realization turned out to be different in the different European nation states.

We can also find evidence that the ways people make use of the existing public spheres have been convergent. Users' strategies aimed at the accumulation and use of specific (economic, social, political) capitals in public discourse (in the Bourdieusian sense) and the construction of one's own public image have shown considerable similarities among public spheres of different European nation states (Heller, Némedi & Rényi 1994, 1995). Both representations ((1) a normative public sphere that exercises control over institutions and public actors and (2) an interest-driven public sphere where participants attempt to maximize their benefits and act strategically) live on in the more and more unifying European public sphere.

But different communication cultures and different historical, economic, cultural traditions generate different needs and uses of ICTs and produce differently structured public spheres on national, regional or local level. I will try to consider here some points of convergence and divergence between different European developmental patterns.

The development of ICTs characterizes the EU as a whole but rather important differences can be found among different EU countries or regions. EU policy papers attempt to foster convergent development,[21] but some underlying problems need analytical clarification. *EU economic strategies* aim at a leading role for Europe in the global economic competition based on continuous growth without considering its possible drawbacks (digital divide, development only in market-related fields, etc.). *EU political strategies*, on the other hand, attempt to achieve more active democratic participation by actors of the civil society, hoping that with convergence a common European public sphere is going to emerge which will help to create and reinforce common European identities. The question of whether these two types of strategies are compatible or how they relate to one another should also be seriously addressed. Do the economic goals, global competitiveness, economic efficiency and the search of unlimited growth foster the democratic development, unification and integrity of the Union, the elaboration of democratic governance and civil participation, the introduction of common norms and meanings, the smoothing of social, cultural and economic inequalities? For the European Union to efficiently function in diverse fields of life, economic differences should be rebalanced. But it is equally important to take into consideration the different models and paces of development of the different regions of Europe, the various European identity constructions, cultural heritages and traditions, and the different communication cultures.

In the following, some statistical data are included to show differences of spread of ICTs and differences in usage. It is without any doubt that both the economic situation of each country and of its population play an important role in the penetration rate of ICT devices, but it is also clear that some differences should be related to social and cognitive factors, to different communication cultures, to more sensitivity in relation to

Table 1. Difference of Internet use in the EU-15 and the new EU member states in % and percentage of increase in three years.

Internet Usage in the European Union

EUROPEAN UNION	Population (2004 Est.)	Internet Users, Latest Data	User Growth (2000–2004)	Penetration (% Pop.)	% Users in EU
Austria	8,022,300	3,730,000	77.6 %	46.5 %	1.8 %
Belgium	10,402,200	3,769,123	88.5 %	36.2 %	1.8 %
Cyprus	950,400	250,000	108.3 %	26.3 %	0.1 %
Czech Republic	10,230,100	2,700,000	170.0 %	26.4 %	1.3 %
Denmark	5,397,600	3,375,850	73.1 %	62.5 %	1.6 %
Estonia	1,350,900	621,000	69.4 %	46.0 %	0.3 %
Finland	5,231,900	2,650,000	37.5 %	50.7 %	1.3 %
France	60,011,200	23,352,522	186.5 %	40.6 %	11.8 %
Germany	82.633.200	47,182,628	96.6 %	57.1 %	22.9 %
Greece	11,208,400	1,718,400	71.8 %	15.3 %	0.8 %
Hungary	10,106,000	2,400,000	235.7 %	23.7 %	1.2 %
Ireland	4,019,100	1,319,608	68.3 %	32.8 %	0.6 %
Italy	57,987,100	28,610,000	116.7 %	49.3 %	14.0 %
Latvia	2,319,200	936,000	524.0 %	40.4 %	0.5 %
Lithuania	3,445,900	695,000	208.9 %	20.2 %	0.3 %
Luxembourg	451,900	170,000	70.0 %	37.6 %	0.1 %
Malta	383,600	120,000	200.0 %	31.3 %	0.1 %
Netherlands	16,254,900	10,806,328	177.1 %	66.5 %	5.2 %
Poland	38,158,100	8,970,000	220.4 %	23.5 %	4.4 %
Portugal	10,389,800	3,600,000	44.0 %	34.6 %	1.7 %
Slovakia	5,381,200	1,375,800	111.7 %	25.6 %	0.7 %
Slovenia	1,954,500	750,000	150.0 %	38.4 %	0.4 %
Spain	41,895,600	14,332,763	166.0 %	34.2 %	7.0 %
Sweden	9,010,700	6,722,576	66.1 %	74.6 %	3.3 %
United Kingdom	59,595,900	34,874,469	126.5 %	58.5 %	16.9 %
European Union	**456,791,700**	**204,050,785**	**119.0 %**	**44.7 %**	**100.0 %**

Source: The European Union Internet Statistics, www.InternetWorldStats.com, last updated: 30 September 2004

status symbols, the priority given to private life and leisure, to carefree entertainment, possession of visible consumer goods, etc. Below, we will try to demonstrate some of the differences and search for possible causes. The Hungarian figures included below in detail are expected to represent central and eastern European peculiarities.

It is interesting to note that new ICTs spread in the different European societies with different speed. The table above permits interesting comparisons of increase in the number and percentage of Internet users in different EU member states.

As it becomes clear from the above statistics, strong economic differences explain part of the different stages of Information Society among the 25 EU member states. But differences can also be attributed to more soft sociological, historical and cultural factors. Several surveys have shown that there are differences of attitude, of expectation and of trust in institutions and in social development between different European societies, as well as strong differences in self-image, identity formation and belief in the future.

Considering the historical model of development of the different European regions, we find that western Europe has known an organic development of civilization, state and institutions and a more peaceful growth of the public sphere in its history of the last centuries. This development resulted in considerably pluralistic national public spheres.

Central Europe and eastern Europe even more have been delayed in social, economic and political development in comparison to the West. This problem has brought about a century-old dilemma of model choice. Social and political cleavages in these countries focus on the problem of what type of model for social development to choose, the three main models being western-type modernization, socialist modernization and intrinsic nationalist models based on traditional (ethnic, religious, national, etc.) values. The historical series of European wars, uprising and ethnic/national animosities demonstrate the weight of the problem. And the dilemma of model choice is still lingering on.

Important differences have always existed between different European countries concerning people's relations to the public sphere and communications in general. The historical path of the nation states in central Europe (and even more so in eastern Europe) did not allow for the development of pluralistic public spheres. Even Hungary, which had the most developed 'restricted public sphere' (Heller & Rényi 1996) among central and eastern European countries in the second half of the twentieth century, is evidence that different communication cultures, different political cultures and traditions may react differently to new developments in communications.

In the footsteps of Norbert Elias, who analysed the differences between the English and French development of civilization and the German development of a different notion of national culture (Elias 1939), Jenö Szücs, the Hungarian historian, described three distinct regions of Europe that have known different models of development (Szücs 1981; 1988). Péter Hanák, another Hungarian social historian spoke of distorted national characters in the case of central and eastern European nations (Hanák 1992) because of their tumultuous past, in the course of which long generations of local populations had to undergo frequent political and ideological changes, subsequent wars and authoritarian political regimes. They had to elaborate cunning techniques of concealment, strong separation between their private and public lives, doubletalk, reading between the lines, etc. Life in this part of Europe could be, and can still be, characterized not only by lower levels of economic efficiency and consumption but also by a lower level of trust in institutions and an increased importance given to private life and consumer goods.

One has to understand that the development of information and communication technology had an important role to play in the recent political changes that occurred in central and eastern Europe. Penetration of various ICT devices[22] that obstructed the smooth functioning of censorship and enhanced liberal, pluralist communication flows accelerated the changes and demonstrated the unsustainability of the former political system.

In the Hungarian context of the Kádár regime, where the existence of a restricted public sphere and people's relatively free private life and slowly growing consumption possibilities were part of a tacit compromise between the political power and the population (as a result of the 1956 revolution), there existed a consensus between the central political power and the population concerning the separation of public and private spheres. The population kept watch of private freedom. In exchange, the political authorities did not expect public participation in politics and kept the masses out of political debates and actions.[23] Private life and consumption were highly valued by the population and sociologists were able to make account of a special sort of 'consumption tourism',[24] when tens of thousands of Hungarian families spent their national holidays going to purchase consumables in neighbouring Austrian villages or nearby Vienna.[25] Information and communication channels free from the control of central authorities exercised a strong appeal for the Hungarian population just as much as western consumables and signs of private wealth and freedom. Products of western technology appeared quickly in Hungary, mostly as private imports. These products (like home videos, Commodore computers in the early 80s) had a clear function of signalling social status, just as did the first mobile phones. These devices were put in the 'saint corner' of homes to be seen by all incoming persons or worn very ostensibly by quickly enriched entrepreneurs.[26]

In central Europe the political changeover of the early 90s quickly abolished the former public spheres. New participants appeared and new rules had to be introduced into public communications. Strong debates emerged on former taboo topics and heated struggle for recognition started among different political and cultural factions. The main topic of debate was about national identity and on what criteria the definition of national affiliation should be based. Debates on EU enlargement and NATO enlargement have to be also evaluated in this very context (Heller & Rényi 2003a, b). The questions at stake included the choice of belonging to the West (at last) or choosing a specific national model of development, and whether economic and political development should better be envisaged in the large European context or by closing up the country. The alternatives included establishing democratic functioning of institutions or re-establishing the rule of a populist, dictatorial nationalist elite. Fifteen years after the political changes, recent media developments and public debates still crystallize around these stakes.

Alongside the political developments, citizens' communication needs and uses have also changed. As it has always constituted an appealing model to many layers of central and eastern European societies, western consumption continued to attract people after the changeover, and pressing needs to acquire the requisites of western lifestyle, including communication devices, became even stronger. New ICTs became the symbols of the newly acquired freedom[27] and also played an important role in

Table 2. Certain consumer goods in the households in Hungary

	2000	2002	2003
Fridge	95	97	95
Deep freezer	59	56	67,7
Microwave oven	NA	47	65,2
Washing machine	NA	99	99
Dish washer	NA	2	5,4
Colour TV	91	96	97
Vacuum cleaner	79	81	84
Video player	52	56	61
Hi-fi	NA	33	43
Car radio	NA	29	39
CD player	NA	25	37
Fixed telephone line	75	74	68
Mobile phone	37	62	67
Home PC	17	26	30
Home Internet	5	11	21
Satellite TV	16	17	12,1
Video camera	3	5	7,6
DVD player	1	4	7,5
Digital camera	NA	NA	5,2
Cable TV	47	53	57

Sources: Tárki Háztartás monitor, 2001, 2003, WIP 2002, GfK 2003, 2004

strengthening contacts with Hungarian populations living outside the national territory,[28] thus re-establishing national and ethnic ties and reinforcing national identity. Communications-greedy populations, however, have to spend a much higher proportion of their income to be able to use the new devices than their western homologues.

In order to understand better the development of ICT penetration in the new member states, let us consider some more detailed figures of access and use of new ICTs by the Hungarian population.

The previous table attempts to show the importance the Hungarian population attaches to devices of comfort and leisure. It is to be remarked that all devices enhancing entertainment and apt to show social status show quicker penetration than devices necessitating active participation and/or user competence.

There was rapid development in the access to home computers: 26% of all households had a home PC in 2002, 30% in 2003 and according to the latest figures, it increased to 40% in 2004. Computers are more frequently present in households with 1 or 2 children: 50% of these households.

Only 23% of the whole Hungarian population used Internet in 2002,[29] of which 79% did so at their workplace (or school) and 31% at home. Among the reasons given for not using the Internet: 44% of the population do not have a PC, 37% are not interested, 22% find it too expensive and 16% claim not to have the basic skills for use. Internet access is also higher in households with children. Broadband Internet access is available in 17% of all households.

Of the main activities through the Internet, 47% look for information in relation to their work, 46% use e-mail, 29% surf on the Net for fun, 22% are engaged in chat, 14% discuss topics on diverse fora and only 7% use e-commerce.

Access to *fixed telephones* was not easy in the Kádár period, people had to wait for years before a telephone was installed in their homes. Today the telephone penetration seems to be at saturation point (since 2002 the number of private subscriptions has decreased), 36% of the population has a fixed phone, 72% of all households.[30]

On the contrary, access and use of *mobile phones* has increased extremely quickly in Hungary, (as was the case of the first Commodore computers or video players in the 1980s). In December 2001 there were 4,923,122 mobile phone subscribers, while in September 2004, there were 8,379,824 – 83% of the population.[31]

This rapid growth of mobile phones can be explained by several factors: the phenomena of fashion and ostensible display of the latest status symbols certainly play a role. As mentioned earlier the Hungarian population is keen on acquiring the latest technological gadgets. But aspirations for individual freedom, the lack of trust in institutions, the former difficult access to landline phones, as well as the possession of summer houses, gardens or agricultural lots might also be of influence (a large proportion of the urban population in Hungary is of direct rural origin and still has parents in remote villages). The fact that a large majority use fancy and interchangeable phone shells, musical rings and op-logos shows that the mobile phone is also regarded as a means of identity expression.

Possession of fixed or mobile devices still does not mean competent use. It becomes clear from several research projects that an important part of new ICT owners use only a limited part of the capacity of their devices. The main reasons for the under-usage are the lack of trust in the safeguard of personal data, lack of sufficient knowledge of languages and the low quality of digital literacy, as well as the relatively high costs.

Most of these reasons also explain the relatively limited use of WAP. At the end of 2000, only 5% of mobile phone users used WAP, and only 7% of mobiles were able to reach WAP services; this proportion increased to 16% in 2001. An important number of mobile phone users report having been deceived by WAP: advertisements gave a more positive image of the services, but users found the accessibility of Internet much slower and usability more limited, not enough content and not easy to manage. The price is also reported to be a hampering factor.

Recent research on ICTs show that their use is very much dependent on social position and it seems that through the management of social capital the use of ICTs also contributes to the strengthening of social position or even enhancement of upward social mobility. The use of different devices is very much dependent on social and cultural factors, as well as economic.

In the light of recent research, more and more evidence can be found about the increasing activity of citizens/users in public debates and civil movements. The regular observation of chats and fora shows that a great number of topics of public concern, either on global, national or local affairs, is tackled by cyber-active citizens. Even if it does not cover all segments of society, a growing communicative activity and more intensive participation can be observed. The range of debated topics is very large: from political to ideological or ethical questions,[32] criticizing decisions on national or local level,[33] as well as more private topics such as dating and pop concerts. The campaign between the two rounds of legislative elections in 2002 in Hungary was marked by an unprecedented intensive use of all ICTs (SMS, e-mail, chats, discussion fora, party politicians telephone calls, correspondence lists) alongside more classical methods (posters, direct mail, leaflets, privately Xeroxed political pamphlets, street manifestations, political meetings, televized delegitimation and mouth-to-ear rumour) (Dányi & Sükösd 2003). It is also worth mentioning that in this Hungarian case wittiness[34] and emotions played an important role in the heated ICT participation of large masses.

It is also clear that new ICTs provide handy communication channels to activities of e-government. There are government and state institutions and municipalities in Hungary with well-designed webpages giving information on local decisions, but also making it possible for citizens to ask questions or react to community affairs. Net polling is also developing.

ICTs also provide comfortable communication channels for all organizing groups as well as for activists trying to mobilize masses for diverse causes. Studying globalization and anti-globalization movements, both Hungarian and international, one can find direct evidence that these movements organise themselves, plan their activities and keep in contact with their activists through ICTs. This is also true in the case of anti- or alter-globalist movements: while attacking globalization, they make use of the fruits of globalization. Serious political analyses, ironical comments, textual, pictorial and film jokes about the Iraq war, the American president, etc. circulate on ICT channels. Pro- and anti-war manifestos, attempts to save Nigerian women from lapidation as well as propositions to smuggle out huge 'black' amounts of money from certain African countries, are sent to either undisclosed recipients or to well-organized networks.[35] These trends might serve as a base for a more active use of devices, not only in private but also in public domains of communication, and feed the hope of a convergent development in the direction of more democracy.

Notes

1. In fact, new research on access and use confirm the re-creation of inequalities through ICTs (access and use highly depending on position in the social stratification and on digital literacy, which itself depends on social position).
2. Need for quick information about directions in an unknown place, etc. Hence, the quickly growing use of hand-held and mobile devices: WAP, PDAs, etc.
3. Accessibility and recordability of music in MP3 format on mobile phones, of video-clips and films on computers, etc.
4. Voice, data, text, picture, film not only on computers but also on mobile phones, PDAs, etc.
5. Passive consumption of cultural products, like watching TV, etc.
6. Cf. the growing importance and the increasing number of e-learning and m-learning projects, of open universities, distance learning, temporary training, recycling or refresher courses, online courses, etc.
7. This is especially characteristic of the central/eastern European societies, where showy consumption competition has been strong in the last decades.
8. The appearance of news radios and news television, media that specialize in political news and which decrease the cycle of information-access (information every 15 minutes) is a clear sign of this phenomenon.
9. Many parents buy mobile phones for their children in order to be in touch with them during the day or during the children's outings for security reasons, but also to be able to control them after school or during their homework.
10. Hotel booking through e-mail after having seen the conditions of accommodation in pictures or film, finding the relevant travel information, etc.
11. See the quickly spreading use of op-logos, personalized mobile phone shells, or the pressing need of certain groups of consumers to possess the latest gadgets with all technological possibilities.

12. According to international research, e-mail traffic is very dense, not only among friends, relatives and workmates but also in interest groups, civil society groups, leisure or hobby groups. A great number of chat and forum talks take place every day on the Net about various public and private topics.

13. This can be proven by such cost-loaded services, where people subscribe for certain ersatz acts of communication: e.g. jokes through SMS, or SMS good-night wishes in Japan, or 'your daily insult' SMS in Norway, etc.

14. Making it possible to pay aggregated monthly bills of various expenses, paying the remote car-parking fee through mobile phone, using Moneo instead of carrying many small coins, etc.

15. Mobile phones tell the time, take pictures and download music; watches can be used as calculators and mini-TV sets, while cameras try to incorporate some functions of the former devices. It is clear that one of the main characteristics of the competing devices is that users wear them on/close to their body most of the time.

16. See various cases of international protest, anti-Bush e-mail jokes before the Iraq war, etc.

17. Many political movements organize their actions through ICTs, there is a dense net of mutually linked webpages of anti-globalization movements, green organizations, etc.

18. The very efficient organization of different world social fora (Rio, Porto Allegre, Genova, etc.) would not have been possible without the use of ICTs.

19. Immediately after Sept. 11th 2001, 33% of American Net users engaged in related online chats and fora. (Horringan et al. 2001)

20. Researchers point to the huge informational potential embedded in social relations. Rheingold, in *The Virtual Community* (1993), emphasizes that one of the main functions of virtual communities is filtering and circulating information. The extremely strong value of these networks lies in the collective reciprocity of participants, which creates efficient basis for trust.

21. E-Europe 2002, E-Europe 2005.

22. Xerox machines, radio-phones, etc. The famous taxi-drivers' blockade in Hungary in the autumn of 1990, which completely paralysed the country for several days, was organized through the net of radio-phones only taxi drivers had at that time.

23. Participation was only expected in rare, highly ritualized mass events of celebrations (e.g. 1st of May demonstration).

24. This is especially true for the last period of the Kádár regime (Wessely 2002).

25. Pictures are famous of the last big 'move': small shabby Trabants carrying on their top huge deep-freezers on the 7th of November 1988 (commemoration day of the Great October Revolution).

26. These gadgets had rather ironical nicknames used by the whole population, like 'blockhead phone', 'bully-phone', etc.

27. See the quick proliferation of satellite dishes and cable TVs.

28. The well-known Trianon trauma, result of the Paris-Versailles treaty.

29. Source: WIP 2002.

30. Source: HIF: Vezetékes gyorsjelentés September 2004.

31. Source: HIF: Digitális mobil gyorsjelentés September 2004.

32. Trust in the results of polling institutes, Hungarian populations in surrounding countries, anti-Semitism, gypsies in the Hungarian society, aesthetic qualities and errors of the new National Theatre, creation of cult films of the former right-wing government, euthanasia, etc.

33. Construction of a new waste incinerator, motorway constructions and prices in certain regions, etc.

34. See the Open Society Archive collection of e-mails and SMSs or the szamizdata.hu webpage of the SZDSZ party.
35. An interesting case of anti-globalization protest of just one person is the widely circulated Nike 'sweatshop' case where Jonah Peretti, a Net-citizen (and MIT media researcher), uses global communication to fight a highly globalized firm.

References

Bourdieu, Pierre (1970), La reproduction, Paris: Minuit.

Bourdieu, Pierre (1979), La distinction, Paris: Minuit.

Dányi, Endre and Miklós Sükösd (2003), 'M-Politics in the Making: SMS and E-mail in the 2002 Hungarian Election Campaign', in Nyíri, Kristóf (ed.) Mobile Communication, Vienna: Passagen Verlag, pp. 211–232.

Dunbar, R. I. M. (1996), Grooming, Gossip and the Evolution of Language, Cambridge, Mass: Harvard University Press.

Elias, Norbert (1939), Über den Prozeß der Zivilisation. Soziogenetische und psychogenetische Untersuchungen. Zweiter Band. Wandlungen der Gesellschaft. Entwurf zu einer Theorie der Zivilisation, Basel: Verlag Haus zum Falken.

Fox, Kate, (2001), Evolution, alienation and gossip. Oxford: Social Issues Research Centre, http://www.sirc.org/publik/gossip.shtml.

Habermas, Jürgen (1962), Strukturwandel der Öffentlichkeit, Berlin: Hermann Luchterhand Verlag.

Hanák, Péter (1992), 'Les traces culturelles d'une histoire discontinue', in: Liber, mars 1992, pp. 14–16.

Heller, Mária, Dénes Némedi and Ágnes Rényi (1990), 'Vázlat a nyilvánosságfogalom értelmezéséhez', in Szabó, Márton (ed): Tükör által homályosan, Budapest: MTA Társadalomtudományi Intézet, pp. 111–123.

Heller, Maria, Dénes Némedi and Ágnes Rényi, (1994), 'Structural changes in the Hungarian public sphere under state socialism', in Seligman, Adam B (ed.) Comparative Social Research, vol. 14. Greenwich, London: JAI Press, pp. 157–171.

Heller, Maria, Dénes Némedi and Ágnes Rényi (1995), 'Populist discursive strategies under state socialism', in: Journal of Popular Culture, 29/2, pp. 129–141.

Heller, Maria and Ágnes Rényi (1996), 'Discource strategies in the new Hungarian public sphere: From the Populist-Urban controversy to the Hungarian – Jewish confrontation', in: Mänicke-Gyöngyösi, K. (ed.), Öffentliche Konfliktdiskurse um Restitution von Gerechtigkeit, Politische Verantwortung und Nationale Identität. Frankfurt/Main: Peter Lang Verlag, pp. 373–392.

Heller, Maria and Ágnes Rényi (2003), 'Public Debate in Hungary on the NATO Alliance. In: Kovács, Andras & Wodak, Ruth (eds.): NATO, Neutrality and National Identity: the case of Austria and Hungary. Wien, Köln, Weimar: Böhlau, pp. 231–280.

Heller, Maria and Ágnes Rényi (2003), 'Joining Nato: The Analysis of a TV-debate on Hungary's alliance with NATO. In: Kovács, Andras & Wodak, Ruth (eds.): NATO, Neutrality and National Identity: the case of Austria and Hungary. Wien, Köln, Weimar: Böhlau, pp. 311–345.

Horrigan, John et alia (2001), Online communities: networks that nurture long-distance relationships and local ties. Pew project,. http://www.pewinternet.org

Keane, John (1995/1), 'Structural transformation of the public sphere', The Communication Review, pp. 1–22.

Noam, Eli M. (1996/4), 'Media trends in the United States. Trends and regulatory responses', Communication and Strategies.

Parks, Malcolm R. (1996), 'Making friends in cyberspace', Journal of Communication 46/1.

Putnam, Robert (2000), *Bowling Alone: the Collapse and revival of American Community*, New York: Simon and Schuster.

Rheingold, Howard (1993), The Virtual Community: Homesteading on the Electronic Frontier. Reading, MA: Addison-Wesley.

Szücs, Jenö (1988), *Nation und Geschichte*, Budapest: Corvina, 1981, or 'Three historical regions of Europe' in Keane, John (ed.), *Civil Society and the State*, London: Verso, pp. 291–332.

Wellman, Barry (2001), 'Computer networks as social networks', *Science*, vol. 293, pp. 2031–2034.

Wessely, Anna (2002), 'Travelling people, travelling objects', Cultural Studies, 16/1.

ePolicies in Europe: A Human-Centric and Culturally Biased Approach

Ursula Maier-Rabler

Introduction

Webster (2002a) states that the concept 'Information Society', which is the usual departure for the development of most European and international ePolicy concepts, is of little use to social scientists, and still less to the wider public's understanding of transformations in the world today. Despite this position, the term Information Society is widely used both within academia and in the wider society. This term, 'Information Society', suggests such a consensual understanding of its meaning that it seems to need no further explication. There are two misleading observations of the concept 'Information Society' commonly used. The fact that there is now a great deal more information available today, more so than a decade ago, and that this omnipresent information, which permeates and influences our everyday experiences, is so readily observable that it has encouraged commentators to declare, more confidently than ever, that we inhabit an Information Society. (Webster 2002a)

A new approach is needed to assist in observing the transformation towards an Information Society: Frank Webster recommends that we should no longer seek quantitative measures of information expansion, but, rather focus on the qualitative changes that have taken place in the ways in which information is used as knowledge. This should be the starting point of our action towards developing practical, innovative and sustainable ePolicies (Webster 2002a).

Keeping this in mind, it becomes evident that we need to shift our research focus back to the people using and/or producing the information. We have to re-conceptualize the concept of development from the popular understanding of economic growth and increases in per capita income, which implies the attainment of a standard of living equivalent to that of an industrialized nation, towards a socially oriented setting in which the capabilities of individuals are taken into account. This means, we need a human-centred approach towards the development of an Information Society (Mansell & Wehn 1998).

This fundamental re-shifting from a qualitative approach to a quantitative approach focused on individuals' capabilities could lead towards real innovation and sustainability within societies.

European policies and national strategies for promoting new technologies within society are subject to qualified critique. We are in the middle of substantial societal transformations. The view of the European Leadership on the transformation processes reduces life to its economic value and is driven by the fear of losing personal, national or European advantages in an accelerated world (Schaper-Rinkel 2003). The question is whether we can find a new quality of social interaction empowered by capable people, and if academic contributions can have an impact on political leadership in Europe.

ePolicies

In September 1993 the Clinton-Gore Administration announced the National Information Infrastructure (NII) Agenda for Action initiative in the US. The primary objective of this initiative was to facilitate development of a national policy that would encourage competition and rapid deployment of new technologies via public-private partnerships. This was to be accomplished by providing a regulatory environment in which the private sector would feel encouraged to make the necessary investments. Despite prior US initiatives (e.g. High Performance Computing Act 1991) and ePolicy papers in other countries (e.g. Singapore's Intelligent Island Initiative 1992/3), the 'NII – Agenda for Action', which was drafted by former US Vice-President Al Gore and Secretary of Commerce Ron Brown, became generally accepted as the world's leading ePolicy concept.

Considering the vital role of the information and communication infrastructure, and realizing that the national telecommunications and information policy had not kept pace with the latest developments in telecommunications and computer technology, the US Administration determined that there was a need for the accelerated deployment of the National Information Infrastructure (NII) Agenda for Action (Malhotra 1995).

The NII Agenda for Action aroused much political debate and made an impact on a global scale. This impact was felt especially by Japan and its Asia Pacific Information Infrastructure (APII) (cf. Harms 1996). Furthermore, many European nations adapted the US paper according to their specific needs, displaying an even more techno-deterministic and marketplace-orientated perspective than the USNII Agenda for Action.

Europe: On its way towards an eEurope

According to Schneider, 'Europe's main handicaps are the fragmentation of the various markets and the lack of interoperable major links. To overcome them it is necessary to mobilise resources and channel endeavours at the European level in a partnership between the public and private sectors' (Schneider 1997). One report launched in June 1994, often referred to as the Bangemann Report, set the tone for most of the subsequently published European ICT strategies. The Report urges the European Union to put its faith predominately in market mechanisms as the motive power to carry Europe into the Information Age.

eEurope as Europe's most elaborate strategy to transform into an Information Society

Since the beginning of the 1990s the importance of the concept of an Information Society for the European Union has increased. In December 1999 the European Commission launched the eEurope Initiative, known as the 'Lisbon Strategy'. Although the strategies and action plans initiated since the Bangemann Report were accepted as successful, new objectives were needed to adapt to the changing conditions (EC 2000b, 5). With the context of the 'Lisbon Strategy' the European Commission committed itself to the objective of making the European Union the most competitive and dynamic knowledge-based economy in the world, with improved employment and social cohesion by the year 2010 (EC 2002a, 2). eEurope reflects the strong belief in the possibilities of potentialities of ICTs to help achieve massive changes within society. The Lisbon Strategy also helps to define Europe's self image as the leading content producer worldwide, identifying its cultural diversity as a strength due to cultural advantages (EC 2000b). Complementary to the eEurope initiative, the European Commission drafted the 'Job Strategies in the Information Society' policy in January 2000. The policy stresses the need for well-functioning capital markets and more competition in product markets in order to foster innovation.

At the Summit in Feira in June 2000, government officials and heads of state committed themselves to a number of practical measures, including target dates, to help bring eEurope forward. This meant that the next step in the elaboration of the political strategies to foster a European Information Society had begun (EC 2000a). Subordinate to the objectives of technological diffusion, by way of a cheaper, faster and more secure Internet, the Action Plan eEurope 2002 placed emphasis on the investment in people and the development of skills while also encouraging broader use of the Internet.

This Action Plan emphasizes the need for developing human capital as a core resource to strengthen Europe's position in the globalized world.

The subsequent eEurope 2005 Action Plan of the European Commission witnessed evidence that many of the objectives of eEurope 2002 had been reached, insofar as an increased number of citizens and businesses are connected to the Internet and, therefore, major changes in society are already visible. The EC proudly states that – as a result of eEurope 2002 – computers and the Internet have been brought into schools across the European Union, governments have been stimulated to go online and attention has been drawn to the need to ensure a safer online world (EC 2002b, 1). The Commission further states that the eEurope programme is providing opportunities for people to participate in society as never before, and it is helping the workforce to acquire the skills needed in a knowledge-driven economy.

Subsequently, the new objectives are now to provide a more favourable environment for private investment and for the creation of new jobs, to boost productivity, to modernize public services and to give everyone the opportunity to participate in the global Information Society. eEurope 2005 also aims to stimulate secure services, applications and content based on a widely available broadband infrastructure (EC 2002b). It seems that the human-oriented objectives to transform Europe into the most competitive economy are perceived as already accomplished, and the needed leadership for successful transition is now focusing again on qualitative technological changes.

This observation becomes more apparent when Schaper-Rinkel states that the European Commission does not actually have a mission to constitute a European Society, rather the mission is to optimize a European market and, therefore, we cannot expect anything other than marketplace-driven ePolicy (Schaper-Rinkel 2003).

This chapter seeks to contribute to finding ways of overcoming the already stated European disadvantage that is a result of its fragmentation in various markets, political and everyday life cultures and the lack of interoperable major links. In the best case the underpinning values of ePolicy could be developed beyond the common understanding of economic growth.

It is the noble goal of all national and international policies to overcome social inequalities. Universal access is seen as the most important prerequisite to increase economic growth and gain competitiveness. This will consequently lead to more wealth, social inclusion and prosperity. Assuming that this simple concept is true, bridging the digital divide would be the most important and only precondition that has to be met in order to achieve a well-functioning and wealthy society. Politicians are very much in favour of this simple linear and techno-deterministic strategy. Clear actions can be taken, such as providing all households and every citizen with Internet access, which is countable and demonstrable. However, it is simply not enough to provide technical access and training on how to operate the technology (Maier-Rabler 2003, 4).

Many hopes have been raised in the context of a movement towards ePolicy on a global scale. The United Nations World Summit of the Information Society [WSIS-Process] narrowly focuses on economic thinking regarding developing ePolicies, wanting to strengthen economic growth and competitiveness through the use of ICTs, along with the general aim of improving lives through alleviating poverty, hunger and diseases, and so, on a more individual level, facilitating one's actions via the new possibilities of public administration (WSIS 2003). The Summit is of interest for this chapter, as the criticism of the rhetoric of the WSIS-Process (e.g. Hamelink 2003) contributes to the re-conceptualization of ePolicy in general.

The re-conceptualization of ePolicy

The network world is malleable. It continues to encourage exchanges of new ideas about how networks can be useful for many people, even though this is still a minority. As Pierre Lévy, a French commentator on the Internet Age, puts it, the power of networks could profoundly reshape social bonds in the direction of a greater sense of community and help us to resolve the problems currently facing humanity (Mansell and Wehn 1998).

This view provides the basis for further work towards a re-conceptualization of ePolicy, whereby Hamelink defines improvement in the field of ePolicy by utilizing two important guidelines, which are that every human being has a right to a decent livelihood and that all people should be allowed to participate on equal terms in decisions that affect their lives (Hamelink 2003).

Mansell broadens the concept from a techno-deterministic approach by coupling the topic of the Digital Divide to the individual capacities on which ePolicy should focus. Ability is not about simply acquiring skills to get on the Internet, nor using the World Wide Web and the services provided. Nor is Mansell talking about the new strategies in terms of eGoverment, eCommerce and so on, which is the main topic of the European Communities and their goals within eEurope 2002 and 2005. The concept of capabilities Mansell is introducing is based on the work of Amartya Sen and refers to acquired cognitive capacities and the ability to discriminate between alternative choices.

Present ePolicy strategies do not provide the right environment for human-centric approaches as demonstrated by the capabilities approach. Such a policy would represent a needs-based approach to new media and the Internet with respect to people's entitlements and human rights. It is therefore proposed that policy actions should ensure that the new media provide electronic spaces where people can acquire new abilities that can assist them in managing their daily lives (Mansell 2001).

Capabilities, in the sense of the meaning proposed by Sen, must not be associated with the development of human capital (skills) in the context of economy-driven, workplace-politic. Therefore, the public sector, if any, and the so-called civil society must be the advocates for the creation of a designated electronic space wherein people's entitlements will be supported. This raises the question of what capabilities people are entitled to acquire. What are the freedoms that people are entitled to in the Internet

Age? Most of the attention of media and communications policy is on markets and regulation, access to technology and on the costs of reducing social exclusion. But, much more is at stake and the necessity is for many more people to acquire new forms of capabilities of the kind Amartya Sen has proposed and what Roger Silverstone calls media literacies (Mansell 2001).

Media literacies are crucial. They go far beyond knowing how to read and understand what we see and hear in the traditional media, or by accessing the Internet. Without the ability to achieve these literacies, problems of alienation, poverty and ignorance, and – indeed – of terrorism, will worsen. This is because relatively few individuals will have the capabilities to improve their own lives or to express their own opinions about what they value. Castells has examined what he calls institutional capabilities, such as those for making policy and for regulating in areas like intellectual property protection, electronic commerce or broadcasting. Often this leads to interesting debates about Internet-related skills, but rarely does it lead to a discussion about rights and entitlements. To delve into this discussion, we need a rather different starting point. In building his idea of capabilities, Sen writes about the concept of functionings. Functionings, he says, are what people may value doing or being. Functionings may be very basic, like being free from hunger or illness. They can also be very complex, such as being able to participate in the life of a community or having self-respect. Sen argues that capabilities are the combinations of functionings that an individual is actually able to achieve (Mansell 2001).

In his critique of the WSIS-Process, Hamelink stated that in their current form WSIS-strategies provide no serious support for social development. The main issues for critique regarding global ePolicy are that it tends to strengthen the world's rich countries and leaves the developing countries behind. The intellectual property rights policies protect the content more than the author and deny access to users. The lack of human rights-inspired conventions permeates nearly every aspect of the official pan-European discourse on the Information Society. This attitude leads to a worsening of social relations and social welfare and does little to promote decent livelihoods or encourage people's participatory function. And, last but not least, this [WSIS] discourse shows also a lack of academic research (Hamelink 2003).

According to Hamelink, the first area of research should be concerned with the design of democratic and pro-active policies and programmes that make it possible to realize the social development potential of digital technologies. It is, therefore, necessary to study the roles and functions that the public and private sector play in the design and execution of these policies, the essential interventions to accord technical changes to social development and the relation between producers and consumers of ICT so that they respond to social needs. The second area should take into consideration a definition of social and institutional changes necessary to maximize the benefits and minimize the risks of the new technologies. Within this area it would be a requirement to adapt the structures relevant for productivity, participation and cultural diversity to the desirable result of a positive social scenario as well as to develop appropriate educational methods and material. Thirdly, it is important to create technologies that reduce the use of energy-intensive resources and to encourage the environmentally sustainable application of digital technologies to strengthen sustainable processes of social development. There are also country studies needed to explore the specific national needs and conditions. The encouragement of relationships between different forces such as politics, the economy, the regions, etc. have to be researched, as well the strategies through which those affected by technological development can benefit (Hamelink 2003).

Old versus new ePolicy

As stated earlier, this chapter wants to contribute to discovering ways to overcome the European policy disadvantage as a result of its fragmentation into various markets, and in political and everyday-life cultures, and in the lack of interoperable major links. It aims to analyse European ePolicy strategies in order to determine which focus is set by governmental activities to accompany the transformation of our societies into the so-called Information Society, both on a national and European level. Therefore, the analysis is driven by the critique of the rhetoric and practice of ongoing ePolicies and orientated towards a human-centred and rights-based approach.

The 'New ePolicy Model' provides the basis for a substantially new orientation in ePolicy, going beyond the mainstream techno-deterministic ePolicy, which is predominately economically driven and targeted to overcome the Digital Divide. The suggested new policy is characterized by the shift from building infrastructure to creating identities. In other words, from bridging the digital divide to closing the knowledge gap (Maier-Rabler 2003).

This means putting the individual, not technology, at the centre of ePolicy, and therefore ensuring that cognitive, cultural and social factors become the determining elements of a new ePolicy. Following Mansell's suggestion to adopt a rights-based capabilities approach, future ePolicy will have to ensure equal chances for access to technology and knowledge in order for people to acquire capabilities in the context of ICT.

The model of a new ePolicy, as depicted below in figure 1, attempts to unify all the relevant factors for a re-conceptualization of ePolicy. The model is a four-fold matrix in which the upper fields refer to the necessity of building infrastructure, both on a technical and on a human/individual level. These fields show how universal access and skills (such as computer literacy) are important foundations for the creation of the electronic space that supports individual entitlement. But access and skills are not enough. As the arrows indicate, the move to the individual identity level is indispensable.

The lower fields of the matrix refer to cognition on the human/individual dimension and to capabilities that can be identified with the technology dimension. Without evoking cognitive processes on an individual level (e.g. awareness programmes), no reasonable choice in order to acquire the necessary capabilities can be made.

The following explorative analysis of European ePolicy papers examines the predominating dimensions: Access, Skills, Cognition and Capabilities. These dimensions have been targeted in most strategy papers. The hypothesis is that access and skills still predominate and that awareness programmes that stimulate cognitive processes are slowly developing.

Another hypothesis is that the distribution of the different main directions of ePolicies follows, among other things, culturally biased underpinnings. These underpinnings are mostly invisible and citizens and politicians are unaware of their power. In the model of a new ePolicy it is indicated as 'Cultural-social Environment'.

ePolicy-Cultures: The socio-cultural environment of ePolicy
The notion of the value of information and the dynamics of actions according to ePolicy concepts differ throughout Europe, which is also partly a result of different political cultures. The main handicaps for Europe's politics are the fragmentation of various

Figure 1. Model of a new ePolicy (Maier-Rabler 2003).

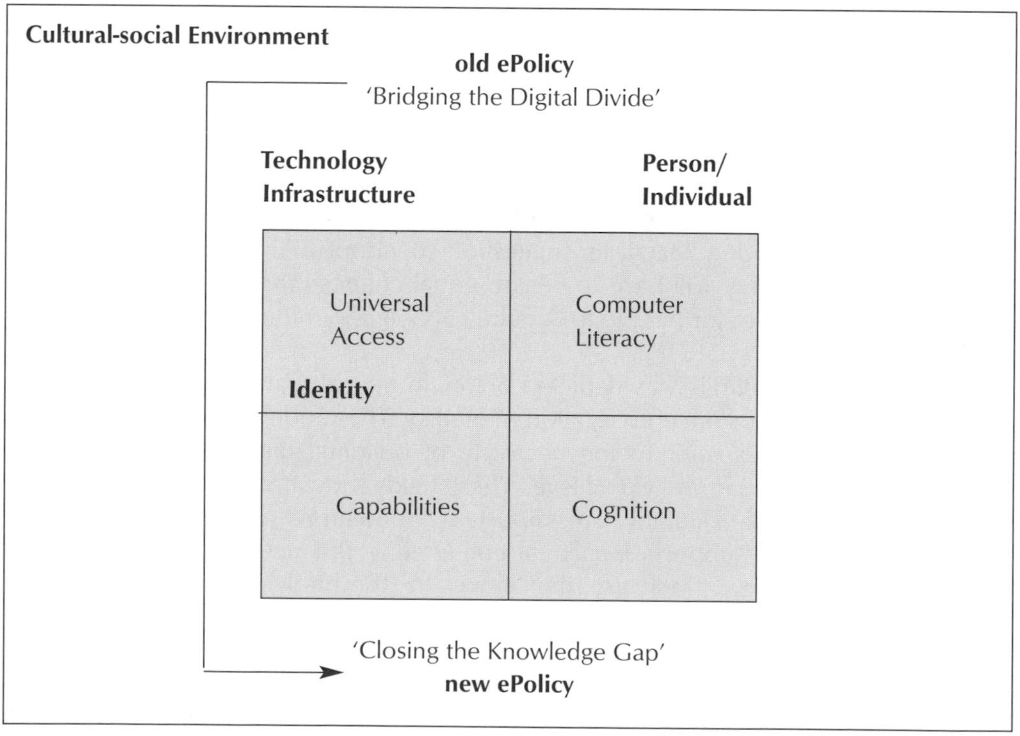

markets, the lack of interoperable major links, the dominance of national governments and the existence of special national policy cultures.

Despite the fact that international institutions, international markets and technology developments are all mechanisms that may constrain national policies, national variations of policy papers seem to persist. 'Policy-makers still have significant degrees of freedom and many choose different solutions to similar challenges' (Storsul 2002).

Policy divergence in Europe

Many different approaches to help explain these policy differences exist. Some are politically driven. For example, Esping-Andersen's approach of different political regimes differentiates between liberal regimes (entitlement rules are strict and often associated with stigma), conservative regimes (rights are attached to class and status and the redistributive impacts are negligible, are typically shaped by the church and committed to preserving traditional family values), and social democratic regimes (emphasis on universal rights instead of proven needs). The ideal is equality of the highest standards, not of the minimal needs (Esping-Andersen in Storsul 2002).

As a result of such different regimes, diverse Welfare State Models constitute the varying state arrangements and the different frameworks for ePolicies.

Other possible approaches based on concepts like 'Dependency' demonstrate how small states and states which are economically weaker and have a geographical disadvantage (e.g. the new member states) may face special challenges as they are dependent on the leading nations within the Union and therefore must adjust their policies to the European mainstream, even if their national policy cultures are different.

It is known that there is a broad body of Policy Studies dealing with the heterogeneity of European politics. For the purpose of this chapter we are looking for a broader approach, including not only political practice, but, also long-lasting and mostly unconscious societal underpinnings.

In the context of research concerned with the formation of state systems and nation-building, Rokkan (2000) introduced a set of more or less stable dimensions which can be perceived as historical crossroads for nations.

Depending on which way a state system was established, and within the context of certain predominating dimensions, up-to-date policies, party systems and political actions can be explained and understood.

The following dimensions or crossroads have been defined by Rokkan: (1) Reformation (division into Catholic, Protestant and religiously mixed parts in Europe); (2) National revolution (differences between centre and periphery, language groups, etc.); (3) Industrial Revolution (cleavages along agricultural and urban industrial interests and along owners and employees); (4) International revolution (cleavages into communism and socialism).

In the context of political development Rokkan is intensely concerned with the ideas of the European nation state and its democratization. He deals with the basic character of new political systems and is interested in the differences of the structural characteristics and developments of each European nation. Rokkan attempts to develop a model in order to explain the complex structure of European heterogeneity. This model is based upon six structure variables, two economic, two cultural and two geopolitical structure perspectives (Rokkan 2000).

The economic structure can be divided into an agrarian and a city-centred aspect with the result of a different economic basis. The cultural structure can be seen from an ethnic and linguistic aspect with effects on the respective cultural unification. The geopolitical structure refers to the early or late installation of governments. Furthermore, Rokkan defines four key variables that are decisive in the process of shaping political systems. Two economic variables, the independence and dependence of city dispersion and the degree of agricultural development, and two cultural variables, independence and dependence of church and autonomy or unification of territorial languages (Rokkan 2000).

This model forms the basis for Rokkan's conceptual map of Europe, which tries to explain the European structure relating to space and time and where he designed a typological interpretation of conditions for the development of political systems (Rokkan 2000).

Rokkan identifies an early formation of centralistic national states in western Europe, federal systems in central Europe and empires in the East. There was a concentration of landed property in Great Britain, in parts of Prussia east of the Elbe, in Danube-Austria and also in the north of France and in the south of Italy and Spain. In Scandinavia, the Netherlands, Switzerland and in great areas of Western Germany the situation was characterized by a dominance of independent farmers. Areas with high concentration of landed property foster the development of strong nation states – first in the West (England, France and Spain), later in the East (Austria, Prussia).

The city-belt from northern Italy to Flanders and the Baltic countries (including the northwest Mediterranean area) developed as a result of intensive trade relations. Dense settlement and powerful cities characterize the west of the city-belt, while the eastern part remained less populous and therefore less powerful.

The Protestant North was dominated by state churches and high religious homogeneity – such as Scandinavia, Great Britain and Prussia. The state churches became the fundamental basis for the formation of states. The Netherlands, Switzerland, parts of Western Germany and Ireland were characterized by different religious beliefs and therefore by religious heterogeneity, although with Protestant dominance. France, the south of Europe and also central and eastern Europe were Catholic areas where the Catholic Church was supra-territorial and also homogeneous. In the south, however, the process of the formation of states was slowed down by the supra-territorial Catholic Church because of the fact that Latin was used as the universal language by the elites. In Belgium, Ireland and Poland the Catholic Church became important only after the French Revolution.

With reference to language, Rokkan distinguishes countries with unitarian systems, in which one main language is spoken, such as England, France, Denmark, Sweden, Portugal, Italy and Germany. A strong language and an early formation of states reinforce each other. On the other hand, Rokkan lists countries with more than one language within the political territory – for example, Switzerland, Belgium or Spain. Rokkan referred to Norwegian, Finish, Icelandic and Irish as '... winning peripheral languages with their one standard and political independence...' (Rokkan 2000).

Rokkan's work supports the hypothesis that the variations of ePolicies follow besides other culturally biased underpinnings. These underpinnings are mostly invisible and citizens and politicians are unaware of their power. In the 'New ePolicy Model' they are indicated as 'Cultural-social Environment'.

Cultural-ethical approach to diversity
In the context of ePolicy, which is also part of a European and national information and communication policy, the underlying culture of information plays a major role in developing strategies and actions.

Attitudes towards freedom of information and access to knowledge had always had a strong connection to the predominating religious, cultural and ethical systems. Therefore, Rokkan's 'Reformation' dimension, combined with the cultural variables, independence and dependence of church and autonomy or unification of territorial languages, provides a promising approach for the development of an empirical measurement of information cultures.

Another attempt to define different cultures of information derives from a prior study conducted by the author. The study measures the degree of transparency in European press statistics compared to those of the United States and Canada (Maier-Rabler & Sütterlütti 1992). The study found correlations between the predominating culture of information transparency and open access to information for all, in relation to the quality of press statistics. Transferred to the problematique of ePolicies in Europe, this suggests that in countries or regions where access to information and freedom of information is a basic human right, ePolicy actions tend to be more elaborated in a human-centred and cognition-orientated manner and thereby less techno-deterministic.

According to the results of the press statistics study, four different types of information cultures were defined based on the European and North American countries included in the study. These information cultures are the following: (1) Catholic-feudalistic information culture, (2) Protestant-enlightened information culture, (3) Socio-democratic liberal information culture, and (4) Socialist-Centralistic information culture.

Catholic-feudalistic information culture

The belief that 'Information and Knowledge is Power' is a guiding principle within this culture, which still influences the invisible underpinnings of ePolicy primarily in the central European region. Information is treated as a scarce resource and its distribution still follows hierarchically defined pathways from top to bottom. There is no general right to gain information. People are not trained to retrieve information by themselves. Who gets which information is still defined by authorities such as government, schools and church. The information provider, and not the user, is in the centre of information design. The Internet is perceived as a tool contributing to further information overload that does not deliver the right answers to questions that are not formulated. Business information is treated as a secret and neither businesses nor governments provide really relevant information. People are not trained to ask for it.

Protestant-enlightened information culture

The guiding principle of the Protestant-enlightened information culture can be described as 'Transparency/Success through information'. This type of information culture is predominant in countries based on economic liberalism, as in the USA, where the free flow of information is a fundamental condition for economic success. A special version of this culture is the socio-democratic liberal information culture, described in the next paragraph. In contrast to the Catholic-feudalistic information culture, economic profits are basically positive and also generously published. Government and political parties make intense use of the Internet in order to bring as much information to the customer/citizen as possible. People are aware that information retrieval is a right and an individual duty. The Internet is the ideal infrastructure for this type of information culture and it is not accidental that the Internet has been developed within this type of information culture.

Socio-democratic liberal information culture

The information-rights of the individual are put at the centre of the socio-democratic liberal information culture that predominately characterizes the Scandinavian countries and parts of the Benelux states. Information is a precondition for the political emancipation of the individual. In this social democratic liberal information culture, free access to information is a basic right and is seen as a condition for the public control of government. Because of their liberal tradition Scandinavia has the most advanced constitutional framework delineating the free access of information. A question-approach describes this information culture, in contrast to the answer-approach of the Catholic-feudalistic tradition. The right of participation as a prerequisite for democracy is a result of this information culture. The diffusion of the Internet in countries with a socio-democratic liberal information culture is favoured, compared with the Catholic-feudalistic tradition; which makes clear that different ePolicies have to be developed according to different information cultures.

Socialist-Centralistic information culture

This type of information culture is more or less non-existant in Europe, but, it is mentioned in order to develop an understanding for the special needs for ePolicy in the new member states. In the former communist eastern states a systematic exchange of information between the centre and the periphery was established. Therefore people, especially employees, were trained to communicate success. This is an important precondition for the successful establishment and usage of the Internet. Besides their eagerness to adopt western European standards (Rokkan's Dependency argument), these countries are favoured as information-friendly compared to some other central European states in terms of information policy (Maier-Rabler/Sütterlütti 1992).

European ePolicy analysis

Within the context of comparative policy research, it is fairly easy to observe that there are a lot of problems regarding international convergences. The development of international economics, cross-border consequences of national activities and the establishment of the European Union in particular, have highlighted the importance of comparative policy research. But, experienced scientists conducting this research consistently remark that similar policy programmes do not have the same consequences and outcomes in each individual state (Feick 1983).

The following are the results based on the findings of a small explorative study conducted at the University of Salzburg, which analyzed ePolicy papers of eight selected European countries according to the fields of ePolicy as we have described in the 'New ePolicy Model'.

The countries included in the study were Germany, the United Kingdom and Spain as representatives of big European countries with different backgrounds concerning information cultures; Finland as a Scandinavian country with a distinct liberal information culture; Austria as representative of a Catholic-feudalistic information culture; Greece as a peripheral EU member state with a low GNP; Hungary as a representative of a new EU member state and Romania as an EU-candidate country.

The ePolicy papers analysed during this study had to be from governmental sources. Most of them were retrieved from government websites, and in some cases directly from governmental officials. The analysis was conducted as an explorative study and is considered to be a model for future empirical research in which major methodological questions will have to be clarified. It was not possible to define the basis (N) of ePolicy papers in the individual countries, therefore, we were not able to evaluate the sample (n). In Romania we included 103 papers in the analysis, while in Spain we could not find more than 19 official papers.

Methodology

Each paper was analysed according to four categories: (1) access, (2) skills, (3) cognition/awareness, and (4) capabilities.

The following definitions of the categories were the basis for our analysis.

Access

Access is the technical prerequisite for people to use new media. Policy papers that aim to improve or create infrastructure and also access to infrastructure have been counted under this category. This includes strategies aiming for universal access, supporting citizens with Internet connections, establishing broadband connections for businesses, schools, households, the installation of public terminals, the equipment of schools, libraries with computers and Internet access. Additionally, actions aiming for regulation of costs and tariffs for Internet connection were counted in the access category.

Technology strategies were not the only variables counted in the access category, but also actions aiming for the creation of content that allows access to institutions and governmental authorities (e.g. eHealth, eGovernment). If the content strategies were targeted not only to provide access to already available information of institutions, but also to create new content, the strategies were also counted under the 'cognition/ awareness' category.

Skills

ePolicies aiming for the transfer of knowledge of how to handle technology were counted under the skills category. Skills are abilities to work with computer programmes (e.g. browsers; e-mail programmes), and how to use existing technology. The category summarizes training programmes (e.g. Internet for elderly people children and housewives) but also subsidized training programmes of local/regional adult education or similar projects. Skills remain a technological category, since skills in the context of this study does not adapt technology to individual needs but adapts people to existing technologies.

Cognition

Cognition means understanding. Projects that were placed in the cognition category were those aimed at making people really understand the impact of new technology and the Internet on their personal lives. Programmes, strategies and actions dedicated to cognition asked for the individual identification of potentials, advantages and disadvantages. Cognition can also be described as an individual learning process, to foster self-knowledge and being aware how new technologies will affect one's personal life. This category is the indispensable precondition for moving forward to the capabilities category.

Cognition can be found in projects and strategies recognizing the necessity of ongoing work, e.g. a network for ICTs research, continuing processes like regular support, keeping the projects vivid so individuals have the chance to be aware of the needs of ICT.

Capability

Capabilities are acquired cognitive capacities and the ability to discriminate between alternative choices. ePolicies which could have been placed within this category, which were non-existent in this analysis, must support the development of capabilities.

This approach allows individuals to categorize the level of importance regarding special technologies, special applications, and special skills in relation to their work and everyday lives.

The goal of this capability approach is to help make people sovereign within the context of new technologies. At this level the individual knows how to adopt technology according to their needs and not the other way round.

Conclusion

Different degree of access and transparency

The access to European ePolicy papers is different from country to country and also to some extent the type of information accessed. In Austria, for example, strategies and actions are hard to collect; there is no general overview paper. Spain, on the other hand, provides detailed information on the Web, but only in Spanish. As not all European policy papers are translated into English, language is one of the barriers that directly affect access and transparency. Although the European Union makes efforts to unify the member countries, the difference of language has a dividing tendency. In some countries there exists only a short version of the policy paper in English, in other countries no translation at all. The official argument to explain this fact is often 'financial problems', but, if something were regarded as really important, the money would not be the problem (e.g. in Romania, where all ePolicies are available in English).

Table 1.

	EPOLICY ANALYSIS	N	ACCESS	SKILLS	COGNITION	CAPABILITY
1	Germany	29	89,66%	3,45%	13,79%	0,00%
2	Romania	103	77,67%	10,68%	16,50%	0,00%
3	Greece	123	52,85%	19,51%	34,96%	0,00%
4	Austria	56	75,00%	26,79%	8,93%	0,00%
5	Spain	19	100,00%	10,53%	5,26%	0,00%
6	United Kingdom	42	78,57%	11,90%	14,29%	0,00%
7	Hungary	49	77,55%	24,49%	6,12%	0,00%
8	Finland	68	64,71%	16,18%	25,00%	0,00%

Therefore the translation of policies into English is more a question of priorities than of finance.

There are two distinct points of view concerning availability and comprehensibility: external and interior transparency.

External transparency

Information is given to an international forum, which includes an easy access and an English translation. Countries that want to establish a profile and show that they are a good partner in the European Union, aim at external transparency. Hungary or Romania, for example, and other countries that want to join the European Union, are quite ambitious about publishing their efforts to catch up to common European standards in the field of information technologies.

Interior transparency

Countries target information predominately at their own citizens to boost the acceptance of IT and to help to establish and reinforce confidence in the new technologies. Important papers are not translated into English and are therefore intended just for the national population. The German paper, for example, contains only a translation of the strategies and single projects were just mentioned as examples without any further information. Finland, one of the front runners, also seems to favour keeping its knowledge within its own borders, as the master paper is only in Finnish and does not even mention any specific project. It is strange that Finland, as a country with a great tradition of the right of free access to information, does not provide any information about its specific projects.

Strategies and actions are hard to distinguish

After observing the countries examined in this study, it is difficult to distinguish between strategies and actions. The ePolicy paper of Greece, for example, makes it quite difficult to distinguish between actions and strategies, as both fields are written without separation. The UK paper sometimes makes this distinction difficult as well. Germany on the other hand gives exact information and a clear division. Finland and Hungary do not give any information about concrete actions, only about strategies. In this case some strategies might already classify as actions. The difficulties in distinguishing strategies from actions are due to the lack of specific information and also to the fact that the English expression 'action' can be translated into German with 'aktion' as well as 'strategie'. This fact reduced the possibilities of our small study, since we assumed that the differences between strategies and actions as strategies would be more homogeneous throughout Europe as, according to the eEurope policy, actions are supposed to express the predominating local/regional/national priorities that are the result of underlying socio-cultural values.

ePolicy is dominated by e-government

The EU and the national governments seem to be convinced that a highly developed level of e-government also implies a high level in the development towards an

Information Society. Online public administration services are a significant cornerstone of the Information Society. Therefore most ePolicies have concentrated on e-government. The reasons are manifold, but two predominate: (1) eGovernment applications are seen as a means to persuade citizens to use the new media, to break down borders between the administration and the citizen and to reduce fears of technology. (2) eGovernment-applications boost eCommerce. Citizens trained by eGovernment applications are good customers for eCommerce. Additionally eGovernment strengthens local and regional hard- and software business and, in its original sense, eGovernment tends to reduce bureaucracy, make administrative work more efficient and helps to save money.

Authentication and security go hand in hand

Authentication and security are two aspects that depend heavily on confidence and reliability. eGovernment and eCommerce depend on a functioning authentication system. As a result of the dominance of eGovernment in ePolicies, the development of secure computing is also a dominating goal of ePolicies throughout Europe. IT security, providing data protection and fighting crime on the Internet are becoming more and more important.

ePolicy characteristics

The new media policy debates widely concentrate on legal issues, regulations and aspects of access. This perspective covers only a fraction of the entire debate concerning ePolicies. As critical authors state, ePolicy is largely dominated by techno-deterministic and market-oriented approaches. The individual human being, his/her cognitive capacities, his/her values and his/her capabilities in the context of new technologies are neglected.

The ICT education programmes that are suggested and supported in most of the existing ePolicies are aimed in the first instance at making people more productive at work, in schools or at the university and not aimed at showing them how to acquire the capabilities needed to become critical and informed participants in the so-called Internet Age.

What remains a methodological challenge is to deliver the empirical evidence of different ePolicy actions in European countries with different socio-cultural underpinnings. Aside from this problematic definition of socio-cultural environments, the difficulties of differentiation of strategies and actions have to be first addressed. Simple observations indicate that the basic political system, and legal, ethical and religious presuppositions, all have influence on new media policies. This means, therefore, that the same ePolicy programmes (e.g. eEurope) will not have the same consequences and outcomes in each individual state (Feick 1983).

References

APII CC (2003), History. Retrieved 7 December 2003 from http: //www.apiicc.org/eng/about/history.html.

Bangemann, M. et al. (1994), Europe and the global information society – Bangemann report. Retrieved 8 December 2003 from http: //europa.eu.int/ISPO/infosoc/backg/bangeman.html.

Castells, Manuel (2001), Das Informationszeitalter Bd. 1. Der Aufstieg der Netzwerkgesellschaft. Opladen: Leske + Budrich.

Castells, Manuel (2001), The Internet Galaxy. Reflections on the Internet, Business, and Society. New York: Oxford University Press.

EC – European Commission (1994), Europe's way to the Information Society. An action plan. COM (94) 347. Brussels.

EC – European Commission (2000a), eEurope 2002. An Information Society For All. Action Plan prepared by the Council and the European Commission for the Feira European Council. Retrieved 21 December 2003 from http: //europa.eu.int/information_society/eeurope/2002/action_plan/pdf/actionplan_en.pdf.

EC – European Commission (2000b), eEurope. An Information Society For All. Communication on a Commission Initiative for the Special European Council of Lisbon. Brussels. 2000. Retrieved 21 December 2003 from http: //europa.eu.int/information_society/eeurope/2002/news_library/pdf_files/initiative_en.pdf.

EC – European Commission (2002a), eEurope 2005. An Action Plan to be presented in view of the Sevilla European Council, 21/22 June 2002. Retrieved 21 December 2003 from http: //europa.eu.int/information_society/eeurope/2002/news_library/documents/eeurope2005/eeurope2005_en.pdf.

EC – European Commission (2002b), eEurope 2005 Executive summary. Retrieved 21 December 2003 from http: //europa.eu.int/information_society/eeurope/2002/news_library/documents/eeurope2005/execsum_en.pdf.

Esping Anderson, Gøsta (1990), The Three Worlds of Welfare Capitalism. Cambridge: Polity Press.

Feick, Jürgen (1983), Internationale Vergleichbarkeit staatlicher Interventionsprogramme. Konzeptionelle und methodische Probleme. In: Mayntz, Renate (Hrsg.) (1983). Implementation politischer Programme II. Ansätze zur Theoriebildung. Opladen: Westdeutscher Verlag, 197–220.

Gandy, Oscar, H. Jr (2002), The Real Digital Divide: Citizens vs. Consumers. In: Lievrouw, Leah A.; Livingstone, Sonia (eds.). The Handbook of New Media. Social Shaping and Consequences of ICTs. London, Thousand Oaks, New Delhi: Sage Publications, 448–460.

Hamelink, Cees (2003), Draft introductory paper for the UNRISD workshop 'Understanding Informational Developments: mapping a future research agenda', Geneva, 26th-27th September 2003. An analysis of the WSIS discourse.

Harms, J. M. (1996), Wirtschaft an der Schwelle zum Informationszeitalter. In: Frankfurter Rundschau (Cebit Beilage), 12.03.1996, 3.

Maier-Rabler, Ursula (2003), Reconceptualizing e-Policy. From bridging the Digital Divide to closing the Knowledge Gap..

Maier-Rabler, Ursula/Sutterlütti, Erich (1992), Pressestatistik im Internationalen Vergleich. Endbericht des Teilprojekts „Pressestatistik und Datenkoordination' im Rahmen des international vergleichenden Forschungsprogramms „Ökonomie und Zukunft der Printmedien'; eine Studie im Auftrag des Bundesministeriums für Wissenschaft und Forschung. Salzburg.

Malhotra, Y., Al-Shehri, A., Jones, J. J. (1995), National Information Infrastructure: Myths, Metaphors And Realities. Retrieved 7 December 2003 from http://www.brint.com/papers/nii/.

Mansell, Robin and Wehn, Uta (1998), Knowledge Societies: Information Technology for Sustainable Development. New York: Oxford University Press.

Mansell, Robin (2001), New Media and the Power of Networks. First Dixons Public Lecture and Inaugural Professorial Lecture. Dixons Chair in New Media and the Internet. The London School of Economics and Political Science. http://www.lse.ac.uk/collections/media@lse/pdf/rmlecture.pdf (Oct. 2004).

National Computer Board, Singapore (1997), IT2000 – A Vision Of An Intelligent Island. Retrieved 21 December 2003 from http://web.bilkent.edu.tr/mirrors/www.ncb.gov.sg/ncb/vision.asp.

Rokkan, Stein (2000), Staat, Nation und Demokratie in Europa: die Theorie Stein Rokkans. Aus seinen gesammelten Werken rekonstruiert und eingeleitet von Peter Flora. 1. Auflage. Frankfurt am Main: Suhrkamp.

Sandfort, S. (1993), The Intellegent Island. In: Wired 1.04. Sep/Oct 1993. Retrieved 21 December 2003 from http://www.wired.com/wired/archive/1.04/sandfort.html?pg=1&topic.

Schaper-Rinkel, Petra (2003), Die europäische Informationsgesellschaft. Technologische und politische Integration in der europäischen Politik. Münster: Westfälisches Dampfboot.

Schmidt, Manfred (1995), Policy-Analyse. In: Mohr, Arno (Hrsg:). Grundzüge der Politikwissenschaft. München/Wien: Oldenburg, 566–604.

Schneider, V. (1997), Different roads to the information society? Comparing U.S. and European Approaches from a public policy perspective. In: The social shaping of information superhighways. European and American roads to the information society. Ed. Herbert Kubicek, William H. Dutton, Robin Williams. Frankfurt/Main: Campus Verlag; New York: St. Martin's Press, 299–339.

Sen, Amartya (2000), Ökonomie für den Menschen. Wege zu Gerechtigkeit und Solidarität in der Marktwirtschaft. München/Wien: Carl Hanser Verlag.

Storsul, Tanja (2002), Transforming Telecommunications. Democratising Potential, Distributive Challenges and Political Change. Thesis submitted for the degree of dr. polit. June 2002. Department of Media and Communication, University of Oslo. Oslo: GCS Media AS.

Webster, Frank (2002a), The Information Society Revisited. In: Lievrouw, Leah A.; Livingstone, Sonia (eds.). The Handbook of New Media. Social Shaping and Consequences of ICTs. London, Thousand Oaks, New Delhi: Sage Publications, 22–33.

Webster, Frank (2002b), Theories of the Information Society. 2nd ed. London, N.Y.: Routledge.

White House, The (1993), National Information Infrastructure: Agenda for Action. Retrieved 28 December 2003 from http://www.ibiblio.org/nii/toc.html.

WSIS – World Summit on the Information Society. Geneva 2003 – Tunis 2005. (2003), retrieved 12 January 2004 from http://www.itu.int/wsis/basic/about.html.

SECTION 2: Techno-Pleasure

The first chapter provides a background to understanding how computer games have come to occupy their current position in our culture. It sets out to suggest a rough theoretical categorization of some of the central pleasures offered by the medium. Focusing on the concept of 'cultural value' is an attempt to address a concern for 'healthy values' in the public discourses about games. However, the emphasis in this chapter is not on worrying effects of violent games nor on the dangers of addiction. It also does not attempt to discuss computer games' direct capacity for instrumental learning, a concern, which – understandably – is becoming more central to parents, teachers and researchers as games become more technologically advanced and an increasingly dominant activity in the lives of young people. Instead, the discussion of values deals with some broader issues raised by different types and genres of pleasurable technological involvements. While they create pleasure, all of these also have to do with learning in one form or another. Any competitive game is, by definition, about challenge, learning and mastery. As an absolute prerequisite for deriving fun and pleasure from a computer game, the player has to learn typical ways of operating the digital machine and typical ways of responding to challenges as they are configured, according to different logics and cultural rationales. Rarely, if ever at all, are these various modes and paradigms of learning given meaning within any pedagogic institutional or cultural framework – and when they are, the rhetoric of sanctioned education tends to take the fun out of it.

The chapter title, 'The cultural value of games', taken as a promise, can be somewhat misleading. Computer games are complex and diverse, and we cannot point to a single and unified set of beneficial values that they are supposed to promote. The aim of the present chapter is merely to direct the attention to some central generic distinctions within the aesthetics of computer games that are mostly overlooked in cultural policy debates. A more precise but somewhat clunky description of this contribution would probably be 'the techno-cultural value of games' in so far as the emphasis is solely on values that relate to the role of technology in the society. Within the broad category of 'computer games' we find various – and largely unrecognized – values that are 'cultural' in a more traditional and literary sense. For further research, it would be interesting to look more into the overlaps and interconnections between, on the one hand, the fictional and narrative worlds of game genres and, on the other hand, their techno-political interpretations.

The second chapter presents a case study in the design of computerized museum visitor support. The background for the project is a growing concern among cultural policy-makers, educators and museum management that museums are getting out of touch with younger generations. At the same time, cultural heritage, and information about it, is being digitalized. It seems inevitable that museums make use of networked interactive media in order to enrich and add to current ways of presenting exhibits. How to shape such new ways of presenting is the main research question addressed. The modest scale of the studies reported does not allow jumping to general conclusions, but they illustrate some meaningful and interesting trends in what museums and visitors want from new media technology in cultural institutions.

One focus of the study is on what Dutch visitors want and do not want from computer support systems. It appeared that they do want more emotionally involving and self-controlled forms of experience and learning. Along with this there seemed to be a wish for some form of customizing of the exhibited content and presentation to fit personal wishes and desires. Our informants were ready to do 'work' in order to get at contents and presentations they wanted. That is, they often preferred finding out what is interesting by active search to being advised by a system in some authoritative way. In addition it was observed that the need for autonomy that might be answered by a support system was not as strong in every visitor category. In particular, student test visitors with a migrant family background and less versed in European culture seemed to prefer more guidance in comparison to student test visitors from traditional Dutch homes, who are more familiar with the Dutch and European heritage. Another focus is on what museums want to offer to, and achieve in, their visitors. The international museums under investigation are keen to use technology to enrich and personalize visitor experiences and to make these more vivid, intense and adventurous. Learning includes both emotion and pleasure, however, entertainment *per se*, as a means to attract visitors, is firmly rejected and left to *theme parks*.

The two contributions in this section share an interest in the role of digital technology in entertainment and learning. They can be seen as two mirroring approaches to the relationship between 'techno-entertainment' and 'techno-learning'. One investigates genres of computerized entertainment, the other explores the possibilities of computerized learning systems. Both are concerned with how specific technologies mediate cultural experiences. The digital learning approach looks at an explicitly didactic institutional framework: the museum. The digital games approach implies a decidedly non-pedagogic institutional framework: the entertainment industry.

The general notion of 'techno-pleasure' that we have chosen as the title for this section indicates that the relationship between entertainment technology and didactic technology is a dialectic one. The pleasurable experience that the investigated museums offer rests precisely on the premise that technologically mediated interactions must be historically and culturally grounded. The typical visitor is motivated by a desire – or at least a vague curiosity – to explore and understand more of the conditions of modern life. In contrast, the typical gamer has no interest in gaining cultural insight or using the games as a means of reflection upon culture, society and self. This fact is part of what defines the attraction of a non-educational commercial computer game.

In other words: it seems that the irresponsible pleasure is the cultural flip side of the serious one, and *vice versa*. However such a dialectic relationship also implies that there are numerous cases where a seemingly simple binary collapses or is curiously reversed. On the one hand, there is a growing niche of computer games that are culturally and artistically ambitious and experimental, as well as electronic art that explores game aesthetics and offers playful interactions. On the other, museums are experimenting with the use of technology to attract younger generations that have grown up in a media-rich world and desire intense and maybe more playful learning experiences.

Even more central in the context of this section's focus on techno-pleasure may be the fact that the 'pure fun' of computer games does not exclude hard work – quite the contrary. The study of computer games in this section argues that the majority of games are not readily available in the same way that, for example, television entertainment or fairground attractions are. They require that the player is willing to invest large amounts of time, concentration, patience and learning. The museum study illustrates how quite similar modes of computerized interaction may be put to use in learning about cultural artefacts. In this case, interactions involve profiling and personal information management, and the particular way artefacts and information are presented. Today the modes of operation of computer systems and of user competence concerned penetrate a range of software-design and work-related practices. In a wider perspective those overlaps may be symptomatic of how the three distinct realms of entertainment, expressive culture and quotidian work practice are becoming more strongly integrated in a computerized and networked society.

The museums under investigation share another characteristic with computer games: Insofar as they delineate a distinct realm of cultural practice in Europe, they operate largely outside established traditions of cultural nation-building. The case studies all indicate that there is a strong sense of community behind the cultural interpretations of visitors as well as producers. Those who enjoy museum experiences seem to be largely in tune with the producers of these experiences when it comes to the fundamental ideas and emotions that govern the understanding of what range of experiences should be central in the modern and technologically 'enhanced' museum.

This sense of community among people of a global cultural elite goes beyond the cultural boundaries and identifications of the nation state associated with the traditional mass media of broadcasting and the printed press. In a similar manner, the majority of avid game players (to a certain extent excluding a broad but unstable and risky segment of casual players) seem to share with the producers of games a common pool of specific cultural resources and understandings that include vocabulary, technical understanding, notions of genre, fictional preferences, repertoire of playing styles and so on. Out of these common interests and resources collective identities are built that are neither national nor European.

Gamers' communities as well as the technological visionaries in museums are playing with the digital technology. As distinct communities across national boundaries they are increasingly growing to become a forceful democratic resource. Both in opposition to and alongside the more traditional cultural elites of cultural and pedagogic institutions, they participate in the development and management of knowledge, especially the kind of knowledge that provides a basis for how we think about the role of technology in society.

THE CULTURAL VALUE OF GAMES: COMPUTER GAMES AND CULTURAL POLICY IN EUROPE

Rune Klevjer

The chapter falls loosely into two parts. In the first part, I look at historical and aesthetic reasons for why computer games rather suddenly – after a more than 30 years' history – are now being considered of cultural and political importance. Particular attention is given to online gamer communities as spaces of social interaction and collective identities. I also discuss the widespread tendency among cultural experts as well as decision-makers to value games mainly as narrative, thereby largely ignoring the cultural significance of play and games. In the second part, I try to give an overview and a brief evaluation of some of some central but often overlooked values offered by a range of different computer game aesthetics and practises. As is also documented and discussed by Tan, Chisalita, Raijmakers and Oinonen in their investigation of museums (section 2), technology has opened up a wide range of diverse and often conflicting 'genres' of information management, entertainment and pleasure.

A European cultural policy for games

On 11th November 2002, on the initiative of the Danish presidency, the Council of the European Union adopted a resolution on 'interactive content for new media'. In his speech to the European Parliament on 11th December, Brian Mikkelsen, the Danish minister for Culture, describes the objective of the resolution as follows:

> The objective of the resolution is to focus on the cultural importance of the interactive media – and on the importance of making the cultural and linguistic diversity in Europe manifest itself in the interactive media content of the future.[1]

The background for the politicians' newfound interest in the matter is, according to the speech, that 'people of all ages all over the world use computer games and other interactive media every day'. And, Mikkelsen adds, the interests of young people are of particular concern. What other kind of 'interactive content' young people use besides computer games is unclear from his speech, so we must assume that games in various forms (PC, consoles, hand-held, networked) are the primary target.

Key words in the resolution are 'cultural importance', 'quality' and 'cultural and linguistic diversity'. Understandably, the resolution does not at this point go into details on what could be the criteria for 'quality' – let alone 'cultural importance' – when it comes to computer games. Presumably, brief references to established and generally agreed-upon values and goals in cultural policy are sufficient at this stage, as an indication of what motivates the politician's efforts.

Obviously, one of the goals is to secure – or if needed, to put into place – frameworks that are able to stimulate quality in the instrumental, commercial sense of the word. The European Union naturally wants the European games industry to compete with the Japanese and the Americans. These economical considerations do not necessarily conflict with the resolution's broader commitments to cultural quality and diversity. Still, in order to follow up the cultural aspect of the initiative, the Council is going to have to seek some criteria for how computer games can have 'cultural importance', aside from more general values of cultural and linguistic diversity. The only further definition of cultural diversity that Mikkelsen can offer us in his speech is, 'We should have more games reflecting European values and stories'.

Parallel to the process initiated by the Danish presidency, some countries in the EU are beginning to establish systems of state funding specifically aimed at computer games. In 2003, in a new initiative announced by Prime Minister Pierre Raffarin, the French government decided to offer pre-production funding to French developers of 4 million euros in total, administered by the *Centre national de la cinématographie*.[2] In Norway a similar system of funding was initiated in 2003, similarly as a part of the existing system for film, administered by the Norwegian Film Fund. From 2003 to 2004 the amount set aside went up from 3 million to 8 million kroner. Also, as a remarkable example of political ad-hoc funding, an extra 2 million was granted directly from the Minister of Culture to a computer game project based on the national folk tales of 'Askeladden'.[3]

Into the media world

It is quite clear from this that politicians in Europe no longer regard computer games only as kids' toys demanding purely pedagogical attention, or as superficial amusements deserving no more attention than amusement parks or fireworks. This attitude reflects a recent shift in the cultural status of computer games in central parts of the cultural elite, most notably among journalists, artists and academics. As once was the case with cinema, computer games are being promoted from the cultural realm of pure fun (where everything is either harmful, harmless or developmental), into the realm of culture proper, along with poems, pottery and rock music.

Academia and the arts

Looking back at games' cultural position through the previous decade, there is a striking difference – particularly in Europe – between their relative isolation in 1990 and their position in academic as well as journalistic media discourses in 2001. In 1990, there was virtually no interest in computer games within the humanities. In the social sciences, research on games was restricted to questions about violence, health and child development. In 2000, a more general interest in the culture and aesthetics of games and their uses was rapidly growing, followed by what can only be described as an explosion during 2001 to 2003.

In the art world, a new interest in computer games is also noticeable. With no extraordinary fanfare, the Barbican Gallery in London set up the exhibition 'Game On' during the summer of 2002, exploring the history and culture of videogames. Following the same trend, the massive commercial game hit *Grand Theft Auto: Vice City* (2002) was recently shortlisted for the prestigious 'Designer of the Year' prize by the Design Museum in London. It is not unlikely that in the next few years we will see something of the same Klondike in the art and design world as we are now seeing in the academic world. Game art and art games could very well be the next hot thing.

Kids who grew up in the 'videogame craze' years of the late 70s and early 80s are now in their thirties. Being mostly men, they belong to one of the dominant demographics in society in economical as well as cultural terms. Against this background, it should come as no surprise how computer games are now being included in dominant cultural discourses and welcomed into spaces from which they were previously banned.

Growing into the mainstream

Paralleling the rapid development in computer technology, there has been an extraordinary aesthetic development during computer games' more than 30 years of history. This development accelerated and acquired a critical momentum during the 1990s, sparked by the introduction of CD-ROM storage media (standard in new computers from around 1994) and 3-D graphics, which hit the market in 1993 with the PC game *Doom* and the *Sony Playstation* game console in 1995. The vastly increased storage capacity of the CD-ROM meant that games became much bigger, with CD-quality music, digitized sound samples and with 'cut-scenes' in Full Motion Video. This expansion of representational forms was accompanied by a transformation from a flat two-dimensional surface to a polygon-based and fully textured three-dimensional space.[4] After the first versions of textured 3-D in the early 90s, the improvements in texture resolution and the growing sophistication of animation, lighting, physics and sound have been nothing less than stunning. Suddenly computer games have started to look a lot like film – at least to outsiders, who have been inclined to overlook the continuity in game concepts and game mechanics that has prevailed through the transition to a filmic space.[5]

The absorption of the videogame aesthetic into mainstream media culture is a reciprocal process. Already during the 'videogame craze years' of the late 70s and early 80s, games like *Space Invaders* and *Pac-Man* achieved status as cultural icons, and videogames started to show their influence in art, music and films. During the last ten years, however, the general influence of videogame aesthetic on film and television has accelerated. This development is in part due to the photorealistic 3-D graphics that games and moving images can now have in common – what Lev Manovich (2000) refers to as 'synthetic realism' – which has grown to become a significant cinematic form following *Terminator 2*, *Jurassic Park* and *Toy Story*. The influence from games on cinema is not just limited to the occasional game-to-film translation, as seen, for example, in the *Tomb Raider* films. Game-like scenes, visual conventions and thematic elements have become increasingly common in action and science-fiction films, as particularly evident in the influential *The Matrix*, released in 1999.

The strong market growth of the industry since the mid-90s, combined with a spiralling technological development, has transformed the computer game industry into a big-budget and unmistakably hit-driven business. At the time of writing, we see considerable growing pains as the developers and publishers are trying to adapt to the economical and industrial logic of mass-market entertainment. Many do not have the financial muscles to meet towering budgets and rapid market consolidation. Through mergers and acquisitions, in which cross-media corporations are the big players, the games industry is being integrated into a wider entertainment industry. Corporations like Sony, Microsoft and Vivendi Universal, along with major independent publishers like Electronic Arts,[6] Activision, Ubisoft and Take-Two, are increasingly controlling the western market, while most of the smaller developers and publishers are struggling to survive. This difficult situation is most felt in the UK, which has Europe's leading computer games industry. During 2003, a large number of independent British developers had to shut down, as did the British publisher Rage.[7]

Participatory media culture

During the period of consolidation of the industry in the 1990s, online Internet gaming gave rise to independent, highly social and self-regulating gamer communities. Games have – at least within a big niche market – introduced a new concept for the production, distribution and consumption of commercial media products, a reciprocal relationship between producers and consumers. The game-genres that have spurred the most distinct and vocal forms of virtual community are the FPS (First-Person Shooter) and the MMORPG (Massive Multiplayer Online Role-Playing Games).

The online FPS gaming culture emerged as a response to the game *Doom*, released by id Software in 1993, in the same year as the breakthrough of the World Wide Web. *Doom* could be played as multiplayer 'deathmatch' either in local networks or – as a result of a later 'patch' to the game – over the Internet. Crucially, id Software released initial levels of the game as downloadable shareware, and also made available the source code of the software tools used for creation of levels, textures and sounds.[8] This invitation to social interaction and co-production among the players has become something of a founding paradigm of the PC-based FPS industry.[9] For every popular game of the genre, there are a vast number of player-made modifications to the original product, ranging from the relatively simple creation of character models and levels to whole conversions like *Counter-Strike*, an amateur 'mod' of *Half-Life* that was eventually bought by the developer and released as a commercial add-on.

More influential as social spaces, however, is the phenomenon of the role-playing virtual community, first emerging with *Ultima Online* (1997), the first game to offer a persistent online graphic world. The game world was based on the highly influential *Ultima* series of fantasy-based role-playing games – bringing to the new virtual world an already established, community-oriented and highly computer-savvy audience. *Everquest* (1999), *Asharon's Call* (1999), *Anarchy Online* (2001) and dozens of others have since followed. In these persistent online worlds, players live what quite accurately may be described as a second life – socializing, trading, building, battling and 'levelling up' the player-character, most commonly as part of organized 'guilds' or clans of players. These persistent game worlds have become much like societies of their own, with elaborate and constantly negotiated social, economic and legal structures. The majority of games are finding their core consumers in the historical and cultural overlap between 'geeky' computer culture and fantasy and science-fiction fan culture, but there are strong signs that the cultural appeal is widening, especially with MMORPGs like *Star Wars: Galaxies* (2003) and *The Sims Online* (2002).[10] Interestingly, there are also a growing number of online worlds on the market that are not primarily game-based but which utilize many of the same principles, like *There* and *Second Life*.

Online gamer communities represent a new form of digital subculture. They are spaces of social interaction that exist in relative independence of – and in relative opposition to – traditional mainstream consumer culture. At the same time we can see strong similarities with more established and familiar fan-cultures – from *Star Trek* and *Lord of the Rings* to Black Metal or Slasher Horror. In his book *Textual Poachers: Television Fans and Participatory Culture* (1992) and in subsequent writings, the media theorist Henry Jenkins has emphasized the creative and co-producing nature of such community-based media use, a form of dialogic media consumption where the power to define uses and meanings is shared between fans and the corporate producers. At the same time, it is increasingly recognized that this co-creative and collective-based pattern of consumption is being integrated as a core element of corporate strategy, a strategy that may be paradigmatic of hyper-capitalist media economies.[11]

The corporate-participatory cultural economy of online-based gamer communities contributes to a fragmentation of media use and media culture. Because of their high level of persistent interaction and self-regulation, they are important arenas for the formation of distinctly sub-cultural identities. These identities work against traditional nation-building strategies of cultural management and engineering on a national or European level. Online gaming is about more than active and participatory consumerism. It is an agent of cultural diversity, and a source of collective deliberation and action that has a cultural as well as a political significance. However, because it is a cultural movement that is carving out its own space within a corporate and consumerist economy, it is by nature both in opposition to and adaptive to global-industrial management and control. The online worlds of role playing are all corporately owned and designed. Corporations like Sony and Microsoft are, in a very concrete and hands-on way, engaged in a new form of social engineering, designing social spaces for communities, economies and identities to develop.

'Europeanness' in games?

Computer games have not historically developed within the frameworks of the nation state, as is the case with broadcasting and the press, and which is also partly the case with film. Therefore, games cannot be expected in any way to play the same cultural role as the established nation-based media. National games produced for a national audience is a rarity, except on the market for developmental or educational games. The notion of 'European games' does not exist at all, other than as a general term for games developed by European-based developers. French developers get 80% of their sales from abroad.[12] More than any other of the big media, games were born into a globalized world, right from the start. In terms of visual aesthetics, they are by nature a cultural hybrid, mixing elements from American and Japanese popular culture with more traditional European imagery (especially of medieval and Celtic/Norse/Tolkienesque type), according to the golden rule of 'anything goes'.

The explanation for this is not just that the medium is relatively new and that it was conceived and developed in the age of computers and telecommunications. Play and games tend to be a culturally very open and generalized form of human activity, with highly unstable cultural boundaries. In computer-based games as in other games, different types of play mechanics follow generic rules that cannot be localized in specific cultures in the same manner as fiction or music. It would, for example, be difficult to culturally situate the basic mechanisms of real-time strategy games, just as it would be hard to explain the cultural specificities of paper-rock-scissors.

In terms of play types and play mechanics, then, it is hard to find consistent patterns of difference between cultural regions. The exception is Japan, which has gaming traditions that are relatively distinct both as fiction and as play forms. Although many Japanese game concepts and game worlds have been exported to the West over the last 20–30 years (and then typically mixing with American traditions and imagery), there are still dominant Japanese game genres that occupy only niche positions on the American and European market. These game types most importantly include console-based role playing, fighting and mecha-games (battle-robots) which all play out in the fictional worlds of *anime* and *manga*, as well as a wide range of simulators (including dating games) that seem eccentric to the western mainstream. In contrast, the differences between American and European gaming preferences seem subtle and inconsistent – except in sport games, where traditions obviously differ.

This is not to say there can be found no distinctive trends on the European market of games, only that they are by no means as immediately evident as is the case in other cultural domains. In general, there is a need for academic research into patterns of cultural specificity, flow and hybridization in the gaming world, research that can compliment the market statistics of the industry. To a certain extent, the industry itself encourages a cultural three-continent model by treating Japan, Europe and America as separate markets, each with separate distribution channels and technical standards (much like the system of region-encoding of DVD films). The most articulated awareness of 'Europeanness' in computer games, therefore, is to be found on the console market (which now accounts for 9/10 of the total market and increasing), where European players share a common position as consumers *vis-à-vis* the European distributors – dependent on their priorities and release dates. A telling response to this kind of 'cultural cultivation' is the influential World Wide Web game portal and community site *Eurogamer*.[13]

Finally, there is definitely a national niche market of commercial PC-games, which are less investment-heavy than games for console platforms, and which do not have to go through the hardware gatekeepers, Sony, Microsoft and Nintendo. There are several examples of relatively low-budget PC titles (low budget compared to big international titles) that have been developed commercially for a national market only. Because of the limitations on budget, these are typically localized modifications of established international games, or nation-specific versions of tried and tested genres and technologies. In Norway, one of the smaller markets in Europe, *Flåklypa Grand Prix* (2000), which is a children's game based on a classical film, has become a big hit and even a moderate commercial success. In the Netherlands, *Amsterdoom* (2000), a generic and rather simplistic First-Person Shooter with recognizable locations from Amsterdam and high fun-factor was released by Davilex Software in 2000, although with no commercial success. However Davilex had great success with *A2 Racer* (1997), a series of localized driving games which were also released successfully in Germany as *Autobahn Racer*, in France as *Paris-Marseille Racer* and in the UK as *M25 Racer* (driving on the left...) – later to be released as *London Racer* (1999).[14]

The narrative fallacy
However, at the moment of writing, aside from these relatively cosmetic 'nationalizations' there are few signs of innovation and diversity in European-developed games (*Flåklypa Grand Prix* being an honourable exception). The Danish EU-initiative can also be read as a sign that policy-makers may have a rather narrow and limited – albeit legitimate – interest in cultural and artistic diversity. The background paper accompanying the Danish initiative, titled 'The Interactive Culture Industry' (Danish Ministry of Culture 2002), defines games exclusively in the category of 'interactive

narratives'. The authors even make narrative into a self-evident part of a definition of the concept of interactivity: 'Interactivity means that the user engages in the narrative in a participatory and active manner' (page 11). There is no hint of alternative ways of understanding 'interactivity', and no mention whatsoever of the meanings and values of games and play – even if the report, in fact, deals almost exclusively with games and the games industry. In the light of everything that has been written within humanistic game theory over the recent years, this approach is quite controversial and, as a way of providing 'background' to the policy- makers, it can be partly misleading.

In recent humanistic computer game theory, there is already a relatively well-established discourse on how to conceptualize the fundamental elements of game aesthetics. The central point of debate has been how to understand the role of narrative in games. As Jørgen Kirksæther (1998) has noted, stories in games are typically constructed as *fictional frames* around the play itself – external metaphors that serve to 'explain' the specific structure of tasks and obstacles facing the player. As a consequence, most games can be enjoyed – and played well – without paying much (or any) attention to the accompanying story, especially if the player is familiar with the genre.

This duality at the heart of most gaming experiences is reflected in the theoretical discourse about computer games. Those who have preferred to approach games within the framework of narrative theory – most typically theorists from literary studies or new media studies – have been labelled 'narrativists' (or sometimes more inaccurately 'narratologists'), while those who advocate a more distinctively game-centred approach have – partly in polemic opposition to the established story-centred traditions – called themselves (or have come to be associated with) the 'ludologists'.[15]

The theoretical premise for the 'ludological' approach (although he never used the term 'ludology') was introduced by Espen Aarseth in *Cybertext* (1997), the first book to suggest a theory about play and narration as two distinct modes of discourse, not only located in literature, but as a dialectic fundamental to human activity in general. Aarseth uses the term *ergodic* to describe what is unique about computer-based literature. The ergodic signifies the general principle of having to work with the materiality of a text, the need to participate in the construction of its material structure. Some ergodic works lead us towards a fixed solution (e.g. a jigsaw puzzle), others can be unpredictable and open-ended (like an experimental hypertext novel). Being a discursive mode, the ergodic can be contrasted to narrative discourse, where the user is invited only to engage in the semantics of the text and does not have to worry about its material configuration. In narrative discourse the user is only a reader, not a co-constructor in the material sense, or, we might say, not a player. While reading narrative is an interpretive practice, playing a game is a configurative practice.[16]

A game is a game?
Even if the ludologist position in its most radical form is largely denounced among computer game researchers today, theorists generally agree that the majority of

computer games are not primarily in the business of telling stories. Narrative in games performs a very different role from narrative in novels or films. Obviously the narrative dimension is particularly played down in certain genres such as sport games, driving games and puzzle games. Still, even in the most story-driven games (adventure and role-playing games) a good story does not make a good game.

If we look at the early pioneers of dedicated state funding for videogames, Norway and France, their approaches differ quite a lot with respect to the role and importance of narrative. Narrative is one of the main criteria for gaining funding from the Norwegian Film Fund, which is explicitly aimed at games for children and younger adolescents. This central concern for national narratives is reflected in the short, basic definition of what it is that they want to support. An interactive production is defined as a computer game (or 'other interactive and non-linear productions') that 'tells stories through moving images'.[17] The message is very clear: games are vehicles for providing children with national stories. The criteria obviously reflect a legitimate and important cultural concern – especially for a small country. However, as a cultural policy it does not recognize games as an art form, or as anything that could be interesting for other than pedagogic and traditional nation-building purposes.[18]

A crucial part of the acceptance of computer games as an art form is a recognition of play and games as forms of cultural expression. Games are more than carriers of 'interactive narrative'. Probably because France has a large and established game industry, their policy states different aims from the Norwegian, and the list of criteria does not adopt storytelling as a requirement. The main motivation for the initiative is that French developers – like the British ones – are struggling in a difficult international market. This does not mean that the government simply wants to support any game project that has commercial potential and needs money. There are artistic requirements. These do not, however, as one would maybe expect, emphasize 'French stories', 'French language' or the like, but refer instead to more general artistic values. The eligible projects must show 'creativity of game design' and 'originality compared to what is already on the market'.[19] In these criteria there is no bias towards narrative whatsoever. On the contrary, 'creativity of game design' is a formulation that will most likely be interpreted as a special concern for non-narrative mechanisms of the game structure. It seems that even for a country like France, where media production and media consumption is heavily supported and regulated to preserve national culture and identity, computer games are – at least for now – an interesting exception from the rule.[20]

What we can see from the Danish EU initiative as well as from the Norwegian and French example, is that a political concern with narrative – typically in a narrow and exclusive sense – is closely tied with the interest to defend and strengthen national traditions, culture and identity. As soon as the focus is expanded to include the structures of playful interaction – the properties that distinguish games from books or films – references to national value become more vague and problematic. The computer game is a medium that, more than any other, seems to resist being appropriated for nation-building and identity-engineering purposes.

This is not to say that games do not have 'stories and values'. There are indeed values of cultural and political importance to be found in games, including – but in no way limited to – what we might call 'literary value'. There is a plurality of values in games, which should be actively encouraged rather than just left to the rather brutal and short-sighted logic of the entertainment industry. The French initiative, although limited by the requirements to commercial potential, gives reason for optimism. In the following, as a contribution to a wider debate about computer games and cultural policy in Europe, I shall briefly point to some of the values in games that might more specifically be labelled 'techno-political'. These are values that go beyond the traditional concerns of industrial competitiveness cultural nation-building.

The techno-political value of games

Computer games are primarily about play, offering pleasures and values that we also find in other forms of play. The general question of the cultural value of human play – including its psychological, developmental, socializing, civilizing or democratic virtues – are discussed in classical works like Johan Huzinga's *Homo Ludens* (1955 [1949]), Roger Caillois' *Man, Play and Games* (2001 [1961]) and Brian Sutton-Smith's *The Ambiguity of Play* (1997).[21] In this discussion, however, I shall restrict myself to the more specifically *technological* dimension of computer-based play. The range of technological pleasures opened up by games should be a matter of heightened cultural and political concern in Europe. The basic premise behind this argument is that technological play is crucially forming culture. Techno-entertainment is not outside art, politics and ideology. How we choose to involve with technology in play is about how we define technology and its relation to ourselves.

Playing the machine

In a far more radical sense than a television set or a radio receiver, the computer game hardware and software constitute a flexible technological toy, constructed for active, hands-on machine-play or techno-play. The computer game is an 'action machine' as well as a representational medium. Other electronic media are also machines that must on some level be operated or 'engineered', but operating them is normally a pure instrumental action (turning the television set on, adjusting the volume, rewinding the video cassette etc.), not a playful bodily engagement. Idle play with the remote control (like switching between channels to the rhythm of your stereo) is not the standard mode of watching television. Looking at computer game aesthetics from the perspective of traditional media theory, the activity of playing the machine will have to move into the centre of attention, as an essential *modus operandi* of the medium. Even if the rhetorical potential of their representations has become more complex and powerful, games are no less playable machines today than they used to be 25 years ago.

To play with a game is to play with a specific configuration or a specific gestalt of a more general technological form. Various game genres are culturally significant as different articulations of technological play, situated within a wider cultural field of technological pleasure. Because they involve archetypical forms of technological pleasure, they play a part in how society develops understandings of how people and technology should interact. These archetypical forms can be described as modes of pleasure, corresponding to relatively distinct and coherent sets of typical operations required from the player. Different game genres emphasize different types of technological engagement, and different players prefer different types of challenges. One man's pleasure is another man's tedium. This diversity is in itself a cultural resource in any society, a diversity that also influences how people approach other digital systems of information and entertainment, for example, those being designed for museums (see section 2).

For the sake of illustrative simplicity, I will propose two broad categories into which we might define some of the dominant techno-based pleasures of computer gaming. The first category, 'software gaming', refers to the typical operations of management and configuration. The second category, 'body-action gaming', refers to bodily sensations, cyborg fantasies and explorative trances.

Software gaming

'Software gaming' represents forms of engagement that are similar to those posed by non-gaming software. These patterns of challenge and interaction are typically involved in the economically productive practices in society and should be of natural interest to policy-makers. Software gaming is a mode of playful interaction which is particularly dominant in role-playing games, strategy games and system simulators. As a form of immersion and engagement, this mode operates independently of, and sometimes works against, the fictional illusions of the game. The primary challenges are *management* and *configuration*. The task of having to control, plan and coordinate a large number of interacting parameters on screen is very dominant in simulation and strategy games, to the extent that pure simulators (i.e. games that feature very little or no battle) are often called 'management games'. Mimicking the operational logic of desktop software, the player is required to play on the surface of the screen, constantly controlling the game through often quite complex commands and menus. Consequently, the 'software pleasure' of computer games is a mode which is tailor-made for the keyboard and mouse interface of the PC platform and converts rather poorly to console and gamepad.

The task of configuration – or personalization – is especially dominant in role-playing games, where growing in the 'role' means building up and configuring (personalizing) your avatar's complex nexus of features, abilities, weapons and other items. In this way, personalization is not only a form of growth management (managing the expanding, dynamic system that constitutes your avatar or group of avatars) but also crucially a form for self-expression – through the language of computerized statistics.

Precisely because the task of maintaining overview, control and balance is such a crucial part of the gaming experience, management gaming naturally also offers the 'wilder' thrills of freely experimenting with the parameters. This *exploratory* mode of technological pleasure includes the chance to upset the balance of the system in various ways, typically with catastrophic consequences within the fictional game world (like, for example, letting a lion loose on the visitors in the zoo management game *Zoo Tycoon* [2001]). Experimenting with the objects and rules of the game world is, of course, a common mode of play in many game genres, one that is not necessarily oriented towards progression or winning the game. As a distinctive pleasure of computer-based play, it can be compared to experimental and 'playful' forms of gaining experience and skill with non-gaming software.

Software gaming presents a very clear example of the blurring of boundaries between work and leisure in our society, between instrumental and playful aesthetics and practices. This convergence can be seen taking place on many arenas of cultural experience. Computer games as well as information systems in museums are evidences of a more general trend: Computer-based mediations and practices open up new spaces for work-like pleasure (or pleasurable work). Therefore, as Ursula Maier-Rabler argues in section 2, ePolicy should not be reduced to a question of access. Work-like pleasures give people reasons to engage with digital technology. Such leisure-based digital practices must be of political concern if we want people to acquire not just the necessary skills, but more importantly the motivation and confidence to be able to take actively part in a computerized and information-based society.

The opportunity to be able to 'play the software' of the digital computer is of great importance to the individual's socialization and empowerment in the emerging digital society. A political concern for diversity and access within this cultural arena is needed. In particular, there are significant economical and linguistic barriers to access, and this is an issue where the decisions of policy-makers can make a difference. Even in the richer parts of Europe, access to more complex and challenging variants of role-playing strategy and management gaming is inhibited by language barriers. With the exception of Germany, France and in some cases Spain and Italy, games on the smaller European markets – for example, in the Scandinavian countries – are not translated from English into the national language. This is normally not a problem with simpler action-games, but it is bound to prevent children, teenagers and other groups with weak language skills from having a go at more complex and intellectually demanding challenges.

From a democratic perspective, such all-pervasive language barriers constitute an unnecessary extra digital gatekeeper, especially to young people who are still forming their fundamental relationships to digital technology. The competence to manage, configure, experiment with and modify digital processes allows the individual to create a space for computer-based self-expression, invention and political action. The cultural and social penetration of 'digital Lego' must be of central democratic concern.

Of particular concern to policy-makers should be the vitality and independence of online gamer communities, which are very distinct practices of collaborative and creative software gaming, creating strongholds of computer literacy and participatory digital culture. Multiplayer computer game role playing in persistent worlds is a virtual variant of social configuration, and in some respects much like an exercise in political distribution and struggle. The collaborative player modifications of the FPS community and in other genres – where players construct their own levels, objects, textures ('skins') and game mechanics – is a radical form of experimental exploration and configuration of games-as-software. Games are transformed into game-building software, based on the modular logic of pre-designed ready-mades.

The strength of such communities has significant techno-political implications. As partly independent and self-regulatory centres of consumer power and production of knowledge, they are playing a particular role in ongoing political negotiations over questions of copyright protection, open standards and user control. At the same time, however, the ideologies embedded in typical practices of software gaming – management, configuration, user control and 'co-creative' practices – can be double-edged swords in a struggle for cultural freedom and diversity. For this reason, the primitive sensations found in gory action shooters may not necessarily be the negative 'other' to cultural policy.

Body-action gaming

While the software logic plays on the surface, expressing what Bolter and Grusin in the book *Remediation* (1999) call the 'immediacy' of digital media, another type of pleasure grows out of the seductive 'transparency' of the medium. Within this general mode of play, the power of the digital computer to create illusions of movement and space takes precedence over the operational requirements of the interface. According to Bolter and Grusin, the desire to 'see through' the surface of the screen and make it invisible has a history dating back to the invention of the central perspective in Renaissance art. Before the Renaissance, painters focused on the immediacy of the surface and the 'play' between its elements. Bolter and Grusin trace these two aesthetic movements and cultural desires through history. While the desktop computer represents today's paradigmatic metaphor for the logic of immediacy, they argue, realist film and 'virtual reality' represent the desire to be immersed 'into' the space of the representational illusion.

Even if Bolter and Grusin's binary interpretation of the history of the visual media might be too all encompassing and too simplistic, their model seems to capture and contextualize a significant tension within computer game aesthetics. In a computer game, illusion and management are conflicting attractions. The direct and bodily challenges and sensations offered by a responsive 3-dimensional virtual space is a form of technological engagement which does not follow the desktop metaphor and has very few non-gaming software equivalents. Consequently, in games where fictional illusions and audio-visual (and sometimes tactile) sensation is supposed to be the dominant attraction, management and configuration on the level of the surface interface must be kept as simple, intuitive and 'invisible' as possible. These 'low-management' and high-intensity games are particularly well suited for the console platforms, which do not use a work-related mouse/keyboard-interface, constructed for point-and-click surface navigation.

Body-action games, in particular classical arcade-action games like *Space Invaders* (1978) or *Robotron* (1982), have particular kind of 'flow',[22] a trance-like quality, due to the simplicity of the interface, the speed and repetitiveness of the action, and the spectacle of the sensations. Unlike the experience of immersion in software gaming (which is also a form of all-encapsulating flow), the real-time cybernetic feedback loop between the expert player and the computer largely bypasses conscious intellectual decisions. In fast-paced and spectacular action games, the typical mode of technological engagement has more to do with some sort of techno-eroticism than with management skills, socialization and progress.

Action games of the 3-D era obviously try to cultivate a notion of 'cinematic' immersion, associating themselves explicitly with the invisible screen of Hollywood cinema. Still, an equally significant historical analogy may be found in the technological pleasures of magic machines, horror houses and motion rides. This analogy seems particularly relevant with respect to one of the dominant action-adventure genres, the aptly named First-Person Shooter (FPS). Most games in this genre illustrate very well the strong tendency in action games to 'double up' or project the pleasure of the concrete and hands-on technological involvement of the physical play-situation into the fantasy of the fictional world. Physical machine-play is translated in real time into virtual worlds of technological operation, fascination and power. What has been called the 'poor man's virtual reality' of the First- Person Shooter seems to be a techno-obsessed genre, a parody of established cyborg fantasies in our culture. The genre presents a modern, violent and excessively techno-fetishist fantasy of power, articulated through the perceptual tunnel vision of the subjective camera-gun. The characteristic first-person perspective is a machine-look, providing a form of pleasure not unlike the sensation of driving (or being driven by) a train, a car or an aircraft. Historically, there are interesting similarities between the technological power play of the FPS and the attraction of the various 'ride-films' from the beginning of the twentieth century, which were shot with a camera mounted on the front of a train (Fielding 1983).[23]

Although motion rides and Hollywood action films are major influences behind contemporary 3-D action games, some recent examples also show modernist and non-realistic inspirations, mixed with strong influences from the more abstract spaces of classical arcade games. Particularly interesting are *Rez* (2002) – influenced by the visual style of the film *Tron* – and *Frequency* (2001), both integrating music and soundscapes into a mix of trance-inducing elements. In this type of body-action gaming, the player navigates a sound space as much as a visual space. On the Japanese market, the 'hippie-game' *Rez* was also released together with a specially designed force-feedback vibrator (named the 'Trance Vibrator'), which apparently could also be used as a game dildo.[24]

Perception and identity

Corporate cultural producers are not inclined to explore the diversity of possible body-action experiences. At the moment, a 'high-concept' game like *Rez* seems to be an exception, and it did not sell well. Similar experiments in the art of technological pleasure risk falling outside the constraints of the corporate world as well as the socially progressive frameworks of cultural policy. An embodied, sometimes regressive and almost drug-like relationship between man and technology has been given no legitimate place within dominant histories of technological rationality and progress. Body-action gaming represents a historical tradition of cheap amusements and technological perversion – in many ways the flip side of modern technocratic civilization. Games like *Rez* prove that this arena can be a fertile ground for art and amusement to meet.

As Tan et al. in the next chapter argue with regard to the diversity of museum experiences, technology is not just a tool or channel of cultural experience. Typical modes and operations of computerized information-systems become integrated parts of the cultural experience itself. In games, one could argue, this is a tautological observation in the sense that there is no cultural artefact external to the game machine itself (like a painting or a sculpture). Precisely because of this 'purity' of technological pleasure, the computer game can be seen as a model. Various game modes and game genres indicate typical perceptual forms of the computer as a medium, different ways of sensing and controlling (and being controlled by) technologically mediated environments. This perceptual diversity – from the chess computer to the horror house – encourages a variety of interpretations and uses of digital technology, laying the ground for diverse patterns of identity formation. Technologically grounded perceptions and fascinations are, however, not mediators of nation-based identities. Neither are they necessarily mediators of productive social and economic competencies. Consequently, a cultural policy of technological pleasure should go beyond the scope of ePolicy – also in the wider sense of the term as discussed by Maier-Rabler – addressing a broader range of artistic diversity and exploration.

Beyond ePolicy

The aim of this chapter has been to consider some of the range and diversity of cultural experiences to be found in computer game aesthetics and practices. I also argue that various modes of interaction and expression offered by computer games are integrated in a wider field of modern practises – in war, in work, in entertainment, in art. It seems that a cultural policy with regard to games will always have to balance and negotiate two general considerations. On the one hand, political strategies and priorities towards this sector are going to be a central part of what has come to be known as 'ePolicy'. ePolicy aims to support and secure access to cultural activities that motivate and enable people to participate and express themselves in a computer- and information-based economy. An ePolicy that wants to turn Europe, in Ursula Maier-Rabler's words, '...into a region of curious individuals eager to engage in life-long-learning' must develop strategies that include the realm of computerized leisure – computer games as well as other forms of computerized cultural experience.

On the other hand, games also have a wider potential of artistic and techno-perceptual innovation. The diversity of challenges and fictions offered by games has an important artistic value in itself, but also widens the cultural space for social and political critique. This may also include forms of techno-pleasures that explore sensual fascinations with spectacle and destruction. Beyond ePolicy, there must be a space for games and game cultures to express their own creativity and their own values.

A cultural policy of games that does not encourage the diversity of technological pleasure risks being an agent of conformism and streamlined social engineering. In a democratic and pluralistic culture, it is important that system-strengthening and 'managerial' modes of digital operation do not grow to become too pervasive. Playful engagements with technology can too easily be caught up in totalizing and instrumentalist techno-cultural forms. Dominant commercial forces are pushing towards ever more narrow and easily manageable practices of computer-based expression and entertainment. In the evolving digital economies of computer databases and networks, there is a tendency for new restrictions and dependencies to be introduced in the name of progress and freedom, embedded in practices of 'interactivity' and 'personalization'. In a dystopian scenario of the digital Information Society, 'personalization' will be the only form of technological freedom – a mode of 'user control' in which mechanisms of continuous feedback, profiling and monitoring (promising 'ease of use' without learning) locks the individual consumer into predictable patterns of interaction and information-seeking.[25]

European strategies

In competition with the much stronger game industries in Japan and America, the cultural and linguistic fragmentation of the market in Europe is a considerable disadvantage. At the same time, this commercial barrier represents a valuable cultural diversity. Europe has a unique tradition of defining expressive culture as a public concern, giving attention to innovation within a less market-dependent economic system. Because of its cultural diversity, Europe is in a good position to produce a range of alternatives both within and outside dominant modes of cultural production. Such projects may involve the exploration of alternative myths and narratives, but should not simply take the form of established game clichés dressed up in 'European' imagery. Rather, it should be about making a contribution to expand the range of techno-cultural expressions in Europe as well as on the global market.

The logics and constraints of a mass-market economy present a challenge to the cultural vitality and potential of the game industry. There is a need for strategies on the European level that can look beyond nation building in order to stimulate experiment and creativity. We must assume that, just as with film, a smaller, independent industry is going to be needed as an alternative to the risk-aversive and conservative mainstream. However, such a development of diversification seems to be slow and uncertain, mainly because of the technological barriers and high costs involved in making games for advanced platforms (consoles and PCs). The French approach is a promising one. It is an attempt to help independent and risk-taking projects get off the ground, by providing crucial support through the initial phases of concept and prototype development. The need for a support to an independent game industry is argued in more detail by Oliver (2003).

At the time of writing, the emerging online game worlds are all under corporate control. Given the cultural and political implications of the development of these communities, the lack of non-corporate alternatives for online persistent societies should be a rather immediate concern for the gamers as well as for public policy-makers. On a very concrete level, public funding would surely give a needed boost to ongoing efforts to develop an open-source, general-purpose engine for virtual game worlds/communities.

The computer game industry, political decision-makers and cultural entrepreneurs in Europe need to establish a discussion of how future developments can be envisioned and supported. The playful relations to technology in society constitute a vital foundation for social development and critique, and a basis from which new ideas about how to live with technology can emerge.

Notes

1. Speech by Minister for Culture, Mr Brian Mikkelsen, in the European Parliament [online], in 2007 no longer available at http: //www.eu2002.dk/news/news_read.asp?iInformationID=25898.
2. Information by the French Ministry of Economy, Finance and Industry [online], in 2007 no longer available at http: //www.telecom.gouv.fr/programmes/jeuxvideo.htm.
3. Press release from the Ministry of Culture and Church Affairs [online], available at http: //odin.dep.no/kkd/norsk/aktuelt/pressem/043031-070141/index-dok000-b-n-a.html.
4. There were 3-dimensional game spaces before polygon graphics, created either with vector graphics (like in the arcade classics *Battlezone* (1980) and *Star Wars* (1983)) or with 2-D sprites 'wrapped' into 'semi-3d' space. Both *Wolfenstein 3D* and *Doom* used this semi-3-D, in which the player could not look up and down.
5. As a parallel trend, sports games have developed a distinct form of 'television realism', complete with commentary, spectator masses and lifelike, motion-captured animations that mimic the look and movement of real-life sports stars.
6. California-based EA is by far the biggest and most successful games publisher and distributor in the world, housing ca 4000 employees and strong in-house development teams.
7. Developers include Hotgen, Kuju Entertainment, Kaboom Studios, Attention to Detail, Silicon Dreams, Lost Toys, Murky Foot, Computer Artworks, Warthog. Source: http: //www.gamesindustry.biz/content_page.php?section_name=pub&aid=2737.
8. For more about the history of id Software and the FPS community, see Kushner (2003).
9. See Morris (2003) for more about modding and the contemporary FPS gamer communities.
10. Daniel Pargman (2003) suggests some interesting explanations for the overlap between computer culture, fantasy fiction and role playing, and gives some useful further references on the subject.

11. For an interesting example of this line of argument in relation to FPS communities, see Sotamaa 2003.
12. BBC News [online] at http: //news.bbc.co.uk/1/hi/technology/3084677.stm.
13. http: //www.eurogamer.net/.
14. In the subsequent years, following the success of the racing games, the company has grown to be an international developer and publisher for both PC and consoles.
15. The dominant representatives of a story-oriented approach to games (and new media in general) are Janet Murray (1997) and Henry Jenkins (Fuller and Jenkins 1995). The theorists who have been most commonly referred to as 'ludologists' are Espen Aarseth (1997), Markku Eskelinen (2001), Jesper Juul (2001) and Gonzalo Frasca (2003) – Frasca being the one who most explicitly advocates ludology as the 'father discipline' of computer game studies.
16. This last point is taken from Markku Eskelinen's article "The Gaming Situation" (2001), a radically anti-narrativist theoretical elaboration of the ludologist position.
17. Presentation by Petter Wallace, The Norwegian Film Fund [online], available at http: //www.filmfondet.no/stotteordninger/presentasjon.pdf.
18. There are ambiguities in the Norwegian initiative that may be seeds of a more thorough debate at a later stage. To the media, a leading spokesperson for the Ministry of Culture says that the government wants to contribute to 'building an industry as we are doing with film', adding that 'Games have become culture and maybe also art.' See http: //www.digi.no/php/art.php?id=93000.
19. Information by the French Ministry of Economy, Finance and Industry [online] at http: //www.telecom.gouv.fr/programmes/jeuxvideo.htm.
20. As a comparison, see the final book chapter by Marcel Machill for a description and analysis of the French policy of public service television.
21. *The Ambiguity of Play* is a very useful introduction to the field, giving a comprehensive overview of the various 'rhetorics' that advocate the benefits of play, and focusing in particular on a critique of adaptive or 'progressive' theories of play.
22. A concept of 'flow' in work and play is developed by Mihaly Csikszentmihalyi (2000).
23. The points on the FPS genre in this section are taken from Klevjer (2003). The situating of the First-Person Shooter within the history of machine-based and visual attractions will be the subject of a later work. The historical and theoretical relevance of Tom Gunning's "the cinema of attraction" is addressed in Järvinen (1999–2000), and (at more length) in MacTavish (2002).
24. For more insights into the dildo-experience of *Rez*, see "Sex in Games: Rez+Vibrator" on http: //www.gamegirladvance.com/archives/2002/10/26/sex_in_games_rezvibrator.html.
25. The relationship between personalization and domination is discussed in Palmer (2003).

References

Aarseth, Espen (1997), Cybertext. Perspectives on Ergodic Literature. Baltimore and London: Johns Hopkins University Press.

Bolter, Jay David and Grusin, Richard (1999), Remediation: Understanding New Media. Cambridge, MA: MIT Press.

Caillois, Roger (2001 [1961]), Man, Play and Games, Chicago: University of Illinois Press.

Csikszentmihalyi, Mihaly (2000 [1975]), Beyond Boredom and Anxiety: The Experience of Play in Work and Games. San Francisco: Jossey-Bass Publishers.

Danish Ministry of Culture (2002), The interactive culture industry. Background paper. Danish Ministry of Culture. Available at http: //kum.inforce.dk/graphics/kum/downloads/Publikationer/TheInteractiveCultureIndustry.pdf.

Eskelinen, Markku (2001), 'The Gaming Situation', in Game Studies, vol. 1, issue 1. Available at http://www.gamestudies.org/ (accessed 25 April 2003).

Fielding, Raymond (1983), 'Hale's tours. Ultrarealism in the Pre-1910 Motion Picture', in Fell, John L. (ed.), Film Before Griffith, Berkeley: University of Calefornia Press.

Frasca, Gonzalo (2003), 'Simulation versus Narrative: Introduction to Ludology' in Mark J. P. Wolf & Bernard Perron (eds.): Video/Game/Theory, New York: Routledge (in Press).

Fuller, Mary and Jenkins, Henry (1995), 'Nintendo and New World Travel Writing: A Dialogue', in Steven Jones (ed.), Cybersociety: Computer-Mediated Communication and Community. Thousand Oaks: Sage.

Huizinga, Johan (1955 [1949]), Homo ludens: A study of the play element in culture. Boston: Beacon Press.

Jenkins, Henry (1992), Textual Poachers: Television Fans and Participatory Culture. New York: Routledge.

Juul, Jesper (2001), 'Games Telling Stories? – A brief note on games and narratives', in Game Studies vol. 1, issue 1. Available at http://www.gamestudies.org/0101/juul-gts/ (accessed 25 April 2003).

Kirksæther, Jørgen (1998), 'The Structure of Video Game Narration'. Short paper presented at the conference Digital Arts & Culture, Bergen 26–28 November 1998. Available at http://cmc.uib.no/dac98/papers/kirksaether.html (accessed 18th June 2003).

Klevjer, Rune (2002), 'In defence of cutscenes', in Mäyrä, Frans (ed.) Computer Games and Digital Cultures – Conference Proceedings, Tampere: Tampere University Press.

Klevjer, Rune (2003), 'Gladiator, worker, operative: The hero of the First Person Shooter Adventure', in Marinka Coupier and Joost Raessens (eds.): Level Up. Digital Games Research conference 2003 [CD-ROM]. Utrecht University.

Manovich, Lev (2000), The Language of New Media, Cambridge, Mass.: MIT Press.

Murray, J. H. (1997), Hamlet on the Holodeck : The Future of Narrative in Cyberspace, New York, London: The Free Press.

Oliver, Julian (2003), 'Developers In Exile: Why Independent Game Development Needs an Island', in DAC98 proceedings [online]. Available at http://hypertext.rmit.edu.au/dac/papers/.

Sutton-Smith, Brian (1997), The Ambiguity of Play. Cambridge, Mass.: Harvard University Press.

Game references

Amsterdoom, Davilex Software 2000.

Anarchy Online, Funcom 2001.

Asharon's Call, Turbine Entertainment; Microsoft 1999.

A2 Racer, Davilex Software 1997.

Battlezone, Atari Inc. (coin-op) 1980.

EverQuest, Verant Ineractive; 989 Studios 1999.

Flåklypa Grand Prix, Capricornus; Caprino Video Games 2000.

Frequency, Harmonix/Treanor Brothers/Crystal Method: SCEE 2001.

Gabriel Knight: Sins of the Fathers, Sierra: Sierra 1993.

Grand Theft Auto III, DMA Design: Rockstar Games 2001.

Grand Theft Auto: Vice City, Rockstar Games: Rockstar Games 2002.

Half-Life, Valve; Sierra Entertainment 1998.

London Racer, Davilex Software; Infogrames 1999.

Myst, Cyan/Red Orb Entertainment: Brøderbound 1994.

Pac-Man, Namco; Midway 1980 (coin-op).

Prince of Persia, Brøderbund: Brøderbund 1989.

Quake, Id Software; Id Software 1996.
Rez, United Game Artists: Sega 2002.
Robotron 2084, Williams Electronics (coin-op) 1982.
Space Invaders, Taito/Midway (coin-op) 1978.
Star Wars, Atari Inc. (coin-op) 1983.
Star Wars: Galaxies: An Empire Divided, Sony Online Entertainment; LucasArts 2003.
Super Mario Brothers, Nintendo 1985.
The Sims, Maxis; Electronic Arts 2000.
The Sims Online, Maxis; Electronic Arts 2002.
Ultima Online, Origin; Electronic Arts 1997.
Wipeout, Psygnosis: SCEE 1995.
Zoo Tycoon, Blue Fang Games: Microsoft 2001.

Learning and Entertainment in Museums: A Case Study

Ed Tan[1], Cristina Chisalita, Bas Raijmakers and Katri Oinonen[2]

Introduction

The problematic of this volume, convergence and fragmentation in a changing Europe, determine current debates on the future of our museums. Questions like the following are repeatedly posed in such debates. How will European museums look twenty years from now? Can they retain their identity as keepers of national and European cultural heritage? Can they retain a central position in presenting more or less unified views of history and culture? Or will they have to change into globally oriented theme park-like attractions in order to survive? Is there a way for them to combine learning with entertainment?

This chapter attempts to shed light on very broad questions like these, concerning the future of museums in the global Information Society. It does this from an extremely confined point of view, namely a case of one single research and development project, SCALEX, aiming at delivering a prototype visitor support system. SCALable EXhibition server[1] SCALEX is not an Internet application. Instead it is a system for use in museums, to enhance the potential of presentations and exhibitions. SCALEX plays sequential presentations of digital or real objects in ways depending on the profile of the particular visitor, and the selections and choices that he or she makes.

The visitor is confronted with the front end of the system only, that is, the displays presenting objects and information, and a user interface that allows him or her to interact with the system in order to make selections and use exhibition support or extension functions. The back end of the system, invisible to the visitor, consists of (1) a knowledge editor that allows the exhibition maker to organise and edit digital resources according to a conceptual plan; (2) a storyliner that is used to define various trajectories through materials and design various modes of interaction with the materials, depending on specific content properties and particular user needs, and (3) an exhibition player that presents materials to a visitor during a visit, according to the general plan made using the knowledge editor: the trajectory defined by the storyliner and input from the visitor. A profiler instructs the storyliner and the player to select materials and adapt presentations to the needs of a particular visitor. The player controls a variety of presentation devices, from monitors and beamers to hand-held computers, and from lighting to sound installation. It also functions as an interface for visitor input. For more detailed descriptions, see *www.scalex.info*.

The design of the system was *user-centred*, meaning that in every stage of development a close approximation is sought to what users want from the system.[2] Therefore, the SCALEX project can function not only as a laboratory for designing museum facilities and exhibition tools, but also as an observatory of current museum policies and museum practices and of views of the future. In this chapter we present results from user studies that are relevant, in particular, to the broader issue of the role of learning versus entertainment in the present, and in an envisioned museum culture. We had interviews with museum staff and visitors about the experiences that a museum visit should target, and tested preliminary versions of a SCALEX prototype in order to identify wishes and views of the same parties with regard to ideal support functions in tomorrow's museum exhibition. In so doing, both museum staff and visitors unfolded their views of the ideal museum visit, and the role of learning versus entertainment in it. In this chapter we give an outline of these views, that offer an impression of the sort of answers that could be given to the questions raised above.

Museums in transition
Museums all over the industrialized world are going through a stormy period of reorientation, due to cultural and political changes. We single out three trends that strongly affect museum culture and, in particular, influence attitudes towards learning versus entertainment.

First, public funding is challenged and the demands of policy-makers have changed beyond recognition over the past decades, stressing access for all at the cost of academic norms of conservation and study by professional experts. So the question arises of how museums can become more attractive to as many visitors, as possible. In many cases this implies that they have to find a new optimum between generalization and specialization of their supply, a choice between convergence and fragmentation.

Second, especially in Europe, demographic changes are rapidly taking place that make it increasingly difficult to address visitors as one group. In a recent past, museums could rely on a knowledge and value background shared among their visitors. It included a set of communalities in terms of national history, religion, lifestyle, education and media use. Mass immigration from countries outside Europe and the industrialized world have created uncertainty about the *why*, *what* and *how* of museum presentations. In particular, it raises the question about the need for convergence of perspectives from various groups into a smaller set of more coherent narratives against allowing for, or even fostering diversity of views, seen by many as fragmentation of address, of knowledge and values.

Third, the global consumer culture, characterised by individual choice, fast dynamics of supply and immediacy of rewards, gratifications and pleasure has become the natural habitus of large segments of the population, not only of the wealthy young. The introduction of ever more competitive leisure alternatives to museum visits, such as shopping, entertainment events and the use of Internet, are a constant threat to the continuity of museums (See e.g. Rojek 2000). The necessity of participation in *high culture* has lessened, since popular culture has been accepted or even embraced by educators, and the status value of the arts and cultural heritage has already diminished. The competitive alternative is almost diametrically opposite to what museums want to convey to their visitors. Global consumer culture tends to replace cultural heritage with less historically grounded content that is instantly invented and enjoyed exactly for its lack of historical charge and weight.[3] This is a form of convergence of content considered by many as transforming museums into theme or even attraction parks.

The three trends are mutually dependent as to their effects. One example is that global consumer culture tends to elevate ethno-cultural differences among inhabitants of one country or of Europe as a whole, substituting culture-specific ideas with goods lacking any cultural specificity and with entertainment deprived of cultural articulation. This results in a further decrease in the attractiveness of museums to immigrants. A government response to this may be the requirement for museums to offer more personal choice and fun in order to become more profitable.

Learning and entertainment in traditional museum culture

Before sketching the future of the museum as envisioned by participants in the SCALEX project we have to settle on a baseline from which envisioned changes are to be projected. Our studies do not include a wide survey of current museum practices from which a general overview might be produced. Instead we characterize the target experiences that current museums aim at in a global fashion.

Of course, museums vary enormously among themselves as to target experiences. If we start from a well-known definition given by the UNESCO in 1996, we may distinguish some ten museum types on the basis of their collection, ranging from art through science and technology, history and ethnography to any other content. The traditional tasks of a museum are to collect and preserve objects in its domain, and to contribute to knowledge of these through classification, description and interpretation of their significance and value through research according to professional academic standards. In the second instance, objects and knowledge are transmitted to the public. This public function of museums has developed throughout the twentieth century, and determines to a large extent the experiences that are offered to the visitor. The essential experiences have to do with learning and, in particular, with learning about the past. What is to be learned is a matter of consensus among experts, e.g., art historians and historians about valid knowledge. As a consequence in general, the knowledge is canonical and intellectual. Professional knowledge is not always translated into terms that non-initiated visitors can understand readily or grasp as relevant to their own life.[4] The visitor experience consists of contemplation of the object and added information received from labels and a catalogue, in some cases complemented by audio support and, in the ideal case, by live explanation from a key person such as a museum guide or teacher. Nevertheless, there are large differences among museums as to what is considered a learning experience. For instance, aesthetic encounters (e.g. discovering structure and enjoying beauty) or historical ones (e.g. experiencing a possibly sensational feeling of communication with a person or community from the past) may be acclaimed by some conservators but not by others (Csikszentmihalyi and Robertson 1990). Emotion and a personal touch to the experience have been introduced in some museums. There are many examples of successful experiments in stimulating the creation of vivid personal memories.[5] The Viking Ship Museum in Roskilde, Denmark, offers its visitors the opportunity to dress in replicas of Viking clothes. Seeing yourself and your company in Viking clothes brings history to life in a first-person *tableau vivant* that facilitates a historical sensation ('Aha, that is how they looked'),[6] an historical imagination ('That's how I would have looked if...') and a personal memory of the experience, like a snap-shot picture ('That's how I looked, then and there'), to be remembered after the visit. Likewise, physically experiencing what a strain it is to serve in combat as a soldier adds a personal touch to the information available in texts, photographs, and films of the First World War, as the Imperial War Museum in London affords its visitors. They offer a hands-on experience in a reconstructed site of trenches, including carrying a backpack as heavy as the ones actually used. In these cases, learning is accompanied by emotions such as surprise, awe and joy. Adding the emotional and personal dimension to the experience is by no means common, and in museum circles it is downright controversial, as some consider it entertainment that distracts attention from the real knowledge. There are large differences within this controversy, not only between museums with different content, but also historically determined ones between countries.[7] Some museums want to remain a place for contemplation and education, more or less against all sorts of pressure from the outside world.[8] Others either do not mind or even aim at presentations that combine learning with strong feeling.[9] But on the whole, entertainment in a narrower sense, that is, pleasurable experiences that are unrelated to serious content, is not offered as part of the actual experience of objects, at least not in regular museums as opposed to theme parks.[10] When pure entertainment is offered at all, it is carefully separated from object presentations in specialized spaces, such as the museum café and shop.[11] Exceptions to the rule may be special events such as the Museum Night in Amsterdam, where visitors were allowed to dance under the

Night Watch, or attempts of museums to attract primary school children offering Halloween-like attractions. It is fair to say that museums judge it necessary to remain clearly distinct from theme parks that integrate knowledge supply – usually simplified in comparison to museums – with entertaining experiences. Experiments with game-like experiences, such as adding reality, enhancing bodily sensations, and virtual historical environments, are met with suspicion by many a curator. In this respect museums act in line with the European tradition that sets fun apart from (national) cultural learning as pointed out by Rune Klevjer in his contribution on games to this volume.

A view from within: Four SCALEX studies

In the development of SCALEX we studied potential users at various stages of the design of the system and its implementation in a prototype. Two categories of end-users have been studied, namely museum staff involved in designing and producing exhibitions, and museum visitors, the ultimate target group of SCALEX whose experiences would have to be enhanced by the system. We present two studies from the user requirements research, initial investigations aiming at the end-users' view of current exhibition practices and views of ideal museum visits.

SCALEX museums research[14]

User-requirement research provides developers with a basis for defining the desired functionality of the system in its appropriate context of use. In the context of this contribution, it offers an insight in how they view the relation between learning and entertainment as target experiences.

The museums taking part in the project are the natural starting point for determining user requirements. As a consequence, the ensemble of museums we studied is small and far from representative of all museums, e.g. as classified by ICOM-Unesco, the international society of museums. Three of the institutions, Ars Electronica, Zentrum für Kunst und Medientechnologie and C3, are *art centres*, that is, institutions facilitating the production of works of art in the first place, and offering public access to the works in the second. AEC and ZKM are also museums by definition, as they have collections, whereas C3 is less so, lacking a collection as it does. It does have a virtual collection. The fourth and fifth museum partners are more or less classical technology museums, the Technisches Museum Wien and the Narodnické Technické Muzeum Praha. They may be representative of the category of traditional science and technology museums (as opposed to science centres), but are traditional museums with an open mind towards cultural innovation.

As part of the research into user requirements of the system, we made an inventory of all museum partners, as to their culture and environment. In particular, we examined their organizational structure and embedding, mission, aims, workflows and procedures, and their usual way of designing and producing exhibitions. For this chapter we report on the analysis of *target experiences*. What museums have in mind when contemplating the ideal visitor experience is illustrative of their opinion on the relation between learning and entertainment. We asked the museums for their mission and main targets and for the methods used to achieve target experiences in their public. In looking for views of the relation between learning and entertainment, we had to take some freedom in interpreting the answers that were originally given, as we did not directly inquire on views of the relation between these two elements of visitor experiences.

Mission and target groups: The mission statements of all museums except C3 have education as an important part. C3's mission involves supporting the production of new ideas and art works, but as the institute is keen to distribute these, we might say that they also tend to support the *reception* of the ideas, which has an educational nature. ZKM's educational mission may be less pronounced than that of the remaining two museums, but it may be that contributing to the discourse on art and technology has educational side effects, in that visitors and interested persons learn about new art views. It would seem, then, that education as a task for art centres is not so much *lifting the masses* as it is *education permanente* of a rather select target group, although the centres differ among themselves at this point, with AEC probably aiming the most at a general public, and attending less exclusively to the artistic dimensions of technology. Pioneering developments in their content area is an assignment shared by the art centres, and this function may guarantee the presentation of innovative content, perhaps in innovative ways as well. If so, this mission implies evoking strong feeling, but not necessarily in all; the art world, a relatively cosmopolitan group of initiated or dedicated and even productive persons may be the primordial addressees of novelties. The technical museums TMW and NTM have a much more clear-cut educational mission, transferring the knowledge of the histories of technology to the general public and to youngsters in particular. *Entertainment* is not part of the mission of any of the museums, but if we consider the term's somewhat broader sense, the strong feelings associated with pioneering trends might make for the kind of superior entertainment that is inherent to savouring novelties and breakthroughs in art. NTM explicitly mentions the importance of aesthetic enjoyment even in its mission statement. The pleasures of media entertainment may be one of the themes of permanent displays and special exhibitions, thus being contextualised and perhaps integrated into an educative discourse. Entertainment taken in its narrower sense, in which pleasure for its own sake dominates, distracting from serious matters, is definitely irrelevant or even inimical to what the museums see as their primary task, which is to further a serious cause.

Raison d'être: In reply to the question as to the *why* of their mission, reasons given are mainly pedagogical in the sense that they involve propagating a set of ideas that are beneficial to society and the individual. Dealing with ignorance (a lack of knowledge, of proper knowledge, knowledge of other disciplines than one's own, government's ignorance or inaction) is the best summary of the *why* of missions. Not surprisingly, entertainment is not included in any of the mission statements that we found.

Methods: Answers to the question of how missions can be accomplished again show a difference between the art centres and the technical museum. The longitudinal perspective of TMW and NTM fits more or less with the academic tradition of chronological historiography followed in schools. Adding other disciplinary contexts and multiple views of history is a more contemporary treatment, emphatically aimed at by both museums. The two approaches allow for effective conventional communication of more or less standardized knowledge through labels and sources of information additional to objects. The art centres start from an almost diagonally opposed perspective, evaluating present developments from the standpoint of a future. Extrapolation of trends and confrontation of viewpoints is far removed from conventional academic traditions of art history, and the methods for conveying knowledge are less obvious than in traditional art museums. Maybe they could be characterized as forms of *deconditioning*. Thematic ordering, unexpected points of view, a surprising and a playful presentation in various spaces contribute to making obvious trends (technological and or artistic) that may go unnoticed in daily life. Involvement with the visitor, by unsolicited encouragement and instruction deconditions the average person, who is used to being left alone in a museum, and may help in overcoming undue embarrassment and fear, as in AEC. As regards emotional impact of methods, the *historical sensation* that is a correlate of understanding the uses of past technology offered by TMW and NTM, finds a counterpart in the regular surprises and occasional shocks offered by contemporary media art, its presentation and accompanying texts. TMW did not mention emotion as a desirable visitor experience (see column 'Make the visitor...' in Table 1), but does stress the importance of strong experience as complementary to information and also sees the desirability of art installations in presentations, and the importance of rich sensory experiences, including haptic ones. The objects provoke lots of emotion by themselves, but nevertheless it appears that emotions are made subservient to awareness of historical significance. NTM has identified aesthetic and other emotions as target experiences, and they express almost literally what a historical sensation should be. The art centres do not explicitly cater for emotion, with AEC as an exception.

Provide what? Information is the major content of the experience, although C3 does not mention it explicitly. However, they declared educational programmes to be one of their aims. Furthermore, they mentioned the integration of arts, science and technology in society as a core objective, and it is hard to imagine how this can be achieved without distributing information in one way or another. AEC and TMW also provide for entertainment experiences. To this end AEC prefers interaction with its objects to static instalments, and TMW attempts to present objects in different contexts and through a variety of media. They both indicated that having the visitor return should be a target of the experience offered, and this implies at least that boredom is actively countered. NTM strives towards offering interactivity and experimentation to its visitors, and as stated, also want to occasion aesthetic gratification.

Personalization

All museums are interested in a form of personalizing their presentations. This is only to be expected, because they all participate in a project that specifically aims at personalization. However, time and again, it has become apparent from the interviews that the structure of the knowledge, about collection and exhibition items that is to be brought home to audiences, is in itself manifold. Perspectives on and ways of contextualizing materials and descriptions are not unitary, as only a quick glance at the 'How' column of Table 1[15] shows. Obtaining the best match possible between the visitors' interests on the one hand and perspectives and contexts on the other is expected to increase visitor satisfaction and to facilitate the museum's educational endeavours.

Conclusions

The conclusion about our main question from this study is that the museums in the SCALEX consortium all promote some form of learning, from more or less straightforward history lessons to an understanding of complex ideas and trends. The target groups range from schoolchildren to art and technology professionals. The contents of the lessons concern serious matters, including the evolution and significance of technology, and the risks of misconceptions of art and technology. There is also ample room for emotion, which is functional in acquiring more profound and lasting insights, or part of the content matter itself, e.g. *the future shock*. It would seem that all our museums deliberately attempt to break with an overly cerebral tradition and are inventive when it comes to answering challenges posed by subjects and presentation. They do not eschew the controversial, and they have a sound fascination for the interactive, personally involving, memorable multimedia exhibits. Solutions to the challenges include spatial, technical and personnel provisions. Technical solutions, art installations, technical devices to experiment and play with, may evoke states that pretty closely approximate the 'techno-pleasures' that Rune Klevjer discusses in the sections *playing the machine*, *bodily sensations*, *Cyborg fantasy* and *explorative trance* of his chapter on games in this volume. Some of the museums qualify these as entertaining, by which they probably mean something like engaging or exciting. However, it is also clear that they all want to stay away from the attraction-like variant of entertainment. In that sense they remain true to the ideals of the conventional museum, however different they are from the average museum, and may be easily set apart from theme parks and entertainment parks.

SCALEX visitor research

The SCALEX system was developed according to principles of user-centred design (van Wely & van der Veer 2000; Mayhew 1994). Before any line of code was written, potential users, that is, visitors of SCALEX-supported exhibitions were consulted about their wishes. Of course, we cannot expect that museum visitors can conjure up for the system designer a picture of what a support system should look like, but they can tell what they expect from exhibitions, distinguishing needs and wishes that are usually met from ones that are not. Interviewing test visitors, while presenting them with a simple scenario or a simulation of a system-supported visit, helps them to consider shortcomings of usual exhibitions and reflect on what they would really want.

Study 1[16]

The aim of this small-scale study was to inspire concept developers, and system and user interface designers, by offering them a structured view of visitor requirements in terms of general motivations and concrete needs, fears, fantasies and dreams. The aim was not to gather data that could be generalized to any population of museum visitors. However, for the purposes of the present chapter, the data illustrate the range of ideal experiences and the individual differences among visitors. Nine test visitors were invited to visit a museum. They were presented with scenarios of a museum visit, consisting of a description of what an imaginary person might see, experience and do on his or her way through a SCALEX-supported exhibition.[17] The persona-based scenarios were read aloud, and illustrations of views of artwork in museum rooms and the touch screen of a hand-held device were simultaneously presented. Test visitors were asked to elaborate on the scenario by indicating what they liked about events and actions and why. Additional interviews were taken in situ (Jordan 1996). In addition, they were asked how presentations might be altered and improved and why. Their contributions were analysed according to various content categories. Here we discuss information needs, desired emotional experiences and the ideal museum experience as envisioned by test visitors.

Information needs, fears and fantasies: It became abundantly clear that most test visitors have a need for information and learning that is insufficiently met by current presentations. A minority of statements referred to information overload, but the vast majority dealt with a lack of information. The knowledge items most needed were information about details of objects (context-sensitive information), information used in comparing or contrasting one object with another in order to detect unique versus generalized features (related works) and stories about the artist's intentions. These findings parallel those obtained in other visitor studies (Marsh 2000). However, what individual visitors wanted to know, and what they considered 'sufficient and clear', varied greatly. This concerned, first, what they found interesting, e.g. historical backgrounds, style, biographical stories etc. Second, there were differences as to depth of information. For instance, a visitor interested in historical background might want to know what a particular costume says about the represented person's status, whereas another might want to see contrasting costumes that are not depicted but would contribute to an understanding of the underlying codes.

Emotion in learning: In this small-scale study the information needed by test visitors may be interpreted as functional for the richness of and personal touch to the aesthetic and historical experience, rather than just contributing to professionally sanctioned 'official' knowledge. To give a few examples:

■ The desired context-sensitive information supports acute sensory experiences by guiding attention to relevant details

■ Information about the artist's intention facilitates virtual communication with a historical person, era or community
■ Clear and sufficient general information about the object enhances intellectual enjoyment of discovering structure, function and meaning of the object

What is less clearly visible from the selected statements is that information needs, wishes and fantasies and information uses seem to be modelled upon experience of Internet use. It is not surprising that our informants, confronted as they were with an imaginary information system, tended to identify system support with the Web, or more precisely, hypertext-functionality. It seemed natural for them to have choices all the time, of using or not using information functions, choosing rubrics, and determining their own depth level of information. This is another manifestation of the coupling of learning with feeling. Self-determination of learning goes along with pleasant feelings of autonomy and control, as has been shown in other qualitative visitor research as well (e.g. Csikszentmiahlyi & Robertson 1990; Marsh 2000). In fact, test visitors often indicated that current museum information lags behind the possibilities that they have come to see as self-evidently useful. These visitors appeared to find it only natural that the information that they want is there, behind the user interface, without wondering about the efforts required to get it there, or considering the problem of choices that conservators and other museum staff inevitably have to make. In addition, the evaluation of proposed SCALEX functions also revealed that visitors seek for ways to make learning less cumbersome – bookmark and route functions were found attractive because they facilitate remembering and planning – and are even fun. An example of the latter proposed by one of the test visitors is that a quiz function would be a great help in intensifying looking and learning. Another proposed a possibility to 'talk back' to the makers of an exhibition, asking why they selected certain items.

Given the observation that our test visitors clearly want learning-with-feeling, it may come as a surprise that, generally speaking, the information that they wanted is pretty close to what museums would want to offer. The artist's background and intentions, related works, context sensitive information and so on, are part of the knowledge that is considered core business, because it relates directly to the collection of objects and the knowledge about these that is valued by the professional museum community. It may be that our visitors had information in mind that looks 'popularized' to some academic expert. An emphasis on 'artist intention' – at the cost of authorized factual information – will be conceived by some as trading valuable art historical knowledge for superficial interpretation and anecdotal storytelling.[18] But there were also clear limits to the test visitor's information needs, unrelated to the works of art and objects. For example, the gossip function offered in one of the scenarios, based on the persona Lotte, an adolescent high school student, was not popular with the informants. Only the lookalike of Lotte, the youngest participant in the study, found it appealing.

The ideal experience according to visitors. Some of the functionality and knowledge needs mentioned by test visitors were manifestations of more profound goals and attitudes relating to their motivation to visit museums at all. This was clear from the way they were stated, or they popped up in the final interview, in which we inquired explicitly about ultimate motives and ideal experiences. The following aspects of desired or cherished experiences were repeatedly mentioned:

- Emotion, including experiencing beauty, authentic objects and personal feelings such as inspiration and involvement with the object and its significance.
- Entertainment, a word used by only one test visitor. Others used words like fun, or 'not boring'. Many statements in the final interviews were about a lively experience, and comments at the proposed support functions also expressed a desire for vividness.
- Learning, varying as to the degree to which 'official' knowledge, is wanted, as we have seen.
- Independent exploration and discovery. This is a kind of learning, but it may be considered separately because some test visitors hinted at an experience of a personal quest.
- Seeking silence was only mentioned explicitly a few times, but is a well-known motive for museum visits. Some people seek an encounter or something like a spiritual experience with historical objects, one so personal that it should be enjoyed in isolation.

These findings may be linked to preferred visitor experiences known from previous research on museum experiences. In a number of studies evidence was found of preference dimensions that can be interpreted as originating in a distinction between more introverted and more extraverted experiences. Introverted experiences consist of comprehension of abstract concepts through observation and thinking. In extraverted ones, concrete impressions gathered by active experimentation prevail.[19] (Note that we are not referring to personality differences, or to quality of experience, when using the introversion-extraversion distinction.) The latter type of experience lends itself more to sharing with others than the former. Seeking silence, personal feelings and perhaps learning the more official knowledge would seem to be more introverted experiences, whereas entertainment, involvement with objects and learning less-authorized knowledge may be part of more extraverted experiences.

Conclusions of Study 1

This study illustrated the variety of needs, fears, wishes and dreams that visitors of museums may have. For many, current museum visits may lack *intensity*. They want more information, more autonomy in learning, a higher rate of impressions, explicit on the spot instruction and vividness of the experience. The sought intensity has a lot to do with emotional experience based on a personal meaningfulness. In fact, the distinction between learning and emotional experience is hard to draw. Emotionally charged intensity of learning may border on entertainment. However, we rarely met with wishes of pure entertainment, obtaining only one expression of it in our youngster. Our test visitor's suggestion, it would seem, is rather that entertainment in the museum is not a side-attraction. It resides in the objects, in the information, in their joint presentation and in an active role of the visitors themselves *vis-à-vis* objects and information. Finally, what the visitors want does not imply a break with traditional museum practice. Canonical stories about what art and heritage objects mean are clearly wanted as well as professional knowledge and explanation. And there should be room for the contemplation and sincere and quiet study of valuable items.

Although the scale of the study was limited, we have conceived the results as a plea for personalization of museum visits. Visitors want to find what they desire, and that may be different from the very general, inter- or impersonal presentation of objects offered currently. In addition we were struck by the impression that the Internet, with its unlimited information and free navigation is the information-cum-entertainment model for visitors, although what is possibly a minority, but an important one, might prefer to be left to themselves, removed from information overload. But it should be kept in mind that our test visitors were not a representative sample of the visitor population.[20]

Studies 2 and 3[21]

Studies 2 and 3 were meant to cast further light on the desire for autonomy in visitors that emerged as a trend from the scenario research. The previous study suggested that visitors want a selection of objects and information that is tailored to their personal interests. It is important, therefore, for system developers to know how visitors should be assigned to the proper subset of objects and to information that matches their needs and wishes. Profiling is a procedure that is becoming popular in Internet business. Customers give answers to a short questionnaire in order to provide a server system with information about them. They are then classified by the system as bearers of a profile that can be further refined by adding data about their consumer behaviour.

We built an interactive simulation of a simple exhibition in a film museum, in which visitors go to rooms where they can view films. Before entering the first room, films and descriptions were selected, using the system. There were three methods of selection:

- The visitor answered one set of questions, resulting in a choice by the system (opaque profiling).
- The visitor chose from a complete list of available items with some explanation (no profiling).
- The visitor made a selection in steps, the system narrowing down choices at each step (medium profiling).

Once in the rooms, visitors could either select and play the movies themselves or they could leave both selection and playing to the visitor support system. We registered satisfaction with the three versions of the visitor support system that varied with the degree of control left to the visitor.

For Study 2, 64 test visitors were selected, varying with regard to age, gender and frequency of museum visits. Thirty-two students of two Amsterdam high schools participated in Study 3. The schools differed as to home background of the students (predominantly Dutch versus predominantly from immigrant families). The results of both studies showed that a large majority of almost a hundred test visitors judged all three interactive simulations more attractive and useful than a traditional exhibition. Furthermore, a majority of test visitors preferred access to the objects without being assigned to any profile by the support system. They also massively preferred autonomy in selecting and playing materials. These results may be taken to mean that, although visitors do want objects and information that they find personally interesting, they dislike delegating control to a support system. However, it turned out that some immigrant students, mostly from Turkish and Moroccan families, preferred more guidance, i.e. they preferred profiling by the system and being presented with pre-selected movies by the system much more often than the autonomous alternative. They also spent more time at actually watching the movies. Finally, the students from Dutch homes played somewhat more with films and options than their immigrant fellows and stated that they wanted to be in control of their visit. They also showed a higher awareness of the simulation, which explains in part the difference in attention spent to the contents.

Conclusions of Studies 2 and 3
The two studies point in the same direction as the scenario research, but they also add some nuance to the picture obtained in Study 1.

First, the craving for personal meaning and learning that we met in Study 1 is clearly not met by telling visitors what they are assumed to like. Profiling without and even with participation of the visitor is not appreciated. Even though one of the test visitors in the scenario research came up with a vision of the computer telling him what he would like to see, confronting visitors with a system that knows best, or makes sequential decisions, tended to created a lack of understanding and even frustration. Informants complained that they wanted to know what was there to choose from, and, once they were profiled, they expressed an urge to know what they had missed. The autonomy motive was, therefore, stronger than the need for guidance, at least as implemented in this experiment. Further research is needed in order to establish what ways of guidance are not experienced as a sort of Big Brother control.

Second, the idea that visitors find interactive exhibitions more attractive and useful than traditional ones is in line with a desire for more involving and self-controlled learning. It was concluded from interviews that attractiveness had to do with autonomy and a potential for free exploration, adding to one's personal involvement and rewarding curiosity. Qualitative evidence for this preference seemed stronger in youngsters than in older informants. The need for autonomy and personal involvement in learning may have been acquired or strengthened by Internet use. The idea of SCALEX is already reminiscent of Web-applications and the method used, an interactive Flash simulation, undoubtedly contributed to the 'hypertext feel' of the test exhibition. The slight differences between younger and older informants in preference for the test exhibition may be explained in part by differential uses of Internet and in part by age related, more profound, motivation factors.

Third, the importance of the immigrant students' different opinion can hardly be underestimated. The effect was of a maximal strength. It may be that cultural differences in the appraisal of the test situation as such have played a role. Also, it is known that immigrant children have less access to Internet provisions than children from Dutch families. But the overall impression was that these students felt a stronger need for guidance. This may also be a culturally determined attitude in youngsters from the cultures represented in our test visitor group, e.g. less resistance to more directive forms of guidance, or a preference for more introverted experiences. These may be supplied by the museum, or alternatively, more effort may be given to invite and stimulate more autonomous learning. But another explanation is a more general lack of common ground between what museums have to offer – including, in our case, the historical movies that were the content of the test exhibition – and what immigrant children know and find attractive *a priori*. In that case guidance may not be the best support to offer, but rather additional information and materials that bridge the cultural gap. Further research is needed to disentangle the two motives. However, we believe that they both deserve to be taken in mind when designing the museum of the future.

The museum meets the visitor in SCALEX
The experiences that museums partaking in the SCALEX project want to offer and the ones demanded by the visitor seem to meet, very globally speaking. The visitors' desire for intense experiences may be answered by the museums' core business: collecting and preserving cultural content that is worth seeing and remembering. For the art centres the content itself has a high-intensity potential because it consists of new, possibly controversial and even provocative views and developments and, last but not least, of intriguing examples of works of art. Finding forms of presentation that maximally exploit these content features seems to be the challenge that has to be met, and technology such as SCALEX may lend a helping hand in achieving the right solutions. The optimistic perspective fits their visitors to the degree that they are equipped to appreciate the developments that are being exposed and produced, that is, a rather erudite audience. To those who are new to the international art culture, e.g. schoolchildren and, *a fortiori*, immigrants from outside the industrialized countries, even the most sensational trends in art and technology may remain devoid of meaning and interest as long as no information is offered that fills the gap, and it remains to be seen whether adding explanation only during a visit can suffice. For these visitors the entertainment is clearly less in the objects and the information, let alone in the discourse informing these. Also, the more challenging ways of presenting objects and information may be lost on them. The technical museum, which is much closer to the prototypical culture-historical museum, has another type of content that is 'sensational' and therefore able to attract sustained interest from its visitors. It is packed with awe-

inspiring examples of lost technology, stories of success, failure and unlimited ambition. The challenge here may be to deepen the learning, for instance, to place less obvious objects within the visitors' experience, and to convey more remote background information, e.g. views from various disciplinary angles. Visitors from other cultures, e.g. schoolchildren with an immigrant home background, may be as impressed as others, but may need extra information, to the extent that they are unaware of relevant local historical facts and trends. TMW have extensively experimented with SCALEX' personalization functions in their exhibition *Wienblick*, where locals and non-locals each got different information on historical buildings and sites. Special interests (historical, architecture etc.) were also served by offering different tours.

We may conclude from our limited studies and our limited viewpoint that both museums and visitors do distinguish entertainment in learning from entertaining *tout court*. In pure entertainment the visitor experience is divorced from learning about and appreciating objects and information. Our museums go a long way in making learning more personal, intimate and even fun. But pure entertainment functions are not appreciated. Visitors do want more involvement, stronger feeling and more immediate reward of curiosity, but fun, which is too remotely associated with the objects, and knowledge, is not sought, except by some youngsters.

However, we have to stress that our test informants did not include people who never visit museums and in order to attract these, or seduce them to pay a visit, the more drastic measure of offering entertainment alongside exhibitions as a side attraction, may be mandatory.

Fragmentation and convergence in learning and entertainment
In concluding this contribution, we attempt to evaluate the relevance of our research for the question of media fragmentation and convergence in a changing Europe, the topic of the present volume. Are the views of learning and entertainment that we observed in the SCALEX museums particular to the countries involved? And how do they fit in larger international trends? The answers that we suggest are tentative and are not connected to our data other than by a thin line of speculative interpolation.

The functions collection, conservation and study that we described as the core of traditional museum culture were once called into existence as a corollary of national agendas. The first museums as we know them today were institutions that served to support the idea of a nation state, by (re-)constructing a common past of a regional community and furthering a shared knowledge and awareness of the past. European and American museums developed as sites of national heritage. During the twentieth century, museums became more international, because of trends in the arts and in the sciences of art and art history. In many cases an exclusive emphasis on the national past gave way to studying international relations in the history of art and culture. Internationalization of organizations is perhaps as important as that of content. Even though national museums have a firm position within their countries and, in part, still function as centres of national heritage, the leading ones are also members of international associations, furthering all sorts of collaboration ranging from exchange of expertise and works of art and culture to the joint production of exhibitions. We can duly speak of a global community of museums, largely informal in nature, but sharing approximately the same values, standards and views all over Europe and the US. The museums taking part in SCALEX are all part of subnetworks of the global museum community. They share the view that a museum is an institute for learning, enabled by communication of knowledge according to professional standards and not for entertainment. It is as probable that our museums are in the *avant-garde* of the global museum community, in terms of awareness of trends in the arts, technology and culture and, also, as their attention to visitor needs and wishes is concerned.

Museum visitors are people who take part in various cultures. One of these is undoubtedly global consumer culture that is in many ways diametrically opposed to global museum culture. Entertainment in a strict sense holds a central place in this culture. According to mainstream conceptions of it, entertainment is primarily geared towards getting pleasure at low cost: one of its conditions is that content lacks personal relevance. We should not run any personal risk in entertaining ourselves, in the first place: gambling is fun as long as you do not walk away from the table with lasting debts. And entertainment drama is less entertaining when actors suddenly start talking as real people to one or more persons in the audience. Art, on the other hand, can have a personal impact that is not always pleasurable, and historical knowledge can, likewise, be the cause of a painful confrontation with shortcomings of our ancestors, of the tradition we live in and even of mankind. Another, related, condition of entertainment is that content should not be official, authoritative or obligatory in any sense. The attractiveness of popular entertainment fare is associated with its entire lack of sanctioned meaning, derived from official knowledge that we have to learn in school. Global consumer culture is a powerful one. The place of national and international cultural heritage with its claims of historical legitimacy is taken by industrially produced popular content, lacking any claim of historical grounding. Study and learning in museums have their often more attractive and more readily available counterpart in entertainment by television, film and games and by Internet surfing.

Museum visitors do not entirely or exclusively identify with this culture, for, if they did, they would probably not belong to the population category visitors. It is not too difficult to identify traces of global consumer culture in our visitor study in the firm expectation that knowledge ought to be just one click away. This expectation may very well be an artefact of the method of study where test visitors were presented with an imagined hand-held computer in a museum visit scenario but we suspect that the need for emotional intensity is not. Neither are expectations of immediacy of service, autonomy in setting goals of instruction, and a certain resistance to official histories the ultimate hallmark of popular entertainment culture. It is conspicuous that at least some of the visitors in our studies were emphatically seeking personal meaning, and that personal meaning and involvement invoked strong feelings, including the need for fun. But it is important to recognize that museum visitors *are* part of global consumer culture, and some more than others.[22] It could be expected that the new Europeans, arriving from Africa and Asia will often more readily become participants in global consumer culture than in global museum culture. However, our third visitor study revealed that at least some of them prefer the traditional museum visit, probably with more explanation, to the Internet-like free surfing and active-choice style.

We have seen that it may be possible to reconcile the two cultures at least in part. A demand for undiluted entertainment cannot be met, but a great deal more pleasure in learning might be achieved when the visitor is afforded more control and autonomy. Breaking up a uniform presentation into those that appeal to a diversity of visitor categories would also be an improvement to this end. The real challenge is to find the optimum between two extremes. One extreme is the same story for all, one that excludes major segments of the population, and the other is everybody's personal story, utterly destroying the idea of a single community for all.[23] Our results suggest that a double bifurcation in the presentation of objects and information may be required. The first is between a guided presentation, which has explanation according to a more or less fixed schema as its main characteristic and free exploration. The second bifurcation is in free exploration only. This consists of a choice between completely free-roaming and discovery on the one hand and on the other, multiple-choice information and presentation styles aimed at special interests, temperaments etc.

Whatever palette of choices is opted for, a lot of mediation is required in order to help the visitor learn pleasurably. Having an army of well-trained guides, knowledgeable about both the museum's subject matter and visitor psychology, would probably be the best solution. An adaptive support system may be second best, for the time being at considerable length, but somewhat cheaper. From our limited view the museum of the future looks like a collection of places, some of them virtual, including a library, a place of worship and a club.

Notes

1. Ed Tan was employed at Vrije Universiteit Amsterdam when Study 1 was carried out.
2. The authors are indebted to a great number of people who participated in the research. We would like to thank the colleagues from the museum partners in the SCALEX project: Sabine Himmelsbach, Anke Hoffmann, Eva Kühn, Otmar Moritsch, Dietmar Offenhuber, Adèle Eisenstein, Brigitte Rauter for their contributions to this paper. The research reported in Study 1 was carried out by Mick de Neeve and Guido Stulemeijer. Tim Voors (Lost Boys) designed the artwork for the scenarios. We are grateful for the support that we received from two schools in Amsterdam, Herman Wesselink College and Hervomd Lyceum West. None of these persons is responsible for conclusions, views, let alone possible errors that this contribution contains.
3. SCALEX (SCALable EXhibition server) is a part of the Information Technologies Society actions of the Fifth Framework programme sponsored by the European Commission. (Number IST-2001-35103.) (For an introduction to the Fifth Framework Programme and its relevance for European museums and other cultural heritage institutions, see Smith (2002).) The project started in April 2002 and was finished in June 2004. The aim of the project was to develop a set of tools for the creation and presentation of exhibitions in museums, adding rich multimedia content. Partners in the project were Fachhochschule Joanneum, Graz;

ASCoR, Univerity of Amsterdam, Amsterdam; Johannes Kepler University, Linz; Joanneum Research, Graz; Lost Boys Ltd, Amsterdam; ADM, Graz; Ars Electronica, Linz; C3 Center for Culture and Communication, Budapest; Zentrum für Kunst und Medientechnologie, Karlsruhe; Narodni Technicke Muzeum, Prague; Technisches Museum Wien; and Institut für Film und Bild in Wissenschaft und Unterricht, Grünwald.

4. This approach is also acclaimed by museum innovators wishing to expand the role of technology; see, for instance, Knerr (2000).

5. There is no 'Europeanness' in computer games, as Rune Klevjer observed in the previous chapter, and there is no national cultural heritage in them either. Instead, they conform to a fictional aesthetics that is by nature a cultural hybrid, mixing elements from mostly American and Japanese popular culture, according to the golden rule of 'anything goes' (Klevjer, this volume).

6. Philip Wright's (1989) complaints about the lack of communication between museum educators and their public have been met in part, but most of these are still valid in a large number of museums.

7. Using a psychological term they could be called *episodic* memories, as opposed to more abstract, categorical memories, usually called *semantic*.

8. The term was coined by the historian of culture Johan Huizinga in his inaugural lecture *Het aesthetisch bestanddeel van geschiedkundige voorstellingen* (*The aesthetic ingredient of historical imagery*), Groningen 1905.

9. See, for instance, Peter Greenhalgh's treatment on the difference between France and England concerning the acceptance of pleasure and entertainment as key elements of a museum visit, already visible in the attitudes towards the great exhibitions of the late nineteenth and early twentieth century.

10. It is illustrative that some museums are reluctant to use temporary exhibitions that they associate with blockbuster policy and with an overemphasis on emotion and spectacle. This view has been very influential, but today it is not common any more. (McCann Morley 2001).

11. Science museums appear to be forerunners in this respect. Many of them are trying out combinations of play, discovery and learning by experimenting. As a consequence, the distinction between science museums and science centres may become fuzzy. Science centres have made emotional experience and entertainment into indispensable conditions of learning (Bradburne 1998).

12. By 'regular museums' we refer to institutions classified by UNESCO.

13. See Stephen (2001) for an overview of attempts to find a new balance between education and entertainment functions of museum buildings; and Greenhalgh (1989) for a historical illustration of the search for a balance in late-nineteenth-century Europe.

14. Reported in Rohde, Haberz and Kipcak (2002).

15. See http://home.medewerker.uva.nl/e.s.h.tan/.

16. Reported in Tan et al. (2002).

17. For a treatment of scenario research, see Carroll (2000). For the use of personas in scenarios, Cooper (2000).

18. See, for instance, Ebert-Schifferer (2002), who considers recent art history books, well written and methodologically sound, as a bridge between art historical scholarship and the general public's curiosity.

19. The following three studies support the relevance of a distinction between introverted and extraverted experiences. From the results of a survey of six hundred visitors of the Metropolitan Museum in New York, by Smith and Wolf (1996), it may be inferred that the introverted style is strongly associated with a higher knowledge of art, more abstract thinking, longer views of single objects and information, less need of entertainment and learning, and

a tendency to plan a visit. An extraverted style is associated with a lower level of knowledge of art, more concrete thinking, shorter views of many objects and information items, a higher need of entertainment and learning, and less planning behaviour. Hinton (1999) carried out a very interesting study of preferences for exhibits at the Victoria and Albert Museum (offering information or affording activity of a more concrete or abstract nature) and visitor behaviour (doing vs. looking). Visitors of a Discovery Area were asked about their learning styles. Hinton found partial support for the validity of two learning style dimensions, active experimentation vs. reflective observation and abstract vs. concrete. A most compelling finding is that those visitors with the most reflective and abstract style had more frequent episodes of uninterrupted looking and less frequent episodes of active exploration, which was afforded by a larger number of exhibits. Simplifying the results of this study somewhat, we may recognize one underlying introversion (abstract, reflection) vs. extraversion dimension (concrete, experimentation). (It should be added that Hinton's starting point was that this dimension is, in fact, an oversimplification if we attempt to cover individual learning styles relevant for museum visits.) Finally, we would like to mention a comparative study of visitors of permanent installations of museums on the one hand and of temporary exhibitions on the other by Zammuner and Testa (2002). It would seem that the visitors of temporary exhibitions (group TE) preferred more extraverted experiences, whereas those visiting permanent (group PE) sought more introverted experiences. Self-report measures revealed that the TE visitors divided their attention more evenly across objects, had a less profound interest in art and in the exhibited works and saw their visit more as an excuse for a small trip and as a fashionable pastime, and less as a natural consequence of being in a city with a rich cultural life and history. When asked to compare the visited art institute with other social institutions, TE visitors more frequently mentioned a social club, a theatre and other institutions more often than PE visitors, whereas the latter ones more often mentioned a church and a library as most similar. Finally, the conceptual association with the visited institute that visitors had also allows for an interpretation of differences between the two groups in terms of introversion-extraversion. The visited museum was more strongly associated with 'worldliness', 'novelty' and 'a crowd' by TE visitors, and more strongly often with art, silence and antiquity by PE visitors.

20. At least one other study has shown that regular visitors of an exhibition prefer authorative historical narratives to multimedia functions combined with a random presentation (Lisus and Ericson 1999). However, due to the content of the exhibition (titled 'Art for a Nation') visitors in this study may have been extremely interested in history and more in favour of a presentation along traditional educational lines than the average museum visitor.

21. Reported in Oinonen et al. 2004.

22. In our studies, we deal with differences among museum visitors in Austria, Germany, Hungary and Czechia. One relevant distinction between them has to do with the establishment of global consumer culture, which arrived only lately in Hungary and Czechia, but has developed since the late 1940s at least in Germany and Austria.

23. This extreme individualization scenario of responding to globalization has been described by Beck (2000, pp. 147–145) does away with imagined geographical communities such as Europe. Beck makes a plea for countering the social fragmentation and exclusion inherent in this scenario (2000, esp. pp. 161–163).

References

Beck, U. (2000), *What is globalisation*, Cambridge, Polity Press.

Bradburne, J. M. (1998), 'Dinosaurs and white elephants: The science centre in the twentieth century'. *Public Understanding of Science*, 7, pp. 237–253.

Carroll, J. M. (2000), Making use: Scenario-based design of human-computer interactions. Cambridge, MA, MIT Press.

Cooper, A. (2000), The inmates are running the asylum. Indianapolis, SAMS.

Csikszentmihalyi, M. & Robertson, R. E. (1990), The art of seeing. Malibu, Getty Museum.

Ebert-Schifferer, S. (2002), 'Art history and its audience: A matter of gaps and bridges' pp. 44–51, in Haxthausen, C.W. (ed.) *The two art histories* New Haven, Yale University Press.

Greenhalgh, P. (1989), 'Education, entertainment and politics: Lessons from the great international exhibitions', pp. 74–98 in Vergo, P. (ed.) *The new museology* London, Reaktion.

Hinton, M. (1999), 'The Victoria and Albert Museum Silver Galleries II: Learning style and interpretation preference in the Discovery Area'. *Museum Management and Curatorship*, 17: 3 pp. 253–294.

Jordan, B. (1996), 'Ethnographic workplace study and CSCW', pp. 17–42, in Shapiro, D., Tauber, M. J. and Traunmuller, R. (eds.) *The design of computer supported collaborative work and groupware systems* Amsterdam, Elsevier Science.

Knerr, G. (2000), 'Technology, museums, new publics, new partners'. *Museum International*, 52: 4 pp. 8–13.

Lisus, N. A. and Ericson, R. V. (1999), 'Authorizing art: The effect of multimedia formats on the museum experience'. *Canadian Review of Sociology and Anthropology*, 36: 2 pp. 199–216.

Marsh, C. (2000), Visitors as learners: The role of emotions. ASTC Resource Center. http://www.astc.org/resource/learning/marsh.htm. First uploaded 2000.

Mayhew, D. J. (1994), The usability engineering life cycle. A practitioner's handbook for user interface design. San Francisco, Morgan Kaufmann.

McCann Morley, G. L. (2001), 'Museums and temporary exhibitions'. *Museum International*, 53: 4, pp. 56–59.

Oinonen, K., Tan, E., Artinger, V., & Wiedner, C. (2004), Evaluation of Input (Visitors), Technical Report SLX-D 2.6.1-UVA-001-01, version 3.

Rohde, T., Haberz, N., & Kipcak, O. (2002), End user requirements document. Technical Report SLX-D 2.1.1-ADM-003-01.

Rojek, C. (2000), Leisure and culture. London, Macmillan.

Smith, B. (2002), 'Digital heritage and cultural content in Europe'. *Museum International*, 54: 4 pp. 41–51.

Smith, J. K. and Wolf, L. F. (1996), 'Museum visitor preferences and intentions in constructing aesthetic experience'. *Poetics*, 24 pp. 219–238.

Stephen, A. (2001), 'The contemporary museum and leisure: Recreation as a museum function'. *Museum management and curatorship*, 19: 3 pp. 297–308.

Tan, E., de Neeve, M., Stulemeijer, G., Raijmakers, B., Schavemakers, F., Voors, T., Nieuwendijk, S., van der Veer, G., Chisalita, C., and Hoorn, J. (2002), Report on scenario-based visitor survey. A qualitative study of what museum visitors might want SCALEX to do. Techical Report SLX-D2.1.1-VUA/LB-007-01.

van Wely, M. and van der Veer, G. C., (2000), 'Structured methods and creativity: A happy Dutch marriage', Collaborative Design. Proceedings of CoDesigning London, Springer, pp. 111–119.

Wiedner, C., Kipcak, O., Oinonen, K., and Tan, E. (2003), Evaluation of Input (Museums). Technical report SLX-D2.5.1-ADM-001-01.

Wright, P. (1989), 'The quality of visitors' experiences in art museums', in Vergo, P. (ed.), The new museology . London: Reaktion, pp. 119–148.

Zammuner, V. L. and Testa, A. (2002), 'Similarities and differences in perceptions and motivations of museum and temporary exhibit visitors'. Visual Arts Research, 27: 1 pp. 89–95.

SECTION 3: ICT AND LEARNING

The mediatization of knowledge and communication

'E-learning' is given much attention in European policies. Aiming at a so-called 'knowledge society', it is generally assumed that – in the words of Peter Drucker – '...knowledge has become the capital of a developed economy, and knowledge workers the group that sets society's values and norms...' (Drucker 1989: 169). In parallel, it is assumed that knowledge can and should be transformed into a commodity within a growing knowledge industry, and that it could be mediatized as something, which, according to this assumption, under the label of e-learning can be disseminated through digital communication channels.

Many of these assumptions are questionable and insufficient. It is still not understood in which way 'knowledge' functions as capital, or how knowledge should be conceptualized in this special context. However, it is quite obvious that knowledge cannot be defined as an essence that can be 'disseminated' through distribution channels. But even though knowledge is being placed in the centre of society, and even though the commodification and mediatization of knowledge are considered to be fundamental means for the realisation of the so-called knowledge society, little has been done in relation to actually understanding the nature of knowledge in this new social context or the effects of mediatizing knowledge and learning.

This section on ICT and learning proposes a communication perspective on these issues. The section focuses on the use of ICT perceived as media in new forms of education. From this media and communication perspective follows a critique of 'e-learning' in 'the knowledge society' along three lines:

- a mediatization critique
- a knowledge theory critique
- an organizational critique

Before summarizing the following three chapters, the European e-learning policy context should be briefly presented.

E-learning policies

Regarding European e-learning policies, the systematic analysis undertaken by research assistant Roxana Ologeanu of the official European Commission and member-state documentation, is revealing. Almost all of these documents highlight what is perceived as a necessary modernization of our education systems; more importantly, they emphasize a range of objectives such as: the development of lifelong learning; the need for partnerships (especially between public bodies and private companies with a view to creating a sustainable content industry) and the desirability of the adoption of a digital culture. Higher education does not come in for any particular treatment, with recommendations here differing very little, despite the autonomy enjoyed by the universities.

For its part, the e-learning programme specifically designed for higher education does take into account a number of objectives, such as employability, the flexibility of labour markets and the reduction of training costs. It should, however, be noted that although e-learning here is regarded as complementary to and not as a substitute for face-to-face teaching, pointing towards blended learning models, the long-term perspective is ambitious. It is an underlying assumption that the many current e-learning projects contained in the programme will pave the way for the realization of the long-term vision of a virtual European university.

Institutional changes of universities

Whether this ambitious goal is realistic and desirable or not, there is still a long way to go before it is reached. A study for the European Commission on *Virtual Models of European Universities* shows that most universities in Europe are 'still at the stage where the use of ICT consists of treating the computer as a sophisticated typewriter', although changes on ICT and learning are on their way (Rambøll 2004: ii). The study concludes that 18% of the 200 replying universities could be characterized as 'front runners' in terms of the use of ICT in their organization and education, including extended co-operation with other universities and suppliers. The rest of the institutions in this survey showed various degrees of co-operation, self-sufficiency and scepticism about ICT in learning. Accordingly, within the institutions ICT is used more often for organizational purposes than for teaching as such (Collis & van der Wende 2003: 31).

This implies that, in the years to come, higher education institutions in Europe will be challenged to integrate ICT more deeply into their core processes and organization, and to develop strategies for effectively educating their students for the new social context (van der Wende & van der Ven 2003). This is the background for the present book section: The dissemination of e-learning in higher education in Europe will be given high priority during the years to come. Consequently, a critical theory of e-learning is required. However, because of the widespread scepticism in relation to these aims, analytical tools have not been developed to critically reflect on this process. In this section, three perspectives are suggested:

Firstly, the dissemination of e-learning will represent a new phase within the mediatization of education. Of course, teaching has always been mediatised, be it through formal lectures in lecture halls, books, notes or examination reports. But the introduction of e-learning, for instance, through compulsory learning management programmes, may not only speed up this process, but also qualitatively change the mediatization of education. In the chapter by Bernard Miège, e-learning is analysed within a communication and mediatization perspective.

Secondly, this process will influence the 'product' of education, i.e. knowledge. Lars Qvortrup analyses e-learning within a knowledge perspective. Knowledge is defined and categorized within a sociological context and the implications for the understanding of e-learning within a knowledge perspective are analysed.

Thirdly, the dissemination of e-learning will affect the organization of universities. In the chapter by Knut Lundby and Päivi Hovi-Wasastjerna, based on a comparative study, different university strategies in relation to the uptake of e-learning are identified, and potential impacts on university culture are discussed.

The mediatization critique

The mediatization process of education, and particularly of the university sector, is not a new development; indeed, it has been around for a considerable time, according to the scholars of the technology of education. Its beginnings go right back to the time when documents and other teaching aides were first used to complement and enhance the educative act. For over a century debate has raged, on occasions acrimoniously, between those for whom the pedagogical act and the transmission of knowledge is defined by and limited to the teacher-learner relationship alone, and those who see technology as an obvious vector of this relationship. This particular difference of opinion became all the more acute when the relevant authorities decided to promote seriously information and communication technologies, more often than not designed and presented as an adjunct to teachers themselves, if not as substitutes.

At university, lecturers are now strongly encouraged to make their lectures available online and to create specifically online lecture materials, as well as all sorts of other electronic resources made possible by the continuous updating of software and other IT tools. Thus innovation is certainly taking place. But we would be wrong to predict a proliferation of especially created online lectures, or of entirely virtual courses; this is a step too far, that no one now dares suggest at present. Forecasts are becoming noticeably more cautious and sober, with a whole host of cultural, socio-economic and political reasons accounting for the fact that the earlier hopes for e-learning, and other educational technologies, have been revised downwards.

It is still the case that the mediatization of university teaching is underway; but we should not expect radical or rapid change. Instead, progress will be slow, contradictory, uneven, and certainly controversial, since the matter is too complex and the technology generally inadequate. The teaching activities of universities are, in fact, simply too complicated and diverse to lend themselves to simple 'modelization' at realistic costs.

The knowledge theory critique

'E-learning' is given much attention in European convergence policies. Also, great changes have occurred, from earlier dissemination metaphors (e-learning as 'distance learning') to contemporary ideas of collaborative learning networks, digital portfolios, interactive simulation applications or virtual classrooms. Still, however, our understanding of e-learning and our ability to distinguish between different types of e-learning based on pedagogical criteria are lagging behind. Which types of learning are stimulated? Which knowledge forms are supported? Does e-learning, in the classical conceptualization of Gilbert Ryle, support knowing-what or knowing-how? It is a basic point that the technological convergence is combined with a pedagogical differentiation of e-learning models and applications. In this article a pedagogical (i.e. not technological) e-learning typology based on knowledge theory is presented, referring on the one hand to the book's initial meta-theoretical considerations, and on the other hand to the empirically oriented articles on e-learning. Also, suggestions concerning the development of European e-learning policies are presented.

The organizational critique

The EU study on *Virtual Models of European Universities* concluded that the existence of an ICT strategy that encompasses the institution as a whole is crucial. The need for management focus and priority setting come to the fore. The management level is important because the fragmented organization of the universities is an obstacle. Universities with an ICT strategy are more advanced in their integration of ICT in their own administration and organization, as well as in their educational setting. The use of ICT in the organizational setting refers to how the EU universities are using ICT administratively (e.g. for supplying course information or enabling course and exam registration) and for reinforcing and supporting their organizational structures and internal and external communication (Rambøll 2004).

The interest in and questioning of ICT and learning might start out from technology or from pedagogy but becomes entangled with organizational questions. They encompass strategies as well as communication practices. In this section, concepts of 'virtual university' and 'flexible learning' are explored as alternative strategies and as communication practices of ICT and learning in universities.

In Europe, universities are intentionally undergoing change in line with the Bologna Declaration, aiming at mobility and flexibility. However, when the two relatively open systems of the universities and the Internet merge, they tend to further restrict access through new market mechanisms. In an inventory for the present book, research assistant Mette Oftebro found that new closed systems are being built; electronic versions of relevant journals on higher education, technology and education, etc. were, to a large extent, reserved for subscribers. The open and accessible journals did not pay much attention to e-learning and institutional changes of universities.

Convergence – fragmentation

The mediatization of knowledge dissemination, knowledge sharing and knowledge creation in higher education and the resulting organizational changes are processes within a broader context. In all European countries universities and higher education institutions are being pushed in order to transform from elite institutions into mass universities.

First, however, this process happens more slowly than was expected by political bodies and manifested in the Bologna Declaration, and with complex organizational results, with some institutions supporting this trend while others resist. Second, the idea that higher education should converge into a business-like educational sector has been rightly criticized, one result being a potential fragmentation between mass and elite universities.

The basic assumption of this section is that in addition to other perspectives the change of universities and the introduction of e-learning should be analysed in a media theoretical context. The ambition of the section is to suggest critical concepts for the ongoing discussion of the complex convergence and fragmentation process of the European higher education sector: From a mediatization perspective, from a knowledge theoretical perspective and from an organizational perspective.

References

Collis, B. and M. van der Wende (eds.) (2002), Models of Technology and Change In Higher Education. An international comparative survey on the current and future use of ICT in Higher Education. Retrieved 26 May 2003, from the World Wide Web: http: //www.utwente.nl/ cheps/publications/downloadable_publications/Downloadablesenglish.doc/.

Drucker, Peter F. (1989), The New Realities. Oxford: Butterworth Heinemann.

PLS Rambøll Management (2004), Studies in the Context of the E-learning Initiative: Virtual Models of European Universities (Lot 1). Copenhagen: Final Report to the EU Commission, DG Education & Culture.

Wende, M. van der and M. van der Ven (eds.) (2003), The Use of ICT in Higher Education. A Mirror of Europe. Utrecht: Lemma.

FOR A COMMUNICATIONS APPROACH TO THE USE OF ICT IN EDUCATION

Bernard Miège

It is customary to offer theoretical and empirical justifications for taking a communications approach to the field of education. Yet there are many articles and studies, relating to various aspects of developments in educational institutions, which focus on communications technologies. In America and in Europe a great number of studies and official reports have attempted to identify the consequences of increased television viewing on the learning behaviours of school age children; they have also studied the impact on children of the use of personal computers once these become used more or less intensively for educational activities, both at school and at home. Similarly, researchers, particularly in the fields of didactics and educational sciences, have intervened regularly in this domain, most often in order to identify the supposed advantages – rarely the disadvantages or limitations – of the new communications technologies in the acquisition of knowledge, and in relations between pupils or students and teachers. These different perspectives all link in some way to the idea promoted in official circles that we are now entering the age of the 'knowledge society'.

It is not within the scope of this paper to evaluate all of these approaches; we will restrict ourselves to noting that most of them are closely related to initiatives or experiments championed by decision-makers at a variety of levels, whose desire to know the results of their ideas and innovations weighs on the research community as if it were hard fact and leads researchers to pose their questions in loaded terms: 'Do personal computers help us to learn better?' 'Do TV images not distort or otherwise disturb the acquisition of knowledge?' In this paper we challenge the assumptions that lead many practioners and researchers to pose such questions. We first question their significance and their scientific relevance, from both a communication sciences perspective and with specific regard to the field of education.

Justifying a communications approach

Communication sciences in Europe, however structured and from whichever institutional stable, began with the study of inter-individual relationships, the public relations of organizations, and, above all, the *modus operandi* of the mass media (with regard to its production, its programming and its reception). Today, these remain the dominant fields of enquiry. At the same time, the emergence of information and communication technology (ICT) and its gradual but as yet selective spread to the various social fields[1] has increasingly drawn researchers towards the study of mediatized communications outside the field of the mass media. In particular, there has been a growing interest in understanding the processes by which new technologies are introduced in society and develop, particularly as this has not been a linear process and has occurred more slowly than had been imagined. Of particular interest are the ways in which uses of these new means of communicating and transmitting information are constructed.

Communication science researchers engaged in these studies have confined themselves to applying analytical frameworks borrowed from the study of the mass media, in that they focus their research on the relationship with the means of communication in what amounts therefore to a media-centred approach. The fact that ICT is more interactive than the 'traditional' media has not altered this perspective, which we deem to be media-centric. We consider that it would be more appropriate to consider the apparent progress of the supposed 'Information Society' from the angle not of the different media themselves, nor that of the communication technologies which are deemed to be the cause of new processes of communication, but from the perspective of the social, cultural and political sites of the mediation process. Our theoretical point of departure is, thus, the study of change in these contexts, especially where there is evidence of new forms of *mediatization* as a result of the use of ICT. We are careful, however, not to artificially separate in our analysis those phenomena arising from mediatized communication from those arising from ordinary forms of communication (involving language, for example, such as body language); nor to assume that the former is replacing the latter.

Yet this perspective does not in itself suffice. ICT (like the mass media) is often seen as a conduit for tighter social control, or at the very least as a channel for the exercise of power – real or symbolic – by dominant social actors. Some authors go so far as to claim that there is evidence, in the first of these scenarios, of systematic control and, in the second, of opportunities for economic and political leaders to manipulate ICT. Even though the discussion regarding the significance of such claims remains open, this dimension of communication is incontestable, contrary to the beliefs and hopes of those neo-utopian thinkers inclined to see ICT simply as a means of social auto-construction. It is equally important to note that this aspect is not exclusive to ICT, since in contemporary societies, mediatized communication is *at one and the same time* the way in which new knowledge and skills are acquired and how increasingly individualized social behaviours are expressed: communications form one of the vectors of the individualization of society.

These are the questions to be borne in mind when setting out to study ICT in the field of education (and training). In one sense, education is affected just like health or culture, or the business world, by what we have chosen to call here *the informationalizing* of society (as opposed to its computerization). But on closer inspection we see that this global notion misses out on essential characteristics of the process. We find the study of the process by field or sector to be more enlightening, especially since the development of ICT cannot be divorced from the social changes with which it is closely linked. In this respect, education is a field that is both distinctive and of considerable interest, for a number of reasons.

First, taking education as a context in which mediation occurs, today and in the past (differently in each case), education has shown itself to be particularly 'resistant' to the adoption of mediatized modes of learning and of the transmission of knowledge. The history of the introduction of modern technologies in education provides us with many examples of this perpetual struggle between those for whom education must only occur within the relationship between teacher and pupil, and those who have regularly championed the introduction of technology, whether as an aide to the pedagogical act or as a substitute. Whilst noting that this clash has generally worked against technology (as was the case, for example, of the last three decades of the twentieth century with the cinema, audio-visual techniques and the first stages of personal computer technologies), present conditions seem more favourable to ICT: social pressures are such that resistance (which we should not assume to be categorically defensive) is no longer effective against the penetration of ICT into the educational field.

The fact is that education is potentially one of the major sectors for the deployment of these technologies, not just the hardware and tools (for distance or face-to-face learning) but also the content. Some educational decision-makers see ICT, not entirely accurately, as a way of saving on the costs of education; others consider it as bringing decisive innovation to the acquisition of knowledge and the training of both the young and adults in lifelong learning. Most of all, however, from a strategic viewpoint, education is essential for the telecommunications, computer and other hardware industries, and no doubt even more so for the 'content' industries, which is a critical sector for the future of the communications industries. The slowdown in economic growth and the fading of the high hopes prematurely placed in what was billed as the 'new economy' have not challenged these trends which, however, can be expected to play themselves out over long periods of historical time.[2] With education, we effectively find ourselves in a field where reticence to technology and especially to its commodification is strong, but which simultaneously offers, via ICT, the most potential for market development.

Finally, our focus on education has its own scholarly rationale. In many publications, approaches based on the communication sciences are mixed or even merged with other approaches, notably pedagogical (do we learn better by seeking information on the Web? Is distance learning as effective as *in situ* training?), or cognitive (what are the psycho-mental processes most favourable to learning? How can they be integrated into learning machines?). These two types of approaches generally find favour with decision-makers who look to them for answers to their questions regarding the wisdom of their choice of, and investment in, hardware and other resources. A communications science approach, however, while not overlooking these sorts of questions, is distinct, both theoretically and methodologically. In what follows we set out to focus on the specificities and originality of the communication sciences.

The communication sciences: a spectrum of research themes
In order to be more precise about what a communications approach to education might (or should) consist of, we first review some of the research themes, which are already being addressed by communication studies experts.

The industrialization of education
This is without a doubt the most talked about and the the most controversial of all questions. It often gives rise to public debates and has recently motivated social movements fighting against the industrialization and, above all, the liberalization of services, as per the World Trade Organization (WTO) agenda. It would however be a mistake to think that the WTO agreement in this respect is the source of such debates. For a long time, teachers' and parent-teacher organizations, students' unions and political organizations have protested (following national patterns) against the privatization of education that they deem would be a consequence of the call on pedagogical resources from outside the education systems, for the most part from specialized firms attached to the 'cultural industries'. In fact, it is not so much the cost of studying (which is highly variable in Europe) or the framework for study and access to knowledge (in some cases mainly public, in others highly dependent on a private sector to which responsibility has been delegated), as the call to commercial or even industrial organizations that is objected to. Furthermore, although such resistance or reticence has existed for a long time (even before the days of obligatory schooling) the pressures are much greater today. In fact, ICT has provided an opportunity to further the industrialization of education and to accelerate this process as no other educational or communications technology has done before. ICT opens up low-risk perspectives to specialized firms, and all that the recent difficulties of the 'new economy' have done is simply to deflate the decidedly overinflated claims intially made for the development of this sector.

But what exactly is meant by 'industrialization' in the context of education? This term has given rise to much confusion, which has not helped in understanding the arguments of the protagonists in the debate. For some – most, in fact, and in keeping with schools of thought that have long been influential in pedagogical studies, 'industrialization' means having recourse to technology. This might complement or facilitate the educational activities of teachers in direct contact with pupils or students, or substitute for teachers (for example by providing remote access, or recordings of the teaching sessions). Other voices, less influential but without doubt more attentive to current trends and the issues taking shape, see 'industrialization' not as limited to the use of technological hardware and resources, but also relating to the large-scale production of reproducible sources, either in their hard copy format (school books, of course, but now also CD-ROMs, DVDs etc.) or, increasingly, in virtual format (notably online access to pedagogical resources, which is not free or will not be once the markets for such products have developed). We can see that there is a world of difference between these two perspectives on 'industrialization'. In the first case, the issue, frequently discussed, is the call on technologies that rationalize the educational act and the new possibilities of seeking information from outside the teaching environment (even where these resources are provided on dedicated networks where no money is exchanged). In the second case, it is a more literal question of the possibility of accessing educational products, generally online, which constitute – or will do so – a partial but significant industrialization of education, or, at the very least, a bypassing of educational establishments. Of course, virtual universities are far from conforming to this model (contrary to the rash publicity of their promoters at the end of the last century); they function thanks to technology, in particular, that which allows networked access to resources that is more or less convergent with educational products (but less so than the advertising led one to believe...); and in this respect these cases demonstrate continuity with the findings of the 'theory of the cultural industries' in relation to commodities in the cultural and information domains.

We should add here that this distinction, which we evidently hold to be vital, does not only concern specialists. It sheds light on different sorts of current changes and allows us to identify the issues more clearly. Following Pierre Moeglin (1998) – whose typology we have nevertheless complemented and modified – we can, in fact, distinguish four types of use of ICTs in education (to be found at the various levels of the educational system):

1. *Distance-learning services*: tutoring, video-conferencing, forums, access to complementary educational resources created by staff within the educational establishment, classroom management. These services derive from current educational practices, but their implementation raises difficult problems regarding the allocation or reallocation of resources. The main factor is the use of additional hardware whose management is left to in-house personnel.
2. *Self-service resources* provided by specialized companies, using dedicated software which allows, in particular, controlled access, and guided learning in conjunction, to a greater or lesser degree, with the educational establishment. Modernized distance-learning centres tend to use this type of product, depending on the type of link – close or not – that they maintain with the educational establishments.

3. Downloadable, standardized *course modules* produced by specialist publishers. These products are akin to old-style textbook publishing which in its time created a specialized branch of the industry that functioned alongside the educational establishments and was assured of their orders. Nowadays these products relate above all to specific types of teaching: foreign language teaching methods; management courses etc.

4. Bespoke products which provide for the individualization of teaching and learning and which do not (in theory) require any human contact. These are the most heavily criticized products. According to their critics, these products effectively create a whole new environment of training and knowledge acquisition that is removed from the control of those who today are responsible for these activities. 'Virtual campuses', say the critics, will have the effect of removing the link (or at least part of it) between the training process and those 'traditionally' responsible for it. They will be accessible from home or the workplace, and consumers of such courses will have to pay for what is effectively an industrially produced educational content.

This typology has used a number of differentiating criteria: proximity to/distance from the educational establishment; socialization/individualization of the educational experience; use of equipment/access to information or content; free/payable; commercialization/industrialization. The main advantage of the typology is that it allows us to differentiate between issues and to relate them to one another, demonstrating what already exists, and what is in its infancy. Thus, type (1) uses are encountered more frequently than type (4), which are to be found mainly in the case of specialized professional training whose spread, at least in Europe, pre-supposes a whole series of economic, political and socio-institutional conditions.

The search (in vain) for the effects (or influence) of ICT
The first theories, which in the 1950s and 1960s inspired research in the communication sciences, and in particular the empirical-functionalist approach to mass media, and the cybernetic model, focused on the media and their foreseeable effects. This process of attempting to match cause (the media; ICT) to effect has since been questioned overall by most researchers and authors (with the exception of psychologists). Yet it remains very present in public debate, particularly in the field of education. Here, not only are teachers readily inclined to see the media and ICT as the 'causes' or 'origins' of the social behaviours of young pupils, working in opposite directions to their own teachings, public sector decision-makers too, in their concern to measure the outcomes of the equipment and resources distributed to teaching establishments, or of teaching methods deemed 'efficient', are avid for studies aiming to identify such results (by means of innumerable evaluation exercises, mostly relating to time-limited [à court terme] and one-off experiments). There is a number of (good) reasons why today's specialist communications approaches are less media-centred, regardless of theoretical differences; let us list them:

- Despite the spread of mediatized communication, communication is not limited to the media;
- The rejection of technological determinism implies making links between technological innovation on the one hand, and social and cultural change on the other. Generally, innovation 'accompanies' or accelerates this change rather than creating it;
- The complexity of the strategies ('real' and symbolic) employed by social actors at micro, meso and macro levels, does not allow us to reflect on these changes in simple or unequivocal terms;
- The constructs to which the media and ICT do contribute are phenomena which play themselves out over long periods of historical time;[3]
- Mediatized communication calls for a *transversal approach*, since it plays so many roles in the functioning and management of social relationships, from the formation of opinions and the functioning of the public space; the acquisition of knowledge and communications norms in society; the construction of 'social time' a motivational force for cultural and leisure distractions; to a role in the spread of skills, and the transmission of knowledge and so on. These questions, it seems to us, can easily be transposed to the question of the relationships between ICT and education. It goes without saying that the field of education functions according to a certain number of 'determinants' of its own; nevertheless, this does not allow us to reject, a *priori*, the 'application' to this field of these transversal lines of questioning, provided, of course, that we do not hold these puzzles to be general, non-falsifiable propositions.

The mediatization of educational communications by ICT

The pedagogical relationship between teachers and pupils, between the 'holders' and learners of skills and knowledge, has been devised as an interpersonal, and inter-subjective relationship, based on body language (voice, gestures, eye-contact); and despite the recourse to more diversified teaching methods which leave more room for pupil or student initiative, these relationships continue to function like this, for the most part. Teaching practices are so heavily marked by this model that the introduction of any new tool or method, even if only an overhead or slide projector, or the use of the press, has been fiercely debated and, sometimes, accepted only with difficulty. Today, any degree of mediatization of the pedagogical relationship thus finds itself under discussion, and its implementation is nearly always a question of volunteers and experiment, with the aim of gradual dissemination. Very often theories of technological innovation are invoked in order to clarify the dissemination process, even to guide it. These same observations can be made for each and every new technology that presents itself.

Mediatization (which assumes the recourse to communications technologies – especially networks – and to systems offering a combination of technologies) has had the effect of putting a certain distance between the protagonists of pedagogical communication and, above all, a (relative) individualization of behaviours. Even if the transition is/will be slow, and slower than is generally hoped or feared, we can agree with the view that the process started by ICT is incomparable, quantitatively and qualitatively, with previous innovations. What seems most likely is that, profound change and challenge to the *habitus* are inherent in ICT, those schemes which both generate communications practices (in the transmission of knowledge and learning) and are simultaneously generated by them.

All lines of questioning converge here to enquire whether this particular mediatization process is harmful or favourable to the transmission of knowledge and learning and, more generally, to training. Faced with such a general question we can only offer incomplete answers...and more questions. First, we note that the uses of ICT are not limited (far from it!) to distance learning[4] and that the individualization of teaching methods is generally accompanied by more robust systems of pupil support (such as tutoring). Second, we see that, in practice, the implementation of modernization programmes is characterized by diversity, if not considerable inequality between countries in the north and south, and also between European regions; in other words, we are not talking about a single or homogeneous process. Moreover, and from a theoretical perspective, we must consider with some suspicion the idea that the technological mediatization of the pedagogical relationship (even with distance learning) eliminates the inter-subjectivity of the exchange. A similar notion was forwarded regarding televised communication, but viewers' 'involvement' in TV programmes (such as debates, or TV shows) demonstrated clearly that there is, or can be, a sense of presence, different from ordinary communication, but there all the same; all the more reason, then, to assume similar processes in the case of educational practices. Finally, this line of questioning is to an extent unanswerable, at least in the short term, since the constructs envisaged are precisely of the type which appears gradually, over time.

Modes of learning ICT
Here there is a paradox which needs explaining: whereas for at least a proportion of the population – notably the youngest, the most educated and those living in large urban centres – ICTs are called upon to play an important role in daily and professional life (with more and more blurring between the two); the process by which ICTs are learned remains relatively unstructured, which leaves a lot of scope for individual initiative (with the exception, it is true, of professional training specific to jobs in IT and networks technologies). There is a striking contrast between the importance of mastering these technologies (which is harder than is often claimed, their very interactivity making for complexity), at least for part of the population, and the *laissez-faire* when it comes to learning, or being taught, how to use them. Educational institutions have included in their programmes introductory courses in the use of IT; but such teaching is usually not integrated into other courses and educational activities, nor into the daily running of courses; moreover, personal computing alone cannot at the current time be seen as representative of ICT. Teaching the use of these technologies is made all the harder to envisage for educational institutions, given that ICT is

incessantly developing – even though usually it is just a question of upgrades – and is designed to be used, and learned, individually. In this way, the bases of education are incontestably challenged by ICT and forced to compete with products and practices that have largely developed outside the educational sphere; in this respect, 'peri-education' is in the process of becoming a real competitor to education *per se*. One example from many is the 'search' facility now available on all sorts of websites and, thus, not only on sources that have been recognized by teachers as relevant or who have verified or authenticated the information. Thus, ICT has created more individualized practices that escape the norms of educational practices in their current forms.

How ICT is marketed and the emergence of habits of use

Despite our observations above, we should not assume that these new markets dominate the field of education: with the exception of certain key products, most are segmented, and those concerned with content are having difficulty establishing themselves, to the point where publishers seem relatively unaggressive in their sales strategies. As we enter the next phase of development, we should, moreover, expect hardware to constitute the lion's share of what is on sale, and that this will be accompanied by the production of 'services', designed and produced within educational institutions themselves, less to take the place of existing courses than to complement them.

This difficulty in creating markets of a sufficient size is undoubtedly not a passing phenomenon; paradoxically, it may turn out to be long-lasting and limit innovation. The educational sector is at one and the same time promising, but difficult to 'mobilize'. Producers and publishers alike, who have on occasions already suffered failures and setbacks, are careful. For the time being, they are leaving the educational professionals to take the lead themselves in a non-commercial environment.

The fact is that, unlike the various discourses of modernity which have taken it upon themselves to promote the supposed 'Information Society', users, and, even more so, consumers, have not proven to be immediately smitten with these new products; in fact, they have been quite reserved and will remain so for a long time to come.

Thus, we should anticipate that the indispensable adjustments between supply and demand will not be left to chance. In the educational sector, as in other fields, the processes by which new uses for it emerge are following a complex path, which we can nonetheless identify, at least in part. Once the initial stage of usage is passed, what is at stake is the stabilization of usage, in other words configurations giving rise, for specific populations, to recurrent behaviours and practices, established over the long term. We should also recognize that knowledge in this respect remains fairly limited, and approximate, since unlike the case of cultural products, educational products still only benefit from approximate know-how. The emergence of patterns of using these technologies is, thus, a question of prime importance for e-learning, as much for products designed for commercial markets and those geared towards educational institutions as a complement to current educational practices.

The socio-organizational management of ICTs

Here we must consider the approach which consists of studying the management of technological and communications innovation in the specific organizations that make up the educational field. With the exception of universities and other higher educational establishments, these organizations still undoubtedly have relatively weak autonomy in this respect. The emergence of ICT is in more or less all cases a site for the clash of opposing interests or which claim to be so. We should even acknowledge the fact that the question of ICT is one that generates not the most debate but the most conflict, sometimes even before the technology becomes available.

A short-range analysis would tend to contrast 'old-timers' and 'modernizers' (a dichotomy that has long been present amongst teachers), technophobes and technophiles; the 'switched on' and the 'switched off' (pun intended). This rudimentary dichotomization is a way of avoiding the recognition of the plurality of interests which are expressed upon the emergence of information and communication technologies. This was the case in recent history when it was planned to install a successive series of communications technologies in schools and universities: closed-circuit television, portable video, personal computers and so on. But with the range of ICTs already available, the problem has taken on another dimension, and the pressure from society that takes many forms, for the 'meeting' of education and mediatized communications, is such today that such inexact approaches are no longer tenable.

In reality, and setting aside the obvious fact that all change, and, thus, all innovation, is for some actors an opportunity to assert themselves and take power that they could not otherwise have legitimately acquired within their institution (by 'merit' formally deemed legitimate); if we exclude (but how can we?) the reflex to defend established interests and situations, the arrival of ICT has seen the emergence of a whole series of other issues, most often at the meso-societal level (as opposed to the micro or macro levels). The list of these challenges is long:

- Classical (presented as fundamental) disciplines vs. those more in tune with modernity;
- Traditional modes of the transmission of skills and the acquisition of knowledge, around since the generalization of obligatory schooling vs. 'new' modes of teaching and learning;
- The different roles assigned to teachers (working individually or in teams);
- The status of written and oral communication in the classroom vs. that of new forms of communication;
- Fundamental vs. a more or less professionalized teaching;
- The monopoly on teaching and training accorded to educational establishments vs. a 'sharing', however limited, with other institutions;

■ Humanist 'values', traditionally disseminated vs. the new norms of communicative activity (see above).

This basic list exaggerates the dichotomies and differences, but does succeed in showing that we are not just dealing with changes in information and communication. Specifically, communication reveals other things, and its 'management' goes beyond its *a priori* implications. Most often, 'communication' incorporates the totality of the adaptation and modernization strategies of schools, colleges and universities; and if this is true, we can understand why research, particularly the communications approach, has much to say on the processes undertaken.

Suggestions for further communications research
It is one thing to outline the research that has already begun into a communications approach, quite another to indicate where we should focus our thinking and analysis. Three perspectives suggest themselves, defined as follows:

A better understanding of the strategies of different categories of users
The examples given above, even where limited to the domain of higher education, nevertheless suffice to show how far the emergence of ICT – at the systems, tools and content levels – involves a significant number of users of varying status. They demonstrate, moreover, that we simply cannot avoid an analysis of the institutional, economic, social and symbolic strategies pertaining to the introduction of these technologies. These products, in some ways, only have meaning with reference to the strategies of which they are part; we cannot understand them solely on the basis of their inherent characteristics. Not only are they largely what those who design, create and use them make of them, strategically, they are also distinctly modified by the uses to which the 'final user' puts them. In this way, the strategies deployed by communications users are not external to the products themselves; they contribute to their existence and their development. Moreover, once these products come into existence, they become the object of usage patterns which considerably modify their original, and apparently set, purpose. The reason that we accord significance to strategies (and even tactics) is that the technological sphere is not clearly distinct from human action; the two dimensions interact in many different ways, as we have shown above.

This is a key point, in particular for information and communication technologies, all of which, to a lesser or greater degree, incorporate software which is nothing other than the representation of mental states or the expectation of social behaviours; what software does is to insert into hardware (sometimes miniaturized) modelized versions of human behaviour. Thus, even in a video-conferencing system, accessible from a personal computer, for example, we can detect modes of action (communicational or pedagogical) which will themselves engender strategies amongst users who will work with or against other users. This is even more true for the more developed tools of distance learning (such as multimedia courses providing 'modular' learning).

Strategic analysis alone must not, however, be considered sufficient. Whilst it provides a subtle approach to the usages of ICT products for teaching and learning, it does not alone provide all the elements that we need to fully understand the subject. This is because this approach allows us to grasp the short and medium term, but not the underlying trends of the phenomenon; this is particularly the case for what we can call the 'social logics of communication', in other words, the structured movements around which user strategies take shape. For example, the intervention of students in class and their propensity to ask questions of their teachers, and to give their points of view, are practices which need to be placed in context as underlying facts of life which shape users in one way or another; and e-learning programmes which fail to take this into account would be doomed to failure (as was the case of the first attempts at computer-assisted learning based on an over-simplistic and over-directive algorithm).

Making the necessary distinction between change and innovation

As an initial analysis, and with reference to theories of change and innovation, we can classify ICT products (technologies and content) into two distinct categories:

- Those which position themselves on a spectrum of continuity with existing pedagogical models (thus, the teacher will continue to dispense a lecture-type class *and* give students access to sites linked to a whole set of documents supporting his or her course);
- Those which, much more rarely, by exploring the possibilities of interactivity and multimedia 'writings', represent a break with the past and escape known 'frameworks'.

This classification is convenient in that it allows us fairly easily to distinguish readily identifiable specialist practices. Both experts and practioners have frequent recourse to this distinction, in the process constrasting the new from the old, the unknown from the known, and that which relates to modernity from that which is attached to tradition.

In fact, this classification merits further discussion; first and foremost because it blends elements of different orders and combines strategies which should be separated. Some of these can be called strategies of *absorption* (such is the case, generally speaking, when transparencies are replaced by slides designed using Powerpoint software); others are strategies of *superimposition* (or accumulation, when new texts are added to current ones); other strategies are simply *additional* (in that they find new potential in the familiar; *a priori*, this is the case of hypertext); finally, there are strategies of *creation* (the product leads to teaching and learning practices which are, effectively, new). But even these distinctions require further analysis, since they could be criticized for their functionalism, in that they link strategy to technological mode.

Beyond these distinctions, furthermore, is the question of how to distinguish *change* from *innovation*. On this point, theories diverge, even if *change* is usually correlated to social and cultural mutation, and *innovation* to the adoption of new technological procedures (or paradigms); *change* also generally implies less decisive modifications than *innovation*. But these are more common-sense explanations than reasoned theory. We can nonetheless note that where *change* most often refers to a movement that is relatively continuous and multifarious, *innovations* are observed *ex post* (they may be 'accidental' and occur, in an almost anodine fashion, after a series of repeated failures; they do not necessarily signify the success of the system that apparently offers the most benefits). It goes without saying that *innovation*, in our view, is more than just technology, even if technology cannot easily be dissociated from the other components of innovation, in particular the communications component of e-learning products.

Three types of case study

For the reasons already given, amongst which we emphasize the (new) norms of communications activity, it is pertinent, in our view, to highlight, amongst the various uses of ICT in the university sector, those which are taking one of the following directions:

- The pedagogical and administrative management of teaching, most often face to face. This includes tutoring systems, individualized course management, the supplying of complementary documentation, and the addition of online forums, exchanges or discussions to courses which otherwise take largely traditional forms;
- The *modularization* of teaching. This, logically, would appear to be a prerequisite for the extension of e-learning but, because of the various forms of resistance from teachers, modularization is instead developing in parallel with the implementation of ICT, according to what is on offer and experimentally so. It is one of the conditions – which we could describe as socio-technological – of the commercialization of such courses.
- The recourse to the possibilities of interactivity and multimedia – which we would define as hypermedia were it not for the fact that, for the time being, this phenomenon tends to be reduced to its strictly technological aspects. In other words it is a question here of emphasizing new forms of text which genuinely take into account the potential of the different modes which are at the heart of multimedia. For the most part, the field of education lies outside experiments and in particular outside innovations in respect of this new technology; it is therefore interesting to detect where there are signs of departure from this ambient conformism.

These are the three directions that we intend to emphasize in our analysis of innovation in e-learning. These perspectives do not as a rule reproduce those advanced by experts or specialists in the field of education (we, for example, do not deem vital the distinctions between face-to-face and distance learning; or between the individualization and the 'collectivization' of training). This is because our approach, as we have shown, is derived from a communications science perspective. The fact that this is still a minority interest justifies our attention, since it holds the promise of renewing the terms of the debate.

Notes

1. The notion of social 'field' is taken from Pierre Bourdieu's 'field theory'. See P. Bourdieu, *Practical Reason. On the Theory of Action* (Stanford University Press, 1998, translated by R. Johnson).
2. The reference to time, here, is conveyed in French by the Braudelien notion of la longue durée (translator's note).
3. See note 1 above.
4. Additionally referred to here in French as *FAD, formation assistée à distance*: assisted distance learning (translator's note). See also the earlier arguments in Bernard Miège, Françoise Séguy et Philippe Quinton, En quoi les TIC innovent-elles? Pour une analyse communicationnelle du recours aux TIC dans l'enseignement supérieur, in "2001 Bogues - Globalisme et pluralisme", tome 3 TIC et éducation, (Pierre Moeglin et Gaëtan Tremblay eds.), Les Presses de l'Université Laval, 2003, pp. 47–67 and Bernard Miege's new book L'information - communication: objet de connaissance, Bruxelles- Paris, De Boeck - INA, col. Médias Recherche, 2005.

E-LEARNING – A KNOWLEDGE THEORETICAL APPROACH

Lars Qvortrup

Introduction

In the field of e-learning, i.e. the use of ICT in education, there is a stark contrast between high policy expectations and a lack of theoretical clarity. The resulting paradox is that a lot is *done* within the field of e-learning, but very little is *known*. European e-learning plans are introduced and e-learning activities at national and institutional levels are initiated. These activities are measured in terms of cost-ratio and evaluation schemes. But we don't know what is measured or according to which criteria evaluation studies are performed because there is a lack of theoretical enlightenment concerning e-learning.

The underlying problem is not that e-learning theories do not exist or that e-learning research programmes have not been supported, but that many incompatible paradigms are at play. One paradigm is used by proponents of e-learning, while others are used by critics. Even worse, these incompatible theoretical positions are not as a rule explained. This results in a state of double contingency. One part supports e-learning based on his or her hidden reasons. Another part is against, but based on quite another reasoning. For me, the problem is not that we cannot judge whether e-learning *per se* is good or bad. This would be an impossible task. The important question is, 'how' e-learning is judged to be good or bad, i.e. according to which criteria this is said to be the case.

Confronted with this situation, the first step must be to actually specify what lies behind the current e-learning debate: what are the hidden criteria? The next step is to elaborate a common framework for discussion. In the present chapter my suggested contribution for such a framework is a knowledge theoretical communication paradigm.

Thus, in this chapter, I first identify and explicate four dominant, but normally non-articulated and mutually incompatible paradigms in the current e-learning debate. Secondly, I suggest that e-learning should be seen in a communication theoretical perspective (cf. the chapter of Bernard Miège in this volume), assuming that education is a specialized form of communication aimed at changing people in accordance with politically defined goals, using oral, print or digital media for this communication. This implies that computers and digital networks are seen as media of communication.

However, in order to further qualify the communication paradigm I suggest that we specify educational communication as knowledge-stimulating communication. The advantage of this approach is that based on a knowledge classification scheme, the impact of different types of computer-mediated communication in e-learning for education can be specified: E-learning is not *per se* good or bad, but different forms of e-learning support different types of knowledge-acquisition.

Current e-learning paradigms

As already said, expectations concerning e-learning, i.e. the use of information and communication technologies (ICTs) for the support of learning processes, are high, and it is generally assumed that the use of ICT will increase the efficiency of training and education activities, both in formalised learning institutions and in the life-long education of the general population.

This, however, stands in contrast to the lack of theoretical clarity regarding the understanding of e-learning. This should come as no surprise, though. E-learning is a new phenomenon, and no consensus regarding the theoretical basis for observing e-learning has as yet been reached. Even the definitions and designations are numerous. The European Commission has suggested the following definition in connection with its so-called e-learning programme for 2004–2006: E-learning includes '...the use of new multimedia technologies and the Internet to improve the quality of learning by facilitating access to resources and services as well as remote exchanges and collaboration.' In itself, this is, indeed, an extremely broad definition. However, the situation is actually worse. Over the course of just a few years in Europe, e-learning has been called distance teaching, technology-supported teaching, flexible learning, computer-based learning and network-based learning. As we shall see, these names contain intended or unintended references to the various theoretical approaches to e-learning which have been around.

The problem with this lack of definitional and theoretical clarity is that the basis is unclear when one discusses e-learning and the expected effects of e-learning. It is often difficult to see what is meant by the concept in one example or the other and to know which forms of e-learning are referred to when expectations of effects are presented.

The lack of clarity is, among other reasons, due to the fact that the approaches to e-learning are based on theoretical positions, which are often not made explicit. It is therefore important to identify the theoretical foundations of the various e-learning strategies. I believe one can distinguish between at least four paradigms with corresponding notions of how to construct e-learning systems: the instructivist paradigm, the body-phenomenological paradigm, the activity-theoretical paradigm and the constructivist paradigm.

The Instructivist Paradigm

The paradigm which dominated the understanding of e-learning from its beginning until the near-end of the twentieth century was the so-called instructivist paradigm, which typically has behaviourist roots. In this paradigm, learning is conceived of as a causal result of teaching or other forms of external influence. Systems based on this position will therefore emphasize and support the possibilities of instructor-led teaching. One would hardly speak of an 'instructivist view of learning' because learning represents an activity engaged in by pupils or students. Rather, one would speak of an instructivist view of *teaching*. E-learning systems based on this position typically support instructor-centred communication, lectures, distribution of materials and possibly aptitude tests.

The instructivist paradigm was closely related to an understanding of ICT as an instrument for transporting or processing data.

From the beginning, i.e. from the 1960s, the understanding of e-learning was based on an entirely traditional conception of tools or technologies, where the computer was conceived of as a tool or a machine for transporting and processing the raw material of the machine: data. Understanding was taken over from the prosthetic technologies, i.e. those technologies whose function is predicated on a physical influence of physical matter. The shovel or the mechanical digger function because they move earth. The lorry or the train transports raw material from one place to another. The centrifuge, the mixer or the chemical plant mixes raw materials, thereby creating new materials.

If new educational technologies were conceptualised as transport technologies, one would speak of ICT-supported learning as 'distance learning'. In the United States in particular large-scale programmes were instituted where lectures were disseminated through the medium of television. It later became the Internet, which functioned as the main transport opportunity. The attractiveness of the new technology was that it allowed for the almost infinite dissemination of data. The idea was that data could be moved around the world.

If, however, emphasis were placed on the computer as a machine for processing data, an example of what was fore grounded would be the effect of repetition relative to the learning of facts. The resulting view was that a computer was valid as an educational technology because it was both more patient and more capable of variations than any teacher and could therefore adapt to the level and standpoint of the individual student on the background of multiple-choice tests. As already mentioned, this approach was based on a mechanical input-output paradigm: Every student is affected by the use of computers. Subsequently he or she answers a question. Depending on the answer, the computer prepares the next stimulus. The process can continue without any limitations, i.e. until the student provides a satisfactory answer and the computer can proceed to the next theme.

In both cases the dominant teaching theoretical perspective was behaviourist. The machine metaphor was applied to the computer, which was seen as an 'artificial intelligence'. But the machine metaphor was also applied to human intelligence, which was seen as an advanced computational device. Based on this, it was obvious to assume that there was a causal relationship between teaching input and learning outcome: The more people data could be disseminated to, the more people learned something. The better the machine was in varying the data relative to feedback from learners, the higher the yield.

The Body-Phenomenological Paradigm

The instructivist paradigm already came under strong criticism in the 1970s, and during the 1980s and 1990s this critique developed into its own paradigm. The basic critical assumption was that there is no reason to believe that learning can be understood as a simple input/output phenomenon. It is more appropriate to consider the pupil or student as a non-trivial system characterised by a given input not resulting in a corresponding output. From here a number of theoretical positions developed, which are far from mutual agreement, each of which has its specific implications for the understanding of learning and e-learning.

The body-phenomenological paradigm developed as a kind of opposition to instructivism. It has its roots in modern phenomenology, with Martin Heidegger as the general reference source (cf. Heidegger 1986 [1927]), and with the French phenomenologist Maurice Merleau-Ponty (1945) as the specific inspiration to understanding the role of the body in psychological and intellectual activities. In relation to digital communication and e-learning, this has been picked up upon particularly by Hubert L. Dreyfus (cf. Dreyfus 2001). The emphasis here is on the bodily dimension of teaching and learning: We do not learn with our intellect alone, but also by virtue of bodily presence. Not least, according to this view, advanced forms of learning are supported by our physical presence in the teaching situation, partly because an intensity is created, which digitally mediated communication does not provide, and partly because the body and bodily emotions are important in imparting meaning to things. On the basis of this position one would therefore recommend that only very simple and routine forms of teaching should take place through e-learning systems, while more advanced forms of teaching should be delivered by face-to-face communication.

In relation to this, the view of computers and the Internet as technologies came to be replaced by a theory according to which computers and the Internet can be understood as media or symbol machines, i.e. so-called non-prothetic tools. According to this, the computer is defined as a device analogous to the clock, which does not work by virtue of its physical influence on a raw material, but by symbolising a phenomenon, e.g. time. The clock and the computer are symbolic media. In extension of this, the computer and the digital network are seen as a complex mediated system through which a programmer communicates with a large number of users via a programme. The Internet in particular is considered a networked medium of communication with unlimited possibilities of feedback.

Many of the pedagogical paradigms in the above-mentioned list attached themselves to this view of technology, among them the phenomenological paradigm. The argument for the significance of the body in a teaching and learning context goes as follows: We do not understand only with our intellect. No, 'Our body plays a crucial role in our being able to make sense of things so as to see what is relevant, our ability to make things matter to us and so to acquire skills, our sense of the reality of things, our trust in other people, and finally, our capacity for making the unconditional commitments that give meaning to our lives.' So writes Hubert Dreyfus (Dreyfus 2001: 90) in explicit extension of this.

The critical conclusion, which Dreyfus draws himself, is that the Internet can be useful in teaching, when it comes to accessing facts and for routine exercises, i.e. for the acquisition of what I call first order knowledge (cf. below). When it comes to improvisation, situated behaviour or what Dreyfus calls the 'expert level', physical presence is necessary. According to Dreyfus, only in a classroom setting, where the teacher and the learner feel they are running a risk in each other's presence and can both expect criticism, are those conditions present which further the development of competent routine and one can only become an expert by acting in the real world. (Dreyfus 2001)

There are two types of objections to this. One is that *all* teaching is mediated and, more generally, that all human collective activity is conditioned by media. There is no such thing as a pre-mediated, 'authentic' presence or being together. When we interact in a classroom we do it through a physical medium – sound waves in the air – and a symbolic medium, i.e. language. When we read books we engage in a thoroughly mediated activity. One cannot distinguish absolutely between embodied and non-embodied presence, but one has to distinguish between *different* types of mediation. Obviously, however, the media spectrum is broader in the classroom than on the Internet.

The second type of objection is media optimistic. It makes the claim that interaction and communication is about bandwidth and that human perception uses a certain, but not unlimited, bandwidth. According to the Danish research journalist Tor Nørretranders, this is 11 megabits per second. '11 Mbps is all we need and all we can use. 11 Mbps is the bandwidth of human sensory experience.' (Nørretranders 1997: 151, my translation) So it is only a question of time before the Internet can completely substitute physical presence.

Between these two positions there is the characteristic middle position, which advocates 'blended learning'. Some teaching activities – the acquisition of facts in particular, according to Dreyfus – can take place on the Internet and at the computer, while others should take place in a physical group. The teaching challenge consists in combining the different types of teaching in an appropriate way, i.e. to create the correct level of 'blended learning'.

The Activity-Theory Paradigm

A third paradigm which has influenced the understanding of e-learning is activity-theory paradigm, which often refers to Lev Vygotsky's work (Vygotsky 1962 and 1978) and which is at times also described as 'constructionist'. This position is, among others, very widespread in the Nordic countries. The basic idea is that learning is a result of the individual and collective activity of students and concepts such as 'collaborative learning' and 'communities of practice' are widely used. According to this view, learning takes place by virtue of learning-orientated constructive work. Systems based on this position therefore emphasize the provision of facilities to support group work, chatting etc., i.e. facilities for collaboration, exchange of experiences, knowledge-sharing etc.

Within the activity-theoretical paradigm, e-learning can be described and classified from the various network morphologies that are formed: Do these networks support collaboration and collective practices, or do they not? This position can be found in the Danish Ministry of Science's 2003 report on e-learning, where four models are proposed:

- E-learning where the learners never physically meet, but only learn through the computer, and where there is no dialogue among those involved.
- E-learning where the learners never physically meet, but where dialogue between the participants is supported in virtual environments.
- E-learning where the learners alternate between learning in a classroom or other form of physical interaction and working independently with their computer, e.g. at home.
- E-learning where the learners only learn by being physically together, e.g. a class, and where the computer is used as a tool in teaching. (Ministry of Science, Technology and Innovation 2003: 6–13)

In addition to a morphological classification as the one suggested by the Ministry of Science, both sceptical and optimistic activity theoretical positions are found. Some emphasize that teaching is best done as an interaction between physically present persons. If that is the case, the use of computers or Internet-based communication would be ill-advised. Others assert that it is the use of computers and the Internet, which can extend the possibilities of interaction, so that they are not only found in the physical classroom or the group of people present, but can be created everywhere, that is to say, as so-called 'virtual classrooms'.

The Constructivist Paradigm

Finally, one ought also to mention the constructivist paradigm, which has many different references, but which, among other sources, is based on Niklas Luhmann and Karl-Eberhard Schorr's works on pedagogy and the education system (cf. Luhmann and Schorr 1982 and Luhmann 2002). The fundamental view here is that education is a structural coupling between two different activities, i.e. teaching and learning. Teaching is seen as a specialized form of communication, while learning is seen as an individual or group-based activity where knowledge is constructed. The basic challenge of education is to overcome the problem that there is no direct input-output relation between teachers and students, i.e. no transportation of knowledge from one to the other. Students can only observe the mediated communication selections made by the teacher and by other students and, based on these and on supplementary observations, the student must construct his or her own understanding. Interaction – and the classroom is an interaction system – takes place as structural coupling between mutually closed psychic systems.

Seen from this position, e-learning systems must both support teaching communication, i.e. the students' observations of the teacher (traditionally through oral and print media, now also through digital media) and individual and collective learning processes, i.e. the self-referential processes of the learning system, and it should first and foremost support appropriate structural couplings between the two activities such as one finds, for instance, in the specialized interaction system of the classroom (cf. Luhmann 2002).

From the constructivist paradigm one would focus on three basic elements: 1) how to meet the demand of supporting teaching communication, i.e. to make communicational selections observable by students, 2) how to comply with the requirement for reflections of the learners, and 3) how to support the student managing his or her competence development.

As regards at least points 1 and 2, the different types of conference-functions accompanying many e-learning systems will be useful: asynchronous conferences have the great quality of formalizing dialogues in order to facilitate reflection and to make knowledge explicit, while the synchronous conferences have the quality of being a forum for spontaneous dialogues and, therefore, a great context for the elaboration of ideas between students.

As a particular interface for the interaction between the individual student and the teacher, among students, but also between the individual student and the educational system one could mention the digital portfolio (cf. the last section of this chapter). Etymologically speaking, a portfolio is a briefcase for carrying personal papers. This is where one keeps one's curriculum vitae, official documents, but also personal notes.

The digital portfolio often contains a private working space and a public working space. In the public working space a differentiation can be made between spaces to which different users have access, for instance, between a space, to which other students have access and one to which the teacher has access. Thus, in a constructivist context the digital portfolio supports both teacher-student communication and individual and collective learning reflections of the students.

Another aspect that is interesting – especially in reference to the point number 3 – is that the student can place all his/her work (materials, notes, assignments, documents, recordings etc.) in a private working space to which, in principle, nobody else has access. This makes it possible to observe one's own learning, because the student regularly has to add new material to already existing material.

A knowledge theory of e-learning

The computer as medium
In the twentieth century the development of the prothetic technologies of industrial society reached its zenith in an almost complete automisation of physical work processes.

At the same time, the twentieth century was the time when the development of non-prothetic or symbolic technologies, i.e. technology that supports knowledge production, knowledge circulation and boundary-crossing processes, was initiated. In 1936, Alan Turing presented the theoretical foundation for the digital computer, i.e. for the universal symbol machine. At around the same time, in 1948, Claude Shannon and Warren Weaver presented the first theory of digital communication, a theory based on a 1938 technical article by Shannon: 'A Symbolic Analysis of Relay and Switching Circuits'. The point is that this created the basis for non-physical machines, i.e. machines whose mode of functioning is independent of their physical basis. The universal computer is a computer, which is independent of a specific medium. It is a multimedia device in the true sense of the word.

This implies that the computer should be conceptualized as a communication medium, not only in the sense that the computer is the basic node in digital communication networks, but in the broader sense that the computer is a symbolic device, a device for the production, processing and dissemination of symbols. Because the functioning of computers is independent of their physical basis, computers are different from other communication media in the sense that they are not restricted by their physical form.

Books, newspapers, blackboards, television sets, video recorders, lecture halls, classrooms are media that are at least partly determined by their physical shape. One cannot do everything with a newspaper or in a lecture hall, but is restricted by the physical shape of the medium. However, a computer is different, because it can imitate any other medium. One can create digital books, blackboards or videos, and virtual classrooms, lecture halls or universities, i.e. imitate books, blackboards, videos, classrooms, lecture halls and universities.

In a limited period of ecstasy it was believed that this implied that digital books or virtual classrooms were identical to printed books and physical classrooms. This is indeed not the case: They are *imitations* of the book and the classroom. They are *mediatizations* of books and classrooms.

Teaching as stimulation of knowledge acquisition

Furthermore, as it has already been noticed, teaching can be defined as a specialized form of communication, i.e. the form of communication aimed at changing persons in accordance with predefined goals. The specific goals are defined in the curricula. However, the general goal is to stimulate pupils' and students' knowledge acquisition. Consequently, teaching can be defined as that specialized type of communication that is aimed at the stimulation of knowledge acquisition.

In accordance with these definitions I will present a knowledge theory of e-learning – or, to be correct, a knowledge theory of e-teaching. This approach builds on and further develops the above-mentioned constructivist approach to teaching as communication. The simple idea is that teaching is specialized communication which must always involve one or more media. Any communication is mediated. With the computer – stand-alone computers and computers linked into digital networks – as a universal medium, i.e. a device that can imitate any other medium, new potentials have emerged for supporting educational communication. The pupil or the student can observe his or her environment – the teacher or lecturer, the other pupils or students, the teaching material – through new dissemination and symbolic media. This may influence the classroom as a complex and delicate interaction system, in which students observe the teacher's communication selections and order to construct understanding, in which students observe each other and in which the teacher observes the students' communicative selections as a direct or indirect sign of their acquisition of knowledge. This may influence the student-to-student interactions, and it may influence the individual activities of the students.

However, as all these activities are aimed at the stimulation of knowledge acquisition, I will present a theory and a categorization of knowledge as the basis for analysing and evaluating teaching as stimulation of knowledge acquisition. This, then, is the foundation of my knowledge theoretical communication paradigm for e-learning.

Knowledge Theory

What is knowledge? According to the theory proposed here, knowledge is a concept to describe the way an individual (i.e. a person or an organization) handles complexity in the surrounding world. Knowledge is a source for transforming insecurity into security, but it is also – and increasingly so – a source for giving shape to insecurity, i.e. maintaining insecurity as insecurity but making it manageable, e.g. by having the ability to identify news, changes etc. and devising strategies to deal with them. In professional jargon, the first form of knowledge is called qualification, the other is called competency. So, knowledge is not a 'store' or an 'essence' but a relationship between internal complexity and complexity in the external world. In a collective organism, internal complexity is created by what Stuart Kauffman calls an autonomous agent, which can be a cell, a plant, an animal or a habitat, i.e. a biological system that takes care of handling relations with the surrounding world (cf. Kauffman 2000). In a psychological system it can be the memory about categorization of phenomena or about adequate strategies in certain situations. In an organization it can be procedures, divisions of labour etc. Such knowledge can be externalized in the form of tools, machines and technologies. A crucial characteristic of knowledge is the fact that it is dynamic, i.e. its interaction with the surrounding world can lead to new knowledge. This is called learning, which is both an individual and organizational process.

Abilities: Skills and knowledge

In a modern society based on print media there is a tendency to confuse abilities with knowledge. One thinks that what we *can do* is identical with what we *know*. The natural scientist and theorist of knowledge Michael Polanyi, in his groundbreaking 1966 book *The Tacit Dimension*, punctured this misapprehension. Besides what we know there is a 'tacit' dimension, that is to say, all the things we can do, although we are not able to account for them. Beside our explicit knowledge – or rather: logically and historically prior to the explicit knowledge – there is tacit knowing.

This insight brings me to a fundamental distinction in the theory of knowledge: The sum total of human abilities can be split into skills and knowledge. Skills may be defined as immediate abilities, knowledge as reflected abilities.

Let me provide an example. Learning to cycle is to acquire a skill. Any parent who has taught their children to cycle knows that it leads nowhere to go over the theory of cycling and then let the child apply the theory in practice. No, one has to fit a broomstick behind the saddle in order to help the child acquire the skill of cycling. Similarly, being able to cycle does not mean that one can account for how we do it.

This type of knowledge is not a knowledge that we 'have' but a knowledge that we practice or 'do'. Consequently, Polanyi does not speak about 'tacit knowledge' but about 'tacit knowing'. It is the processive nature of tacit knowing, which makes me designate it as a 'skill'.

From this Polanyi concludes that tacit knowing precedes explicit knowledge, i.e. skills precede knowledge. First we 'can do', then we 'know'.

This, however, does not, as some seem to believe, mean that 'skills' or 'tacit knowing' are especially deep or authentic. They are merely one side of the distinction between skills and knowledge, which make up the concept of ability. In modern society an increasing number of activities are knowledge-based. The very fact that we have to go to school to acquire formal or reflexive abilities demonstrates that in modern society it is not sufficient to imitate the skills of one's parents and immediate surroundings. The differentiation of an education system is, therefore, the institutional expression of the fundamental division of abilities into skills and knowledge.

But this, on the other hand, means that knowledge – reflexive abilities – does not exist without skills, i.e. immediate abilities. Among other things, this has implications for the theory of learning. If learning something means to develop knowledge about something, this knowledge cannot exist or be generated without its twin: the skill, the immediate ability.

Concerning teaching and learning this means that there are limitations, not only to e-learning, but to any kind of mediated teaching – and as already said any kind of formal teaching is mediated. Important things cannot be taught in so far as teaching means communication. They must be practised. On the other hand, other things can not be learned by doing, but only by communicating, i.e. as the result of formalized teaching. The difference is not, as Dreyfus believes, between simple and complex types of knowledge, but between skills and (explicit) knowledge.

Forms of knowledge – a systematique
Early in his academic career, the British philosopher of language Gilbert Ryle (1900–1976), inspired by the phenomenological discussion of Descartes (cf. Husserl 1987 [1929]), criticized Cartesian dualism, i.e. the distinction between *res cogitans* and *res extensa:* the human intellect and the physical world. Ryle called the notion of a special thinking device that was not of this world the idea of 'the ghost in the machine' (cf. Lyons 1980). The human mind is not something outside the world, but it is itself part of the extensive world.

In 1949 he drew the conclusion from the critique of the Cartesian paradigm that we have to describe knowledge differently than we have been used to. The implication is that knowledge is not, and cannot be understood as being, something – a substance – in the human mind referring to something different in the external world. In Ryle's famous formulation in his main work *The Concept of Mind*: 'knowing-that' presupposes 'knowing-how' (Ryle 1949).

In accordance with Ryle's critique of Cartesian dualism, in the 1960s the American anthropologist and epistemologist Gregory Bateson suggested that learning and communication can be divided into four categories: first-, second-, third- and fourth-order learning (Bateson 2000 [1972]).[1] Taking inspiration from Bateson's categorization and elaborating Ryle's distinction of knowledge into knowledge forms, one can identify four categories of knowledge. First order knowledge is simple knowledge: Knowledge about something or 'knowing-that'. Second order knowledge is knowledge about knowledge, i.e. reflexive knowledge. This category corresponds to Ryle's 'knowing-how'. Third order knowledge is knowledge about knowledge about knowledge, i.e. knowledge about the preconditions for reflexive knowledge. Finally, one can identify a fourth-order knowledge, which represents the social evolution of knowledge or experience, i.e. the collective and perhaps unconscious knowledge process and the total knowledge potential. This corresponds to what Edmund Husserl calls the meaning horizon of society.

The theory proposed here builds on this idea. Its main claim is that a mundanized subject (i.e. a subject which is always also part of the world that he or she observes) observing the world in order to know about the world, that is to handle complexity – and all subjects are mundanized subjects – must make the following forms of observation:

- It must observe phenomena in the world as objects of observation (1st-order knowledge)
- It must observe itself in the world (2nd-order knowledge)
- It must observe the world as a precondition for observing the world (3rd-order knowledge)
- In addition it must be presupposed that the world, including the subject observing the world, exists as a precondition of knowledge (4th-order knowledge).

Where the first three forms of knowledge represent observation-based forms of knowledge, i.e. relations between subject and world (including the subject's knowledge of itself as a subject in the world), the fourth form of knowledge is not knowledge about the world but the world as knowledge.

First-order knowledge is knowledge about something. For instance, I know that from where I am sitting I can see a beautiful bed of rhododendrons, and I know that the large plant in the middle is a Rhododendron Cawtabiensis.

Knowledge category	Knowledge form	Knowledge designation
1st-order or simple knowledge	Knowledge about something	Factual knowledge
2nd-order or complex knowledge	Knowledge about the conditions of knowing	Reflexive or situative knowledge
3rd-order or hypercomplex knowledge	Knowledge about the conditions of the reflexive knowledge system	Systemic or creative knowledge
4th-order knowledge	Society as dynamic knowledge horizon, i.e. the knowing society	World knowledge

Second-order knowledge is knowledge about the knowledge situation, i.e. the capacity for self-observation. Not only do I know that the shrub out there is a Rhododendron Cawtabiensis, but I also know that I know it because I had to elaborate my wishes to the owner of the nursery I bought it from. I also know that the fact that I consider it beautiful maybe because I planted it myself. In other words, I am not only capable of categorizing what I see, but I also have the ability to stand next to my own observation and consider it.

Third-order knowledge is knowledge about knowledge about knowledge, i.e. knowledge about the systematic of knowledge that my knowledge is part of. It can, for instance, be knowledge of the botanical systematics, which lead to the designations of species that I employ. Or it can be knowledge of the aesthetic criteria for beauty, which makes me find my garden beautiful. My aesthetic preferences could be caused by a predilection for English garden aesthetics rather than the more formal French or Italian classicist garden aesthetics. This is also called 'creative' knowledge, because knowing the systematic preconditions of my present knowledge is a precondition for changing this knowledge system into a new one. This is related to, but not identical with, Kuhn's notion of paradigm change.

Finally, fourth-order knowledge is knowledge about the preconditions for the knowledge systematic represented by the entire cultural system, into which these knowledge forms and judgements of taste are embedded. For Bateson, this fourth-order knowledge is a very particular form of knowledge, which cannot be contained within one person but resides in the social community of which the individuals are members.

Knowledge technological forms of media

If one defines the computer as a medium rather than a machine, in accordance with the knowledge categories elaborated above one can identify four knowledge technological forms of media, because conceiving of the computer as a medium means considering the totality of the computer as a symbol-producing and symbol-communicating medium:

1. *The computer as representation and simulation medium (1st-order knowledge medium).* Here, the computer functions as a medium that represents phenomena in the world, be it as simple references to facts, as interactive multimedia simulations of dynamic world phenomena or as representation of communication selections of the teacher.
2. *The computer as a feedback medium (2nd-order knowledge medium).* Here, in classical terms the computer delivers a programmed feedback to the student's input. With the computer as medium the student can observe the effects in old and new contexts of what he or she already knows. His or her knowledge is 'reflected' back into the student by the computer.
3. *The computer as interaction medium (3rd-order knowledge medium).* Here the computer system can function as a medium, for instance, for teaching as classroom

interaction, both between student and teacher and between students. This approach makes it possible to support and/or to mimic the very complex communication processes in the classroom, i.e. the teacher's communicative stimulation of learning processes, the student's observation of the teacher's communicative selections and of the behaviour of other students, and the teacher's observation of student behaviour as an indirect expression of their comprehension. These processes can be mimicked regardless of whether the classroom is a physical space, i.e. independently of whether the parties to the interaction are physically present for each other. More importantly, however, the classroom is simulated as an arena of knowledge, i.e. as a community that has agreed upon certain paradigms or basic assumptions.

4. *The total computer system (e.g. the Internet) as a representation or simulation of world knowledge (4th-order knowledge medium).* Here the computer is used to simulate phenomena in the external world, among them – by virtue of the computer's feedback potential – as a medium to simulate phenomena in the external world where the learner is an acting subject him/herself. Particularly, the Internet, or the World Wide Web, is a dissemination medium with a structure that combines global accessibility with self-generated addressability. This means that it functions as a semi-autopoietic knowledge system, i.e. as a structural simulation of the dynamic and self-developing system of world knowledge.

The computer as simulation medium: Social simulation

As long as knowledge technology is conceived of as a simple observational medium or as a mechanical stimulus/response medium, one is at the level of first-order knowledge. The computer and the digital network can make knowledge accessible for observation and it can stimulate the cognitive processing of facts.

Only when one conceives of knowledge technology as a feedback and an interaction medium, one moves to second- and third-order knowledge, not least because knowledge technology provides a very effective simulation of the phenomenon that the 'I' is itself a subject endowed with agency in the world that is being simulated, and conversely that the 'I' is always already integrated into this world, that is to say that it is a mundanized subject.

This connection can be made intelligible in the following example, where I use the example of the computer as a social simulation medium. The example must be sketched out first, though.

My case study is one among many products from the Danish e-learning company Zenaria. It is a training system for a Danish bank's in-service training of staff involved in credit business. The system is based on interactive video and multiple choices. One follows simulated situations such as where a young couple approach the bank's credit adviser in order to apply for a loan for their newly opened bar. They require 10,000 euros for a music system, which in their view is a precondition for the bar to achieve its essential customer base.

In the interactive video the user acts the role of the acting subject, the credit adviser. After each line from the couple applying for the loan, the user has to choose from four possible responses and, depending on the response chosen, the dialogue continues. In other words, the conversation is split into turns, and in each turn the user has to place him/herself in the position of the credit adviser.

When a credit advice sequence is concluded, one can follow the customers home, where they comment on the advice given. Comments from the credit adviser's colleagues can be heard or one can see the credit adviser's psychological profile as expressed by the answers given.

This form of teaching through interactive, social simulation contains learning potential in relation to all of the four levels described above.

Firstly, factual knowledge is transmitted. The user sees how credit advice takes place. One is presented with the guidelines, according to which one has to operate in the bank in question. Factual observations are made.

Secondly, situational knowledge is transmitted. This is where the main emphasis lies. The user is placed in the position of the credit adviser and has to respond to an inquiry within short but realistic time frames, i.e. handle a situation with its situationally based but unpredictable developmental path.

But the system also provides an opportunity for third order observation. One does not act only in an I/you relationship, but one also observes this I/you relationship from the outside, i.e. one observes ones own 'I' as an element in the relationship between ego and alter. This happens implicitly in the use of the video itself, as it constantly gives cause to self-observation ('what should I do in this situation?' 'which of the four answers is the most appropriate choice?' 'what would I do, if I were in their position?'), but it also happens explicitly, because one can observe the other party's reactions to the interaction and one is thereby forced to observe oneself through the eyes of the other, as happens through the comments of colleagues and in the psychological profile drawn up as a result of participation in this simulated social interaction.

Finally, one might claim that interactive simulation constitutes a fourth-order knowledge system in itself. This means that the user's observation of the system of simulation itself is a world observation, but with the proviso that one is not observing a world but a simulation of a world. In reality, one is observing a second party's observation of the world one has to believe in, identify with and interact in. The other party can either be the bank's self-presentation through the producer, Zenaria, or it can be Zenaria and the premises of simulation, upon which Zenaria bases its productions.

To sum up, one might say that systems such as the one analysed do not only make factual knowledge accessible to immediate observation, but the medium also makes

Knowledge levels	Knowledge technological forms of knowledge: The computer as a simulation medium
First-order knowledge	Factual knowledge: ■ Factual knowledge is made accessible to immediate observation
Second-order knowledge	Reflexive/situational knowledge: ■ Visuality (spatial recognizability) ■ Narrativity (temporal recognizability) ■ Interactivity (the I/you relationship)
Third-order knowledge	Systemic knowledge: ■ Possibility of system observation: 'the I/you relationship' observed from the outside ■ Possibility of system transformation: simulated relearning
Fourth-order knowledge	Metasystemic knowledge: ■ Possibility of context observation. ■ Possibility of observation of organizational and cultural conditions for knowledge forms 1–3

situational recognizability possible. As a user one can recognize the situation one acts in, and one can in particular develop interactive competence in the I-you relationship. It makes systemic observation possible, because one can observe one's own interaction with the other from the outside, i.e. as an acting element in a system-embedded I-you relationship. It also makes possible a metasystemic reflection, because the medium provides possibilities for observing one's own situational and systemic being from the outside, i.e. from the position, which the organizational and cultural conditions for situational and systemic practice constitute. It is not least in this sense that the new usages of the computer as a knowledge-industrial medium constitute an interesting addition to the possibilities inherent in traditional media of education.

The computer as interaction medium: Digital portfolio
There has been significant development in recent years with regard to the application of computers as media for classroom interaction. Thus a number of experiments have been conducted using portable computers to support class interaction, both in the physical classroom as well as in the 'virtual' class, i.e. between teacher and students or between students outside the classroom and after school hours (cf. Mathiasen 2002).

At this point I would like to mention the so-called digital portfolio as a particular interface for the interaction between the individual student and the teacher and for the interaction among students. Etymologically speaking, a portfolio is a briefcase for carrying personal papers. This is where one keeps one's curriculum vitae, official documents, but also personal notes.

The basic structure of a digital portfolio is such that the student can access a server through the interface. The server contains the student's private working space (the portfolio) and a public working space. In the public working space a differentiation can be made between whether one is working in a space to which other students have access or one to which the teacher has access.

The basic point of the digital portfolio is that the student can place all his/her work (materials, notes, assignments, documents, recordings etc.) in a private working space to which, in principle, nobody else has access. This does not only provide unique multimedia work facilities, where e.g. digital video recordings can be combined with notes, sound recordings, scanned and downloaded materials etc., it also makes it possible to observe one's own learning, because the student regularly has to add new material to already existing material. If learning is defined as the process through which a system – in this case a psychological system, but it can also be an organizational system – stimulated by external influences changes its present way of functioning on the basis of its own preconditions and with a view to maintaining its present way of reacting (this is where it differs from 'socialization', which is change stimulated by external influences with no regard to comparison between before and now, i.e. without memory and without any consciousness of the change, i.e. of the development as 'learning'), then a portfolio constitutes an interesting medium for the observation of changes of self. In other words, the portfolio makes it easier to separate learning from development and/or socialization.

Already through this the portfolio constitutes a medium, which makes it possible to observe second-order knowledge. Of course, one observes 'facts' first and foremost, i.e. world observations in the form of sound, image and text, but one also observes 'facts' in a temporal sequence between before and now. What is relevant to add to the already recorded knowledge of the world? What do I know today that I did not know yesterday? In other words, the portfolio makes it possible to observe learning.

But it must be added to this that the student always has to reflect upon what private knowledge should be made accessible in the public knowledge space. When is the knowledge I have accumulated and elaborated relevant as a source for other people's knowledge? When is it worked into a form that can be passed on to the teacher? To carry out these operations, the teacher has to place him/herself in the place of the other, whether this other is the students or the teacher. This stimulates the student to observe his/her own knowledge from the outside, i.e. in relation to the collective knowledge system represented by the class, or in relation to the knowledge system of teaching represented by the teacher.

	Private	Student public	Teacher public
Observation	Observation of material (observation of world representation, i.e. first-order observation)	Observation of development of the other (observation of collective learning)	Observation of expectations of the education system (observation of learning expectations)
Reflection	Self-reflection: Observation of material in a before/after perspective (observation of individual learning, i.e. second-order observation)	Comparative observation of the 'I' in the I/you relationship: 'I' observed through the collective other, i.e. third-order observation in the I/you context	Comparative observation of 'I' in the I/system relationship: 'I' observed through the education system, i.e. third-order observation in a systemic context

There could be a particular public space, which could be called the 'assessment' or 'career selection' room. Here the student makes the material that he/she wishes to put forward for assessment available for observation and communication. The implicit precondition for doing so is for the student to judge when the knowledge generated by himself/herself corresponds to the education system's expectations of acquisition of knowledge. In other words, the student has to place himself/herself in the position of the system and observe himself/herself through its horizon of expectations.

Conclusion

In this chapter, I have argued for the following conclusions:

Firstly, I have argued that the current situation of e-learning in Europe is hampered by a lack of theoretical clarity. There exist at least four mutually incompatible and normally non-explicated paradigms. Each one has its specific criterion of success and failure, and its specific understanding of the nature of ICT as a tool or medium for teaching and learning. I do not claim that theoretical consensus can or should be reached, but I do suggest that theoretical conditions should be made explicit.

Secondly, I have argued that the understanding of the relationship between ICT and teaching/learning depends on whether ICT is conceived of from a tool or media perspective. I argued in the chapter that teaching should be conceptualized as a specialized form of communication. This implies that the media perspective is the most relevant. This also implies that simple views of causality cannot explain the effect the new media have on teaching. It is, therefore, not reasonable to apply a simple cost-benefit consideration to e-learning.

Finally, I have tried to illustrate that in a teaching and research context it is appropriate to conceive of the new technologies as knowledge technologies and to apply a knowledge theoretical communication paradigm to e-learning. In this way it becomes possible to differentiate different forms of knowledge and processes of knowing. As I have demonstrated, this presupposes distinctions between forms of knowledge, which are different in nature. This might constitute a basis for e-learning analyses and evaluations across existing, incompatible theories.

Note

1. See also the detailed review of Bateson's categories of learning in Qvortrup 2001.

References

Bateson, Gregory (2000) [1972], "The Logical Categories of Learning and Communication." In: Gregory Bateson: *Steps to an Ecology of Mind.* The University of Chicago Press, Chicago and London.

Bell, Daniel (1973), *The Coming of Post-Industrial Society.* Basic Books, New York.

Brown, George Spencer (1971), *Laws of Form.* George Allen and Unwin, London.

Craig, E. (1990), *Knowledge and the State of Nature.* Oxford.

Dewey, John (1997) [1938], *Experience and Education*. Touchstone, Simon & Schuster, New York.

Dreyfus, Hubert L. (2001), *On the Internet*. Routledge, London.

Heidegger, Martin (1986) [1927], *Sein und Zeit* [Being and Time]. Max Niemeyer, Tübingen.

Husserl, Edmund (1997) [1907], *Fænomenologiens idé* [The Idea of Phenomenology]. Hans Reitzels Forlag, Copenhagen.

Husserl, Edmund (1987) [1929], *Cartesianische Meditationen* [Cartesian Meditations]. Felix Meiner Verlag, Hamburg.

Kauffman, Stuart (2000), *Investigations*. Oxford University Press, Oxford.

Luhmann, Niklas (2002), *Das Erziehungssystem der Gesellschaft* [The Educational System of Society]. Suhrkamp Verlag, Frankfurt a. M. (means Frankfurt am Main – in contrast to Frankfurt an der Oder)

Luhmann, Niklas (2002), *Das Erziehungssystem der Gesellschaft* [The Educational System of Society]. Suhrkamp Verlag, Frankfurt a. M.

Lyons, William (1980), *Gilbert Ryle. An Introduction to his Philosophy*. The Harvester Press, Sussex.

Mathiasen, Helle (2002), *Personlige bærbare computere i undervisningen* [Personal Portable Computers in Education]. Danmarks Pædagogiske Universitet, Copenhagen.

Merleau-Ponty, Maurice (1945), *Phénomènologie de la perception* [The Phenomenology of Perception]. Editions Gallimard, Paris.

Ministry of Science, Technology and Innovation (2003), *Perspektiver for kompetenceudvikling – rapport om e-lærning* [Perspectives for Competence Development – report on e-learning]. Copenhagen.

Nordkvelle, Yngve (no publication year), *Forelesningen som undervisningsvirksomhet* [The Lecture as Educational Activity]. Unpublished manuscript Highschool of Lillehammer.

Nørretranders, Tor (1997), *Stedet som ikke er. Fremtidens nærvær, netværk og Internet* [The Place which does not Exist. Future's Presence, Network and Internet]. Aschehaug, Copenhagen.

Polanyi, Michael (1958), *Personal Knowledge*. University of Chicago Press. Chicago.

Polanyi, Michael (1983) [1966], *The Tacit Dimension*. Peter Smith, Gloucester, MA.

Qvortrup, Lars (2001), *Det lærende samfund* [The Learning Society]. Gyldendal, Copenhagen.

Qvortrup, Lars (2002), "Cyberspace as Representation of Space Experience: In Defence of a Phenomenological Approach". In: Lars Qvortrup (ed.): *Virtual Space. Spatiality in Virtual Inhabited 3D Worlds*. Springer-Verlag, London, Berlin, Heidelberg.

Qvortrup, Lars (2003), *The Hypercomplex Society*. Peter Lang, New York.

Qvortrup, Lars (2004), *Det vidende samfund* [The Knowing Society]. Forlaget Unge Pædagoger, Copenhagen.

Ryle, Gilbert (1949), *The Concept of Mind*. Hutchinson, London.

Vygotsky, L. S. (1962) [1934], *Thought and Language*. MIT Press and Wiley, Cambridge MA.

Vygotsky, L. S. (1978), *Mind in Society*. Harvard University Press, Cambridge MA.

Zahavi, Dan (1997), *Husserl's fænomenologi* [Husserl's Phenomenology]. Gyldendal, Copenhagen.

Zahavi, Dan (2003), *Fænomenologi* [Phenomenology]. Roskilde Universitetsforlag, Frederiksberg.

'Virtual' and 'Flexible' University Learning: Comparative Convergent Strategies for Communication Practices

Knut Lundby & Päivi Hovi-Wasastjerna

Positioning and delimitation

As knowledge and competence are crucial to the changing Europe, media scholars should study communication practices in education and learning and strategies behind these practices. Universities are among the changing institutions of Europe. They have been carriers of thought throughout European history, depending on oral, written and printed media for centuries. Today, computer-mediated communication is used by the universities and by the learners as part of the adaptation to a new market of education. Digital networked media invite 'virtual' and 'flexible' teaching and learning strategies. These terms carry on from distance learning. Information and communication technologies (ICT) open new options of virtuality and flexibility. The contrasted terms of this study, 'virtual university' versus 'flexible learning', are among the most used and relevant as ICT and learning in present European universities are concerned. The idea of this chapter is to compare these contrasting conceptions within a similar socio-cultural context of Europe. The selected Nordic countries of Finland and Norway, however, take different stands on the European integration process.

ICT and changing media should be regarded as integral elements in larger structural changes. In Europe they are initiated by governments, companies or by European bodies. Global networks and global competition make the context for institutional changes of universities. Their application of ICT in education and learning could be understood in terms of 'knowledge, markets and management' (Robins & Webster 2002). These are critical aspects of today's universities, and they need to be studied within a critical perspective. However, we do not look directly at industrialization of learning and business, rather, we focus on the changing universities through their learning strategies for communication practices, which are critical to their 'production' of knowledge. We look at opportunities and limitations with ICT-mediated learning in universities. We are not doing a study on learning as such (processes, outcome), but on strategies and plans for communication practices at universities.

Life rarely fits the hype. The institutional changes of universities due to ICT are gradual and slow (Collis & van der Wende 2002: 7). 'Virtual universities' are less often just virtual. So-called 'Net-based' learning does not happen on the Internet alone. But when computer-based networked media are taken on board in strategies and practices, institutional changes occur.

Research questions

Finland and Norway are among the most extensively connected or networked countries in Europe in terms of Internet and mobile phone access and use. The development is based on a good infrastructure. The two countries are both part of the Nordic region, have a fairly distributed population of some 5 millions each, share many cultural traits and have a similar and strong social-democratic political tradition. Methodologically, to compare two countries of similar size and background helps focusing the key variables: Finland and Norway differ in policies of Europeanness as well as national and institutional strategies on flexible or virtual learning in higher education. The implications of these differences are the focus of this research: How do these distinctions influence the ICT-mediated teaching and learning practices of universities in Norway versus Finland? And for further understanding of this complex situation, how is the role of communication conceived in such ICT-mediated education?

ICT-mediated learning: 'flexible' or 'virtual'

All education is mediated, as is all communication. Artefacts like textbooks, chalk and blackboard, even the lecturers and institutions of education could be considered parts of the mediation apparatus. Mediation, in this descriptive sense, refers to 'any acts of intervening, conveying or reconciling between different actors, collectives, or institutions' (Mazzoleni & Schulz 2003). This chapter takes a more specific look at computer-based media in the mediation processes of universities under change.

Today's 'digital' media are 'networked' media. Our focus is on these 'new' media as they are included in changing strategies and practices of higher education. The Internet is a main infrastructure of computer-mediated education. To stress this networked character of the information and communication technologies, we employ the concept of 'ICT-mediated learning'.

The digitalization of mediation in education is a radical technological shift. However, processes of mediation with the computer-based tools are not activated until they are being applied in the social and cultural life of the universities, i.e. in their communication practices.

By ICT-mediated *learning* we direct attention to the learner, to the student who is the user of digital and networked media in his or her studies. However, learning in a university setting is structured activity. Hence, ICT-mediated learning presupposes ICT-mediated *teaching*. Together, they make up the concept of ICT-mediated *education*.

The use of digital and networked media are still combined with face-to-face and classroom situations; the virtual is mixed with the physical. We still apply the concept of ICT-mediated learning for this 'dual mode', 'blended' or 'combined' learning as the use of ICT is crucial or significant in these communication set-ups.

Here two concepts of ICT-mediated education are contrasted: the 'virtual university' versus 'flexible learning'. They both offer flexibility in time and space due to the application of digital and networked media. The 'virtual university' implies a stronger organization or degree of institutionalization, where 'flexible learning' rather refers to looser networks and individual initiatives. This is expressed in the first by the term 'university' while the other focuses 'learning'. The two categories are, of course, not all inclusive but fit the purpose of this research.

The concept of virtual university as well as the concept of flexible learning has a certain ideological aspect attached, a flavour of future optimism. The metaphors of virtuality and flexibility both have these connotations. The future will, of course, turn out to be neither very virtual nor fully flexible. The 'virtual society' has to be researched with a question mark (Woolgar 2002).

'Flexible learning' comes out of the distance learning tradition, but with added learner choice as well as computer-provided options (Collis & Moonen 2001). For 'virtual university' Ranebo (2001) found a number of definitions being applied: First, a *vision* that anyone, anywhere, anytime, can get access to university-based flexible learning opportunities with the help of ICT. Second, *full virtual universities* offering flexible Net-based options for learning with help of ICT (i.e. Open Universities). Third, there are corporate university joint ventures or a *denomination for university organizations* (i.e. consortia of universities). Fourth, 'virtual university' could also mean a *national education authority* on Net-based education – co-ordinating and offering support to research and development to higher institutions.

Here, the concepts of flexible learning and the virtual university will not be further defined, as it is part of this research to investigate how the concepts are being used and understood in the Finnish and the Norwegian cases to be compared.

Research focus

This research aims at an understanding of *communication* in the context of the selected cases, to be presented below, as in 2004. The focus is on communication *practices* as they develop at universities. However, the material in this particular study goes not much beyond the development of 'virtual' or 'flexible' learning *strategies*. This implies teaching and learning where ICT and digital networked media play a defined role. ICT do not function only as tools in learning processes. The metaphor of 'tool' is not sufficient. ICT function as media in the communication processes of these universities.

The strategies and practices of flexible or virtual learning at a given university are related to the converging media technologies and the converging institutional practices employed. However, the range and variety of available media and the 'flexibility' of the learning strategy may at the same time imply fragmentation or divergence.

This chapter gives specific attention to visual communication, as digital multimedia open new options for the active use of visuals in teaching and learning. To what extent – and in which ways – are visual forms and visual media being applied in the said communication strategies and practices? How is visual communication understood?

Methodology

The methodological approach of this study is pursued in four steps. First, we assess the degree and character of Europeanness in the institutional context of the two cases. On this background we, in the second step, investigate aspects of convergence-fragmentation in the flexible/virtual learning strategies of the selected universities. Thirdly, we identify and analyse aspects of digital, networked communication practices within the institutional learning strategy of each case. Finally, we discuss possible relations between the said university strategies and practices of flexible/virtual learning as well as the degree of Europeanness these universities relate to.

Cases

The selection of Finland and Norway for comparison depends on the national base of the two authors and on their universities: The University of Art and Design Helsinki (UIAH), in Finland (Päivi Hovi-Wasastjerna) and the University of Oslo (UiO), Norway (Knut Lundby).

The two universities are both higher educational institutions in small countries of northern Europe with a similar infrastructure of converging media. The two universities and their institutional policies are, however, sufficiently different to provide this research with significant distinctions. Their differences in size and scope offer a larger variety of relevant dimensions, even if it makes a direct comparison harder.

There are problems as well as benefits following the choice of cases so pragmatically linked to the workplaces of the two authors, however, the research could benefit from local knowledge of the own setting. We have both been involved with the development of institutional strategies in our own field under study and are much aware of the need to establish a critical distance for the analysis of one's own university, which has been helped by the co-author.

The empirical material to be analysed from the two selected universities is from the academic year 2003/2004. The study then offers a comparison in space (UIAH in Finland versus UiO in Norway), but not in time, except the closing discussion of future prospects.

Europeanness as context

In a research programme on 'Changing Media – Changing Europe', the degree and character of 'Europeanness' in the institutional, political and economic context of the university policies, is an important variable. By 'Europeanness' we understand the orientation to and participation in European institutional structures, usually but not necessarily through the EU.

Finland is an active member of the European Union while Norway so far has decided to stay out of the political institutions of the Union. While not a member, Norway, however, takes part in the Economic Area of the inner market of EU through a special agreement. Norway also fully participates in the education and research programmes of the European Union. The 'eEurope' plan and concept – which both countries relate to – gives the overall reference to Europeanness as policy. 'E-learning' strategies are part of eEurope policies.

The European identity of Finland and the Finns develops with major reference to the European Union. A European identity is becoming stronger in Norway and among Norwegians as well, along with expanded institutional co-operation and exchange in a growing number of sectors of society. Still, Norwegians to a large extent relate the concept of Europe to continental Europe. As long as Norway stays outside the EU, Norway is often considered outside Europe – or at the outskirts of Europe. Table 1 roughly summarizes the difference between Finland and Norway in terms of Europeanness.

Table 1. Europeanness of the institutional and national context.

	Finland	*Norway*
European identity	Develops within EU	Fairly weak European identity, however, being strengthened through institutional exchanges
Government relation to EU	Active member state	Non-member, but part of the Economic Area and participant in EU research/ educational programmes

The two countries of Finland and Norway are both part of an initiative for a Nordic Research and Innovation Area (NORIA) encompassing plans for a Net-based Nordic virtual university (White Paper 2003). This initiative will possibly be squeezed in-between the various programmes on a European level.

The 'Bologna Process'

In Europe, the Bologna Declaration, adopted 19 June 1999 by 29 countries, has summarized challenges of higher education in a globalized economy as well as defined parameters of ongoing changes in universities in Europe.

This Europeanization is at the same time an Americanization, as a key idea of the 'Bologna Process' is to create a system of comparable and convertible degrees. The selected Bachelor, Master and Ph.D. degrees match not just the British but the American system as well. More precisely, the 'Bologna Process' changes continental European degrees into an Anglo-Saxon system. At the core is the joint European Community Course Credit Transfer System (ECTS).

The Bologna Declaration challenges each signatory country to reform its own higher education system 'in order to create overall convergence at European level', while still respecting 'principles of autonomy and diversity.' The Bologna process, then, is one of accepted convergence in institutional development. Diversity in terms of mobility and choice is part of these 'convergent reforms' as the other side of the coin.

Finland and Norway are both implementing the Bologna demands but the Norwegian government is ahead of the Finnish. Norway launched its 'Quality Reform' during the last half of 2003. In this structural change of the higher education system the Anglo-Saxon degrees as well as the ECTS marks are being implemented within new study programmes. There are much tighter demands on teachers and students alike to deliver teaching and supervision as well as degrees on time to a changing work market in need of up-to-date competence. For the institutions this is a big challenge. The University of Oslo had to re-create or establish anew all its courses on all levels in order to comply with the reform.

Finland plans to convert to the ECTS as part of the European university system probably from 2005. As already implemented in Norway, one academic year will then mean 1600 student's work hours, which gives the credit of 60 student points. A master's degree (5 years) is 300 credits. So the new system means Europeanness.

ICT-mediated learning in the Bologna process

The Bologna process includes demands of mediated learning strategies. The simultaneous aims of convergence and divergence could not be reached without large computer and information systems, applied for administrative as well as substantial learning purposes. The 'European space for higher education' defined by the Bologna Declaration presupposes the use of ICT-mediated learning, but does not define how.

This has been further defined under the heading of 'eBologna'. The eBologna objectives are (Bang 2003):

- New pedagogical models for competence development.
- Flexibility in a lifelong learning context.
- E-assessment, individualised study support and collaborative learning.
- E-learning and blended learning to make European higher education more accessible from anywhere.
- Virtual mobility.

One country, as becomes apparent in the present study, gives priority to 'virtual university' while the other stresses 'flexible learning'. In Norway and Finland alike the implementation of the Bologna process relates to the national programmes on ICT-mediated learning, but these programmes differ.

Mobility of students is an alternative as well as a supplement to virtuality in the implementation of the Bologna process. Rectors of all twenty Finnish universities signed in June 2003 an agreement on 'student mobility and flexible study rights among all Finnish universities', linking mediated learning technologies and physical mobility.

The aim of the Finnish authorities is a leap forward in virtual education. When the transfer to the ECTS is undertaken in 2005, traditional teaching, face-to-face in classes, should make up a maximum of half of the teaching time. The other half should consist of different learning forms. They could be virtual or new forms of face-to-face exercises etc, depending on the university. Norway has no similar high aim of virtual or Net-based activities in higher education. The present national programmes of ICT-mediated learning will be explained below.

The irony of mobility and the ICT-supported learning in the Bologna process is that the flexibility hence offered to the learners is introduced in order to establish an institutionally more convergent system. Convergence always has a flip side of divergence or fragmentation. Flexibility for learners – be it virtual or not – offers a bit of leeway for diversity in lifestyle and life situation within a tighter and more coherent educational system made possible through technological and economic convergence. ICT, then, allows for control through convergence as well as for diversity through divergence.

Convergence in learning strategies

The Bologna process aims at institutional convergence. This intended outcome depends on the economic as well as the technological convergence. The 'analysis of convergent media use requires both a technological and economical definition of convergence', Schorr (2003: 15) maintains:

> The EU defined convergence as (a) the ability of different network platforms to carry essentially similar kinds of services, or (b) the coming together of consumer devices

such as the telephone, television, and personal computer. This definition should be complemented by a third aspect, namely (c) the convergence in media use (e.g., Web surfing over cell phone…). The principle prerequisite for an increase in new forms of 'convergent media use' requires a basic fitting of convergence-capable media which is different in each of the European states (Schorr 2003).

ICT-mediated learning involves convergence in media use. This comparative study investigates differences of 'convergence-capable media' in university education in Norway and Finland. However, we do not go into the actual media use of the learners. This study is limited to the strategies and planned communication practices for ICT-mediated learning. Hence, this study relates primarily to the institutional level, as does the Bologna process in general. However, intended for student flexibility through ICT-mediated learning, the institutional convergence of the universities relate closely to the technological convergence inherent in their ICT-mediated learning strategies and practices.

The term 'convergence' in the context of this study covers institutional as well as technological convergence. There are different forms of technological convergence (of networks, of terminals etc.), but for the purpose of this study it is not necessary to go into such specifications. Similarly, 'institutional convergence' is here a general term covering economic, organizational and social convergence. By identifying technological convergence separately, we employ a certain technology focused perspective. We are much aware that there are social and cultural presuppositions for the technology, and we will later focus on aspects of the social and cultural distinctiveness of its use. However, the focus on ICT-mediation requires a specific eye on the technology aspect, as necessary in all 'convergent media studies' (Drotner 2002).

Discussing the dimensions of convergence in the 'Changing Media – Changing Europe Programme', Ib Bondebjerg (2001) identifies convergence at three levels:

> first, at the level of *economic and organizational structure*, the growing horizontal and vertical integration of media companies, and their integration into wider corporate structures; secondly, at the level of *social institutions*, the convergence of communications with other spheres – work, education, family life, leisure, and thirdly, on the level of *aesthetics*, and the new forms and genres of multimedia, the Internet and other interactive forms of communication.

Our concept of convergence – and divergence – covers all three levels. However, we object to the term 'level of aesthetics': visual communication has experienced convergence before today's new media. The concept of 'aesthetics' is not suitable in this context – because it refers to cultural value. We do not need to go into this value aspect of convergence. We rather use 'visuality' or visual communication. This will be handled in our analyses below.

National programmes of ICT-mediated learning

While in Norway as well as in Finland the existing national programmes on ICT-mediated learning in higher education are closely related to the Bologna process, there are, however, significant differences between the two countries in terms of overall policy context in this area.

In Finland the national ICT policy is co-ordinated by Government Policy Programmes. The Information Society Policy Programme is headed by the prime minister himself. The preparation and monitoring of the programme is delegated to a ministerial group. Administrative decisions relating to the policy programmes are made by the Government in accordance with agreed procedures and with the help of existing organizations, and the representation of the universities is weak. The president of Finland, Tarja Halonen, speaking at the UN World Summit on the Information Society, Geneva 10.12.2003, stated that '...Within the information society, the significance of the information itself is central. Every human being must have access to information and it is the job of governments to guarantee this access. Information is the very basis of democracy.' There is an eFinland programme (http: //e.finland.fi) and specific, coherent ICT programmes in various sectors under this strong governmental co-ordination.

Norway has a weaker co-ordination of the national ICT policy, but there is an eNorway plan (http: //www.enorge.org) reflecting the eEurope ambitions. In Norway the various sector ICT-plans become less coherent compared to the Finnish, due to the softer policy co-ordination.

When it comes to the national ICT-mediated learning policy, Finland constructs a national 'virtual university' (VU) as a network connecting all university institutions. The comparable higher education programmes in Norway are more loosely built around

Table 2. National ICT policies of relevance for higher education (2004).

	Finland	*Norway*
National information society (ies) policy	Strong, dedicated. Finland had the EU-commissioner for IS	Weaker, not as dedicated
National policies of ICT-mediated learning	Explicit plans by Ministry of Education. All universities into a national Finnish Virtual University consortium	No all-encompassing national policy for ICT-mediated activities in higher education. Specific, limited initiatives.
Key terminology in ICT-mediated learning plans	Virtual university (VU)	Flexible learning (FL)

the concept of 'flexible learning' (here abbreviated FL). In terms of terminology of the national ICT-mediated learning policy, 'flexible study rights' is part of the strategy of the Finnish Virtual University. On the contrary, Norwegian agencies of 'flexible learning' in higher education do not apply the virtual university concept. Before discussing the two national programmes, the general differences between the two countries on relevant ICT policy are summarized in Table 2.

Finland: Virtual University

Finland has since 2001 a Virtual University programme (www.virtualuniversity.fi) initiated by the Ministry of Education. The Finnish Virtual University (FVU) is a consortium of all universities in the country aiming to act together as one network of learning and teaching. The development objectives of the FVU are in line with the objectives in the Bologna process for removing obstacles to student mobility, for increasing the comparability of university degrees, and for developing quality assurance procedures for the provision of education (FVU strategy 2003). According to the consortium, FVU together with its member universities should carry out the following activities:

- develop high-quality network-based education and study services
- co-ordinate online education provision, student counselling and research network activities
- develop records and databases for curricula, student info and study registries
- produces publications
- draft agreements needed to facilitate the activities
- found the necessary operational bodies
- collect fees for financing its activities

The vision of the FVU in the strategy is, by the year 2005, to have established high quality, ethically and economically sustainable modes of operation in network-based education and research, in widespread use at Finnish universities. There will be a permanent structure from the end of 2004, when the project activities and the service production of the present strategy is completed. The universities have been told they will have to fund VU programmes themselves after 2005.

The purpose of the FVU is to make virtual education practices and co-operative networks a natural part of the entire Finnish system of higher education. Strategic objectives in the FVU are, for example, networking, equality of access to educational and research services, elimination of barriers of the co-operation between the universities, development of mobility of the students in Finnish universities and saving university resources in the long term. In the FVU the educational use of ICT means the use of new technology in a pedagogically sound manner. ICT are used in both teachers' and students' work in ways that are flexible in terms of time and/or place (FVU strategy 2003).

Norway: Flexible learning

Norway does not have a similar explicit virtual university plan. National policies for higher education are about co-ordination and support of networks and local initiatives rather than strong national programmes. However, recent policies link separate agencies and initiatives into the new 'Norgesuniversitetet' (http: //nuv.no). Norway has, since 2000, co-ordinated information of online courses at the higher education level in The Norwegian University Network for Lifelong Learning. The new 'Norgesuniversitetet' was established from 2004 when the Ministry of Education merged the former university network with The Norwegian Agency for Flexible Learning in Higher Education (SOFF). From the start in 1990, SOFF concentrated on 'distance education', but at the turn of the new millennium re-conceptualized the activity under the 'flexible learning' label. This is still the key term, as 'Norgesuniversitetet' should support the development of 'flexible and lifelong learning'. This implies strengthening and developing networks between higher education, working life and other sectors of society – hence, not limited to the universities. Still the institutions of higher education should be the primary focus of this new national agency.

Comparative critical assessment of national strategies

Compared to the Finnish Virtual University consortium, 'Norgesuniversitetet' has fewer and weaker means of power to put through a national strategy for ICT-mediated learning. In these matters, Finland follows a top-down strategy while Norway employs a bottom-up strategy. Norway creates in 'Norgesuniversitetet' a 'meeting place', informing about flexible and lifelong learning, and developing analyses of this approach to education. This agency will be able to fund and stimulate the development of flexible, ICT-supported courses and programmes at institutions of higher education in Norway.

For the objective of gaining money, Finland is able to work very efficiently with EU funding through the FVU structure. FVU has government funding, but FVU applies for other programme funds. Norway is part of the same EU research and educational programmes, but the institutions of higher education in Norway will have to apply to the EU system separately since there is no unified national structure to work through.

Finnish universities insist they are independent, but they need to go where the funding is and the teachers also will be forced into going where the funding is. But even if the Finnish universities are part of the national consortium, they can apply their own virtual university strategies and create their own learning practices. All teachers are asked to do their courses in a 'digital way'. There is only one vision of the change of learning in the FVU, one future of learning, linked with a tendency towards technological determinism. It is, then, a question of convergence more than of fragmentation, but it is too early to say to which extent the system will be covering the universities. This is still 'hype'. The virtual university process is still at the beginning. There are difficulties of communication and collaboration in interdisciplinary programmes. Still, the Finnish Virtual University demonstrates some of the strengths of a centrally defined programme: It develops a high level of ICT competence, could rely on state funding for a start-up period, provides good coverage of the universities network and also offers research of the learning environment.

There are similar positive reasons given for VU in Finland and for FL in Norway:

- it helps motivation
- it creates new tools/new possibilities in learning
- it creates a new role of the teacher
- it increases mobility of the students
- it encourages long-distance learning (real needs, e.g. minimize student travelling)

The barriers are in both cases understood to be technical, related to copyrights and to lack of digital material. Finnish universities, under the more coherent system of the FVU, regard the strict result objectives of the universities set by Ministry of Education as another barrier, as well as economy of the activity when government funding ceased after 2004.

But is ICT-mediated learning improving the quality of learning? This is a matter of bigger change than just the technological one. However, the universities often concentrate on providing technical skills instead of increasing the understanding of the possibilities ICT offer in learning. VU and FL should provide more than simple tools for learning. This is not just a question of new ICT-supported pedagogical models, but also a question of communication. Pedagogical models of ICT-mediated learning demonstrate in fact a new way to communicate in teaching and learning. Is flexible learning only communication with a variety of tools or does it change the meaning of communication? To pursue this question, we will go into the strategies and communication practices of ICT-mediated learning at the two case universities.

Strategies at the two universities

The two selected universities follow their national strategies in this matter, too. The University of Arts and Design Helsinki (UIAH) relates to the virtual university strategy, which applies to universities all over Finland. The University of Oslo (UiO) is in line with flexible learning thinking of higher education in Norway. This makes it possible to use two different types of universities as cases. However, as stated already, there are differences in size and scope of UIAH and UiO.

'Virtual university' strategies at the UIAH

The University of Arts and Design Helsinki (www.uiah.fi) is part of the Finnish Virtual University (FVU). VIRTU is the responsible unit at UIAH. The objectives of the strategy of VU at UIAH (http: //www.uiah.fi/virtu) are the following:

The operation concept of VU at UIAH is to support the development of flexible teaching and teaching pedagogically and technically. Part of the concept is to support and produce Net-based study periods and learning materials as well as to function innovatively and as a network.

VIRTU supports the development of research services online and works in co-operation with the information service unit, education administration and library. One of the focus areas of 2003–2004 is to create a tutor organization: training and organizing tutor help for Internet environments, suitable solutions and support for the teacher and the student.

The key idea of VU strategy at UIAH is to support in production and in the whole concept of the course. The focus areas of development work and support in production are internal development work of the university; inside departments, between departments, co-operation between networks and international co-operation.

Production types:

■ course and teacher/materials bound to person
■ independent materials
■ a mixture of the two above
■ Teacher/realization VIRTU teams responsibility
■ Teacher & students/VIRTU team
■ Teacher carries out/VIRTU team supports
■ Students carry out, teacher expert/VIRTU team supports

The VIRTU production team at UIAH consists of a project manager, producer, graphic designer, visual designer (Web), sound editor. In 2003, the Ministry of Education issued quality awards in the virtual university category for the development of online teaching. The Virtual University of the University of Art and Design Helsinki received an honourable mention for its producer-based support model for teachers.

UIAH is involved in the scientific networks of the Finnish Virtual University. Among them is the University Network for Communication Sciences (http: //www.uta.fi/viesverk) and IT-Peda – Network for Enhancing Knowledge on On-line Teaching and Learning in Finnish Universities (http: //www.uta.fi/itpeda/).

The strategy of the Finnish Virtual University does not mention 'flexible learning', but the universities practice flexible learning, e.g. VU in UIAH. Due to the independence of the Finnish universities the convergence of the FVU strategy level is not the same at the university level, as each university has its own VU strategy.

Strategy of 'flexible learning' at the University of Oslo
The University of Oslo developed in 2002 a strategy of 'flexible learning'. UiO is a research university as well as a 'mass' university of 32,000 students under the Ministry of Education (www.uio.no). The said strategy of flexible learning was based on ten years of small-scale experiences of distance learning activities, with the new opportunities offered by Web technology, and pilot projects on 'digital learning environments'.

The term 'flexible learning' was used about learning activities which are flexible in terms of various uses of ICT, regardless of whether the learners are located on or off campus, and whether they are in basic study programmes or in further, 'lifelong' learning. The harsh reality of changing the study structure completely through the 'Quality Reform', however, forced the University of Oslo to concentrate on students in BA and MA programmes on campus. The 'flexibility' kept, then, relates to the use of ICT or mediating technology for teachers and students in ordinary study programmes. The students should, however, be able to take part in their undergraduate or graduate training even when they are not present on the campus.

The strategy of UiO aims to:

■ integrate ICT as 'tool' and pedagogical support in the teaching programmes
■ develop staff competence and motivation to use ICT support for their teaching
■ give the students general competence in use of ICT and digital knowledge resources
■ prepare the institution to learn from its own flexible learning activities
■ make it possible for the students to take part in learning programmes while on or outside campus.

The strategy of flexible education or learning at the University of Oslo was evaluated in a thesis on public administration (Skarstein & Toska 2003). The authors point out critical factors for this strategy to be carried through. They stress factors related to language and culture; they see as a prerequisite that flexible learning does not conflict with basic values of the organizational culture of the university. This observation invites us to understand the mediating learning strategy within a communication perspective. Communication, then, could not be defined as a transfer of knowledge or information, but should be regarded through the defining processes within the community of learners and the community of staff at the university.

Convergence and fragmentation?

How could the strategies at UIAH and UiO be understood in terms of the convergence dynamics, involving divergence or fragmentation as well as the clustering of convergence? First, let us summarize key aspects of 'virtual university' and 'flexible learning' at the two universities (Table 3).

European university structure is still fragmented but moving towards convergence. ICT helps to streamline and speed up this development. But convergence produces and demands new flexibility and mobility. The Bologna process creates a more convergent system of university studies. To accomplish this convergence with the diversity it aims at, these programmes need components of ICT-based flexibility and mobility. This is coming strongly through in the Quality Reform in Norway even with the softer strategy of 'flexible learning', compared to the tighter structure of the 'virtual university' in Finland.

Table 3. Convergence-Fragmentation in university fl/vu strategies.

	VU at UIAH	FL at UiO
Part of national virtual university programmes	Yes	No
Defines itself as a 'virtual university'?	Yes, the VU activities. VU unit at UIAH	No
Strategy for flexible learning	Not under term of 'flexible learning', but in practise as part of VU activities	A specific strategy for 'flexible learning' under implementation
Organization within university	VU co-ordinator under rector	A central 'team leader' to co-ordinate support units and local activities
Specific programmes for digital learning environment etc.	Develops the learning management system FLE3 for specific use	Yes, pilot development of 'Digital learning environments'

ICT-mediated learning presupposes some technological as well as institutional convergence, because these are big systems. FVU is converging more than FL in Norway. The FVU vision is to be fully established by 2006. It is too early to know how wide or deep the convergence will be in higher education.

A top-down strategy (like FVU) might converge quickly, but a bottom-up strategy (like FL in Norway) might be better grounded, even if convergence takes longer. The national FVU strategy aims at networking and convergence. The universities, however, are independent, which means that they can themselves decide their own system. The fragmentation occurs within the universities. Some teachers have adapted ICT mediated learning, others not, to a large extent depending on the available support system of the university in question.

Technically there are no big differences between Finland and Norway. Both countries have established basic technical convergence in terms of infrastructure (networks: Internet, mobile telephony etc. and equipment: PC, cellphones). Of course, it could be further developed, and software in particular is not yet good enough for real convergence. However, the focus should be on the organizational and cultural challenges to convergence, i.e. institutional convergence. The FVU strategy gives an impression of more convergence than is actually the case at the university level. The universities are quite well networked under fairly well-developed ICT strategies for learning, but practices vary. What could we learn about convergence and divergence from looking at communication practices of ICT-mediated learning in the universities?

Communication practices of ICT-mediated learning

The communication practices of mediated learning at the two universities under comparison are based on plans and experiences under the pressure of structural changes of the university sector on the national as well as on the European level. The analysis does not, however, follow these practices deep into the actual implementation, where ideals and realities easily diverge.

The material analysed in the two universities is of somewhat different character as the programmes of ICT-mediated learning differ, but it is still possible to compare the material. For the UiO we analyse those 15 active flexible learning projects funded by the university for 2003/2004, which was the first year of this strategic initiative at UiO. At the UIAH we analyse the 22 courses – as presented on the Web – under the FVU; 16 of them ongoing and 6 courses started in the academic year 2003/2004. In addition UIAH offers one general guide on how to study on the Net and one Net-based guide for foreign students. They are both omitted here. Cf. Table 4.

Virtual university courses at UIAH 2003/2004 are offered by five different schools: School of Motion Picture, Television and Production Design, the Media Lab, School of Design, School of Art Education and School of Visual Culture. The flexible learning projects at the University of Oslo 2003/2004 relate to seven of the eight faculties. In particular, they are carried out at departments or units of theology, law informatics and public law, health education, East European and Oriental languages, Spanish, media and communication, biochemistry, pharmacy, chemistry, informatics, political science, teacher's education and special needs education.

All courses at both universities are part of the ECTS system. At UIAH this system gives 1–3 credits with the number of students ranging from 25 to 160. The projects or proposed courses at UiO will offer modules in new BA or MA study programmes within the 'Quality Reform', numbering from a handful of students to large classes. A few of

Table 4. Characteristics of ICT-mediated courses UIAH – UIO 2003/2004.

	VU at UIAH	FL at UiO
Number of courses/projects	22	15
General characteristics:		
The kind of courses	Small modules, 1–3 credits	Modules or lab resources
The teacher(s)	UIAH teachers + tutors	UiO staff
The students	BA and MA	BA and MA

the projects are developing databases or other infrastructure for flexible learning rather than creating courses as such.

We set the analytical focus, first, on the *patterns of social interaction* (the teacher-learner relationship, the role of face-to-face and group interaction, and the extent of making things and creating material as part of the study). Second, we ask if and how these processes are *mediated by ICT and networked media* (the use of digital media in learning communication, the appliance of learning management systems and the mediated forms of the learning material – visual, text, multimedia etc). Finally, we concentrate on *visual communication* (the use of and understanding of visual communication as part of the mediated learning practices). This is because we regard visual expressions to be of growing importance in the media-rich learning environments of tomorrow's universities.

'Virtual university' practices at the UIAH
The University of Arts and Design Helsinki concentrates on subjects implying design, visual communication and art education. This university has been doing courses as part of the Finnish Virtual University since 2001. UIAH should, as a university of art and design, be able to handle these aspects of ICT-mediated learning.

1. Patterns of social interaction

It is a question of how these courses are constructed. Twelve of the 22 courses are constructed so that they can be studied virtually. It is not possible to categorize all courses in three different groups as to whether the course is face-to-face (F2F), virtual or the combination. Already in 2002 some of the courses were purely virtual. By 2003 only one course is 100 per cent virtual, Visual Communication, which is used in the courses of the University Network for Communication Sciences (http: //www.uta.fi/ viesverk). The course on Photography was ready during 2004. It can be used also as a purely virtual course. Many of these courses use flexible learning.

- *The teacher-student relationship* in many courses is based on an active interaction, e.g. Picture Analysis. The tutor system for supporting teachers is being extended at the departments of UIAH. Tutors, between the teachers and students, give support for learning. This support is pedagogical, technical or content-oriented.
- *The role of group interaction* (face-to-face vs. mediated) depends on the course. The same course can be used for different teaching purposes.
- *The extent of making things and creating material as part of the study* depends on the course.

2. Mediation by ICT and networked media

The concept of virtual university involves mediation by ICT.

- *The use of digital media in learning communication* is flexible. Many media are being used.
- *Use of learning management systems:* LMS used in August 2003 at UIAH are FLE3 and WebCT. (WebCT was suspended in UIAH as well as in several other Finnish universities in October 2003 because of the high costs.) FLE3 (=Future Learning Environment) is a Web-based learning environment, depending on and designed by Media Lab at UIAH (http: //fle3.uiah.fi). FLE3 is designed to support learner and group-centered work that concentrates on creating and developing expressions of knowledge and design. The EU/IST project Innovative Technologies for Collaborative Learning (ITCOLE) (http: //ww.euro-cscl.org) is also coordinated and designed by Media Lab at UIAH.
- *Mediated forms of the learning material* are visual, text, multimedia, films, videos, videostreaming, animations, maps, sounds. Some courses are based on the students producing their material in the FLE environment or in digital form, e.g. courses in illustration of children's book and history of art education.

3. Visual communication

Visual communication is one of the main issues in ICT-mediated learning at UIAH. It is a question of using the visual materials as well as visual productions. Visual communication is not just about 'illustrations'. It is a primary focus.

- *The use of visual communication* is a basic question in the university of art. Visual communication plays a considerable part of the learning and teaching practices in the virtual university courses at UIAH as well as in conventional courses at this university.
- *The use via visual production by students* is already quite common in the virtual university courses at UIAH. See the previous paragraph.
- *The understanding of visual communication* is a basic objective of the education at UIAH and so it is well understood.

'Flexible learning' practices at the University of Oslo
The 'flexible learning' strategy of the University of Oslo was launched in 2003 through a call for the development of flexible learning forms for the academic year 2003/2004. Thirty project proposals competed for a limited sum equivalent to 250,000 EUR in support for the said academic year. This analysis concentrates on the fifteen projects awarded and actually established. Most of the actors of these flexible learning projects are well aware that programmes to implement the Quality Reform of the Bologna process imply larger institutional changes. Here, as part of this larger picture, we ask how they handle the challenges of relationships, interaction and communication focused in this study. The analyses are based on applications, progress reports and websites of the projects.

1. Patterns of social interaction

None of the fifteen flexible learning projects at UiO are purely virtual or Net-based. They all rely on ICT-mediated as well as face-to-face (F2F) social interaction in a variety of combinations. In general, the use of digital and networking media comes as an add-on to the basic structure given in F2F study programmes. However, two departments at the Faculty of Education, as well as the Faculty of Theology, implement ICT-mediated systems on the whole to such an extent that the ICT-mediated system might lay the premises for configuration of the study modules. This is more a matter of organization than of technology.

■ *Teacher-learner relationship*. For some of the departments ICT-supported learning means teacher support, as these projects offer opportunities to let the students interact with machines and learning programmes rather than with teachers in the flesh. However, most projects try to build new kinds of collaborative structures between learners and teachers by adding ICT-mediated communication.
■ *Role of group interaction* (face-to-face vs. ICT-mediated). Some reflect in their project proposal justification for the continued and renewed role of face-to-face communication within flexible learning programmes. In most flexible learning programmes there is still a classroom aspect. However, the group interaction is at the same time carried onto the Net.
■ *Extent of making things and creating material as part of the study*. Nearly all projects do involve making or creating something as part of the learning process. Some stress the opportunities to use ICT resource bases for practice with 'real' calculations and cases etc. Others aim at the use of portfolios of assignments for evaluation. A few invite the students into a more coherent use of the Net-based multimedia options, such as the media studies assignment on creating newspapers on the Web as part of their training.

2. Mediation by ICT and networked media

'Flexible learning' in this context implies the use of ICT for mediation between learners and education providers. But which ICT tools or media are being used and for what purposes? In the UiO-projects it came to vary quite creatively, even if the university had given priority to the use of one specific Learning Management System (LMS) for handling the virtual part of the new study programmes.

■ *Use of digital media in learning communication*. Nearly all the flexible learning projects explore the Internet and the web for their purpose. They are all networked, but a few also include stand-alone learning resources like a DVD. Streaming video in MPEG4 format is integrated in some of the projects and a few plan to explore MPEG7.
■ *Use of learning management systems*. About half of the projects apply the Learning Management System (LMS) advised by the University of Oslo, which is 'Classfronter'

from the Norwegian company Fronter (http: //www.fronter.com). However, one successful programme insists on the competing Norwegian LMS 'IT's Learning' from the company IT Solutions (http: //www.itsolutions.no). Chat option is frequently used. About one third of the projects stick to the Web without exploring LMS systems at all. Some of them use available software in creative combinations.

■ *Mediated forms of the learning material* – visual, text, multimedia, etc. Most resources made available in these flexible learning projects are text-based. Some of them are innovative, such as the project 'Rich Text' (http: //www.hf.uio.no/east/riktekst/), making a variety of East European and Oriental languages available in their correct alphabets. This project, as well as a text-based course in Spanish, add radio over the Internet to their learning resources. A few employ visual and multimedia material, to be explained below.

3. Visual communication

In this research we are specifically interested in the use of visual communication. At a full-scale university such as UiO text-based material is the most relevant in many subject areas. However, we are interested in the multimedia potential in ICT-mediated learning.

■ *Use of visual communication*. Two thirds of the UiO-projects use visualization. A majority of them simply want to explain material by the use of graphs, video demos etc. Just a few of the projects enter into visual *communication* as something more than *presentation*. These few do, however, go into reflection on how visuals work in interaction between those involved in the education processes.
■ *Use via visual production by students*. Almost all projects employing visualization and visual communication produce this *for* the students, not with them. The exception is the course on newspaper production for the media studies and the digital media programmes. In this course, the students learn by creating a Net newspaper.
■ *Understanding of visual communication*. With some exceptions, which are primarily the two projects at the Department of Media and Communication, the applications for the flexible learning projects at UiO demonstrate limited understanding of visual communication. In some projects they simply add a video demo without any integrated understanding of this in relation to the subject to be taught. But there are also examples of professional filming, integrated in multimedia cases, even employing the options of choice and selection in MPEG4 streaming.

Comparison of the two universities
For the academic year 2003/2004 the ICT-mediated learning projects at the University of Arts and Design Helsinki and the University of Oslo could be compared and summarized as in Table 5.

Table 5. ICT-mediated communication practices related to the flexible/virtual learning strategies at the selected universities.

	VU at UIAH	FL at UiO
Social interaction patterns:		
The teacher (teaching) – learner (learning) rel.ship	Many courses based on an active interaction	Some FL-projects establish distance teacher-students, others shape collaboration
The role of group interaction in F2F vs ICT	Depend on the course. Some use only ICT others both ICT and F2F	Group interaction carried into the Net, but not much reflection on F2F vs. the Net
Making things, creating material as part of study	Production team	Nearly all projects invite students to create and make various deliverables
ICT-mediation:		
Use of digital media in learning communication	Fairly advanced use of new media	Internet and networked media in all projects, some advanced streaming media used
Learning Management Systems (LMS)	Developed FLE (Future Learning Environment)	Half the projects apply the Norwegian LMS ClassFronter
Learning material applied (visual, text, multimedia)	A variety of media most commonly used	Most text-based courses, some of them innovative, with radio. Also projects with visuals.
Visual communication		
Use of visual communication	More and more; depends on the actual learning environment.	Some, but more as illustration or presentation than as reflected communication
Use via visual production	Some courses	Produces Net newspaper in media studies course, otherwise little such production
Understanding of visual communication	It is one topic of VU in UIAH	In general little reflection on visual communication in the FL projects

The patterns are not uniform. In general, Finland and UIAH follow a top-down strategy while Norway and UiO has a bottom-up approach. However, in the use of learning management systems, the Norwegian Classfronter strategy is top-down compared to the open source Future Learning Environment (FLE) developed at UIAH.

Visual communication is used where the need is perceived, or where the role of visual communication in teaching is understood. At the outset this will be needed and understood more at a university of art and design like UIAH than at a mass university like UiO. But in relevant study programmes, as in media studies at the UiO, they are coming close to UIAH in this respect.

Concluding discussion

The political mission of eEurope is taken seriously in the national political strategies of Finland as well as in Norway. How could the distinctions in Europeanness and ICT-mediated learning strategies influence the ICT-mediated learning practices of selected universities in the two countries? The immediate context of Europeanness is the same as both countries are deeply involved in the Bologna process and in pursuing the eBologna objectives. However, Finland is, as a member of the EU, organizing national programmes to fit eEurope and Information Society policies more effectively than Norway. The Finnish Virtual University (FVU) strategy advances this convergence and networking on the institutional, national level. Norway does not have a similar converging institutional strategy, bringing all institutions of higher education together in a joint approach to the European programmes.

However, the Norwegian bottom-up strategy and practice of 'flexible learning' is more realistic and sustainable than the Finnish 'virtual university' in the slow processes of institutional convergence. Over time, the bottom-up and the top-down approaches possibly will meet. This relates to university culture. The roles of the teachers change slowly. This is also a generational question. ICT-mediated learning has divided the role of the university teacher into many different roles (producer of learning material, tutor, supervisor, lecturer etc.). It will probably influence the communication between teachers, as well as between students. The traditional communication between student and teacher has changed. ICT- mediated learning supports this intercommunication. Flexible learning offers alternatives in learning as well as in teaching. This adds different ways of learning and encourages the use of various kinds of materials (not only digital).

The understanding of visual communication supports ICT-mediated learning and ICT-mediated learning gives more opportunities for the use of visuality. The use of visual communication and visual material requires the development of the learning environments and not only for transfer of text. The use of visual material in learning requires that teachers understand visuality (which is not only a technical question). In the adoption of ICT-mediated learning, usability is most important.

The differences we find in visual communication between UIAH and UiO relate to the different profiles of the two universities (art & design vs. 'mass university'). However, visual communication could be used much more in all universities. New tools give the options for these ways of teaching and learning. Traditional teaching itself is not without visuality. The challenge is to re-capture this in ICT-mediated learning.

How, in general, has ICT-mediated learning understood the role of communication? In the rhetoric of the strategies of virtual universities and flexible learning the terms 'technological and pedagogical' are used, but not 'communicative'. However, the main challenge relates to changes in the role of communication in learning and teaching.

The focus in this chapter is on communication practices as they develop at universities from 'virtual' or 'flexible' learning strategies. This implies strategies and practices where ICT and digital networked media play a defined role. ICT do not function only as tools in learning processes. ICT function as media in communication processes.

The strategies and practices of flexible or virtual learning at a given university are related to the converging media technologies and the converging institutional practices employed. However, the range and variety of available media and the 'flexibility' of the learning strategy may at the same time imply divergence or fragmentation in actual communication practices.

For a long time there has been a drive for change in the university culture. ICT for its part responds to this challenge. The main questions are about accessibility and usability; e.g. today's universities do not have the resources to respond to the costs of the worldwide education business. The issues of accessibility and usability are very important when higher education is going to widely adopt ICT-mediated learning.

The strategies of ICT are written from a political point of view. When they are written with political rhetoric, they are usually no alternatives. They go for one future, the IT future. One has to keep in mind that even the e-Future depends on social relationships and social interaction. Traditional face-to-face teaching can be very interactive – while interactivity with ICT might be merely rhetorical.

The technical side in itself is not the most important, but 'changing Europe' in this field depends on a certain converging stage of 'changing media', a certain infrastructure and available equipment – but also on competence in use – which points to the cultural and communicative presuppositions. They are as important as the technological presuppositions.

References
Bang, J. (2003), "E-Bologna – Progressing the European Learning Space", Opening speech, 6 November, EADTU Annual Conference, Madrid.
Bondebjerg, I. (2001), "European Media, Cultural Integration and Globalisation. Reflections on the ESF-programme Changing Media – Changing Europe", *Nordicom Review* 22: 53–64.

Collis, B. and Moonen, J. (2001), *Flexible learning in a digital world. Experiences and expectations.* London: Kogan Page.

Collis, B. and Wende, M. van der (2002), *Models of Technology and Change In Higher Education. An international comparative survey on the current and future use of ICT in Higher Education.* Retrieved 26 May 2003, from the World Wide Web: http: //www.utwente.nl/cheps/ publications/downloadable_publications/Downloadablesenglish.doc/.

Drotner, K. (2002), "New Media, New Options, New Communities. Towards A Convergent Media and ICT Research". *Nordicom Review* 23: 11–22.

Jakubowicz, K. (2003), "Convergence (Keyword)" [CMCE Team 2 keyword project].

Mazzoleni, G. and W. Schultz (2003), "Keyword: Mediatization" [CMCE Team 2 keyword project].

Ranebo, S. (2001), *Mapping of the Virtual University.* Helsinki: Nordinfo.

Robins, K. and F. Webster (eds.) (2002), *The Virtual University? Knowledge, Markets, and Management.* Oxford: Oxford University Press.

Schorr, A. (2003), "Communication Research and Media Science in Europe: Research and Academic Training at a Turning Point", in: Angela Schorr, William Campbell and Michael Schenk (eds.): Communication Research and Media Science in Europe. Berlin and New York: Mouton de Gruyter 2003, pp. 3–55.

Skarstein, S. and J. A. Toska (2003), *Det umuliges kunst? Kritiske faktorer i strategisk satsing på fleksibel utdanning/læring ved et norsk universitet.* Master thesis in Public Administration, Handelshøjskolen i København.

Woolgar, S. (ed.) (2002), *The Virtual Society? Technology, Cyberbole, Reality.* Oxford: Oxford University Press.

Finnish Virtual University strategies 2003, www.virtualuniversity.fi.

The strategies of the Ministry of Education in Finland, www.minedu.fi.

The Government Polity Programmes in Finland, www.valtioneuvosto.fi/english.

Information Society Infrastructures in Educational Finland – Survey Results 2001, Ministry of education committee reports 20: 2002. (Finnish).

Studies in the Context of the E-learning Initiative: Virtual Models for European Universities (lot 1). Final Report to the EU Commission, DG Education & Culture, Annex G, December 2003. (q: /projekt/dg education and culture/e-learning universities lot 1/analysis and reporting/draft final report/rep).

SECTION 4: POWER, TECHNOLOGY AND POLICIES

How is the political economy of media and communications changing in light of technological and market developments? To what degree are established political objectives and measures under pressure? How can politicians and regulators respond to the current challenges?

These are some of the main questions addressed in this section which takes a closer look at some challenges and opportunities within current media and communications policies. The focus is on Europe. Many of the trends discussed are, however, not specifically European but of a more general character.

The starting point of this section are the changing technological and political environments within which media and communications policies are formed – and which challenges these developments form for political goals about promoting media diversity, democratic equity and cultural values.

The digitalization of media and communications networks and production processes give new openings to new and independent media actors as, in principle, all can become media providers as the threshold for entering the media market is a lot lower than for analogue media. But at the same time, digital technologies enable multinational companies to standardize and diversify their products across borders. And, as contents, programmes and productions will all be in digital form, it can be reused between media platforms. In this way, it is not only the small media actors that get new openings, but also the big media houses get new opportunities to expand and control the big markets. Thus, current nationally oriented regulatory approaches to promote media *diversity* may be challenged.

Digitalization of networks for electronic services also implies that these networks can be used for multiple purposes. As more and more information and social participation depend on electronic services, access to electronic networks becomes a key question for social and democratic *equity*. The political challenge is how to ensure universal access to the services that are important for social and political participation. Will the market ensure this, or would some political interference be necessary to ensure an inclusive Information Society?

These processes also affect television policies. Digitalization of television networks enables the transmission of more channels than ever. The question then arises that when people have more channels to receive, do we need public service television at all? Or should the role of public service television be extended to the Internet in order to ensure the protection and promotion of *cultural values* in new digital environments?

These challenges are not only technological. They are experienced and formulated within an era of *political neoliberalism* and *economic globalization* in which the role of the state in any market is constantly questioned. National and multinational companies have pushed for less national regulation to enable global markets – and to a large extent this route has been successful. This has caused serious changes in the political framework for media and communications over the last decades. In western Europe, telecommunication was typically regulated as state monopolies, and the main broadcasters in most countries were public. The press was less regulated, but the markets were national or local – and so were the owners of the newspaper industry. Since the 1980s, these markets have undergone large changes. Telecommunications and broadcasting markets have been liberalized, and competition has replaced public monopolies as a governing mechanism and the owners in both telecom and media markets are increasingly multinational.

These political liberalization and globalization processes were reinforced by the rhetoric of the new *technology*. By the mid-1990s, both the EU and several national governments presented ICT policy document in which technology was described as a driving force for social change.[1] This was described as a self-driven process, which could not be stopped, hence political adaptation was required. Although technological determinism has been abandoned by most scholars, it was a frequently used argument to legitimize policy reform. Arguments about the transformative power of technology played important roles when the decisions were taken to fully liberalize telecommunications – and they continue to play a role in debates about further deregulation of broadcasting and media markets.

These challenges and processes of policy change are partly conducted on a European and partly on a national level. The EU provides a quite detailed framework for telecommunications policy. The EU plays a weaker role in broadcasting and other media issues. The EU offers incentives for European media production (quotas, film support etc.), but basically the principle of subsidiarity means that the states are allowed to protect their public service broadcasters and develop their own cultural policies. Nevertheless, as the economic policy of the EU is pervasive – it often interferes with the states' cultural and media policy – and the pressure for change is, therefore, often towards economic objectives of deregulation and liberalization. Thus, there may be tensions between the economic ambitions of the EU and the national media policies focusing more on cultural objectives.

In the following chapters, this framework of technological developments and political-economic forces forms the background for three studies of changing structures and networks of power in Europe. These studies relate to questions about convergence and diversification in terms of media conglomeration, political convergence and developments within broadcasting. The contributions put a special emphasis on not only discussing the challenges and their current solutions – but also gives room to discussing possible routes forward.

The chapter by Werner Meier takes up the theme of the globalization of the media industries through the lens of media ownership. The industrial structure of the media affects who may access the 'marketplace of ideas'. Concentration of ownership continues to matter and requires scrutiny. The article proposes 'Media Governance' as a model of co- and self-regulation on a national as well as on a European Union level.

The second contribution, written by Tanja Storsul, focuses on policies and prospects for universal provision of telecom services in liberalized markets. This is a key challenge to make the Information Society an inclusive society. However, market interference for distributive purposes is contested by strong networks of industrial interests. The article discusses how this is handled in three small European states and how the EU should allow multiple responses to the challenges in order to promote an inclusive Information Society.

In the final chapter, Marcel Machill discusses the role of public service in broadcasting policy. Many critiques doubt in general the 'raison d'être' of publicly financed television in the era of multiple channels and digitalization. In this regard, France is an interesting case study because French media policy has taken some unexpected measures that can add fruitful discussions for media policy decision processes in other European countries.

Note
1. Such as the Bangemann report.

MEDIA GOVERNANCE: VALUABLE INSTRUMENT OF RISK DISCOURSE FOR MEDIA OWNERSHIP CONCENTRATION

Werner A. Meier

Introduction to a fundamental social problem

Media concentration is not a new phenomenon. From the beginning of the industrialization of the press, as a result of the technical-economic changes in the nineteenth century, certain social forces have repeatedly attempted to promote the monopolization of the media and to realize entrepreneurial interests (Hale 2003, p. 142). Against the background of processes of concentration at national level, and in view of the media enterprises operating transnationally, the concentration of ownership in both the print and the broadcast media has reached a degree hitherto unknown and resulted in legitimation deficits in the area of policy relating to society and democracy. The causes of the development described may be numerous but they are hardly secret:

- The growing horizontal and vertical integration of media and cultural industry organizations, and their integration into a wider corporate structure has paved the way for the globalization of markets
- Global competition has engendered a new competitive wave that cuts across national and cultural borders
- The increasing integration of the telecommunication-, the media/cultural and the computing industry has opened up a new range of new forms in production and distribution.

It is possible to identify a number of economic advantages deriving from the increasing interpenetration within the media sector and the growing concentration. In the literature on media economics these are covered by the keywords 'economies of scale', 'economies of scope', 'economies of multiformity', 'cross-promotion' and 'reduced transaction costs'. As a rule, integration and ownership-concentration strengthen the leading media corporations, which are successfully defending themselves against every attempt to limit their growth economically and politically. This means that state measures aimed at controlling media concentration and reducing the power of the media have little or no effect, inasmuch as they have been implemented at all. If one looks at the deregulation measures in the area of the media, one can even talk of the state promotion of concentration. Since the 1990s and across Europe, politicians and policy-makers have favoured the deregulation of media ownership rules without having looked deeper at the social consequences of such moves. Politicians – always with a keen eye on careers, influence, reputation and prestige – try to prevent dissent in relation to corporate interests and ambitious media owners: 'Because politicians are increasingly driven by the desire to accommodate the wishes and aims of influential media groups, the extent to which competing public interest goals for media ownership regulation (of any sort) can make any impression on policy decisions is diminishing' (Doyle 2002, p. 177).

It is, therefore, hardly surprising that its consequences are neither sufficiently well identified nor appropriately assessed, given that the media themselves are part of the problem. While the heads of media companies seek to reassure the public, disconcerted by mergers or takeovers, politicians react ambivalently: They tend to consider the power of the media to be highly problematic; when it comes to it, however, most of them are amenable to the growth strategies of the leading media corporations and hope for a strengthening of the media sector at regional and national level. Only a minority of politicians lay the primary stress on the risks for the economy, for the economic order and for democracy, and call for a clear and unequivocal limitation of media ownership.

In brief, the state and its subordinate authorities tend rather to promote mergers and acquisitions than attempt to prevent them. In this context, Gershon and Alhassan talk about the deregulation paradox: 'In principle, deregulation is supposed to foster competition and thereby open markets to new service providers. The problem, however, is that complete and unfettered deregulation can sometimes create the very problem it was meant to solve' (2004, p. 2), namely the lack of competition and increasing concentration. However, the current situation in Europe favours transnational media conglomerates. In addition and more specifically, the media and audio-visual sector has to play an important role in realizing the main objective of the Lisbon agenda, making the Continent the most dynamic, knowledge-based economy of the world.

However, the continuing concentration within the media can in no way be blamed for all the sector's weaknesses and the current crisis. Media concentration is just one –

albeit prominent – dimension of growing media power; the latter, however, has hardly been analysed scientifically, let alone overcome politically.

Despite all the failings, a free and pluralist media sector is an essential requirement for the full respect of the right of freedom of expression and information as well as for democracy: '"Political" pluralism is about the need, in the interests of democracy, for a range of political opinions and viewpoints to be expressed in the media. Democracy would be threatened if any single voice, with the power to propagate a single viewpoint, were to become too dominant'. "Cultural" pluralism is about the need for a variety of cultures, reflecting the diversity within society, to find expression in the media. Cultural diversity and social cohesion may be threatened unless the cultures and values of all groupings within society (for example those sharing a particular language, race, or creed) are reflected in the media' (Doyle, 2002, p. 12).

Lack of empirical research and insufficient evidence

Very few scholars research the problem of media ownership and concentration holistically. Few complain about the lack of analyses and debates within the scientific community (Doyle 2002, p. 13). As Sterling (in Compaine & Gomery 2000, p. xvii) observes: 'Surprisingly little research has been done – only marginally more than we could draw on two decades ago. Too much is assumed or anecdotal, merely suggesting results from ownership changes.' According to Picard (2001, p. 66), the primary reason for the absence of research in this area is the lack of adequate data and funding. Compaine and Gomery, editors of Who Owns the Media, disagree with this observation about neglect. Gomery (2000, p.507) argues that 'no research in mass communication can ignore questions of mass media ownership and the economic implications of that control' (Compaine & Gomery 2000, p. 507). Unfortunately, mainstream communication researchers are seldom able, and seldom willing, to analyse the implications of media ownership and concentration. McQuail (1992, p. 116) argues that 'despite the amount and ingenuity of research, it is hard to avoid the conclusion that it has failed to establish clear general effects from monopoly conditions on the balance of cost and benefits, in performance terms. Where there is evidence, the effects seem to be quite small.'

However, some academic media economists are at least able to provide some figures measuring concentration. According to Alan Albarran, the Herfindahl-Hirschman Index (HHI), the CR1, CR4 and CR8 ratios as well as the Lorenz Curve (Albarran 2002) have been used to measure concentration within media and cultural industries. Concentration ratios can also be applied to measure across industry (Albarran & Dimmick 1996). In contrast to the United States, there is no agreement over the particular measures to be used in assessing concentration processes in Europe. Concentration ratios, the HHI and the Lorenz Curve are not recognized as usable instruments across European countries (Albarran & Mierzejewska 2004).

Concerning local media concentration figures in the United States, Eli Noam tracked the HH-Indices from the year 1984 to 2001/2 providing trends for five local media in 30 American cities, and he recently produced the following findings (Noam 2004):

- All local media (radio, local TV, multichannel TV, local newspapers, city periodicals) are strongly concentrated, with most HHI values well above of the Justice Department classification 'Highly Concentrated Market' (<1,800). Local concentration in 2002 is significantly higher than it was in 1984.
- The local newspaper industry shows an upward trend in concentration, from 7,219 to 7,621. The print media are among the most highly concentrated, while Radio and TV are in relative terms the least concentrated, with an upward trend in the former and a downward trend in the latter. While most cities must be content with one newspaper and one local magazine (if at all), there are likely to be half a dozen or more TV stations.
- Radio manifests the fastest rate of concentration, but remains, in absolute numbers, well below most other local media. The weighted average share for the top 4 firms (CR4) rose from 939 to a highly concentrated 2,400 for big cities.
- The local concentration of TV has declined over the past 2 decades, from a CR4 of 90% in 1984 to 73% in 2001/2. The HHI declined from 2,460 to 1,714.

The concentration in the sector of new media and Internet is higher than in the print and broadcasting sector. The Internet concentration is likely to increase in near-term, because of economies of scale and the profitability potential of oligopoly.

Albarran observed new cross-industry trends at the national level, based on the revenues of the top eight firms in the cultural industry: In just five years – between 1995 and 2001 – the share of the top four companies nearly doubled from 25% to 49%, while the share of top eight firms grew from 40% to 66% (CR8). In summary, the data is very clear in describing the United States as an increasingly consolidated media market (Albaran & Mierzejewska 2004).

It is one thing to have justifiable worries about the possible results of an increasing worldwide concentration of the media; the simple fact remains that it is empirically much more difficult to identify and describe the actual negative effects of this concentration. It is not at all surprising that the dominant view doesn't deny the ongoing process of concentration but presents the results as trivial. Indeed, the ambiguity of the findings that almost every market structure produces positive effects as well as negative ones, confirms such an assessment. Moreover, the absence of a public debate on media concentration indicates an increased acceptance of powerful commercially operated media companies and of flamboyant media moguls in the era of neo-liberalism. In the United States in particular the primacy of competition policy by regulatory bodies favours big, highly integrated media corporations and stimulates ownership concentration on a national and global scale. The dominant media firms in the American market are an oligopoly and a global cartel at the same time. According to a study by Aaron Moore, News Corporation, Disney, Viacom and Time Warner have 40 interlocking directors and the dominant 5 media conglomerates have a total of 141 joint ventures, which makes them business partners with each other (Bagdikian 2004, p. 9). But market power is also political power. 'The five dominant media firms ... have that power and use it to enhance the values preferred by the corporate world of which they are a part' (Bagdikian 2004, p. 25).

However, governments and corporate power elites are keen to relax media ownership rules, whereas the majority of the public fear a devastating loss of localism, diversity, quality and journalistic competition between different media outlets. Although every member state of the EU and the Council of Europe have the political, legal and moral obligation to ensure that the rights of all European citizens to a diversified and pluralist media are respected, governmental agencies invariably fail, because they are either unable or unwilling to take adequate media policy measures.

Media concentration in Europe: Some facts and figures concerning leading media companies

In order to obtain a preliminary picture, the following questions at least should be addressed: Who are the major players in and from western Europe in the different media markets? In which media sectors are the leading media companies involved and dominant? In which European countries do the leading media companies have a marked presence and actually play a strong role?

Looking at the media groups with the highest business volume worldwide, one can state that either American enterprises or European enterprises with a strong presence on the American market are dominant. The French concern Vivendi, which is active in six

	TV	Cable TV	Newspapers	Magazines	Books	Online	Radio	Other media markets	Other industry sectors	Media volume 2003 (billions US$)
Time Warner	x	X		X	X	X	x	x		**39,6**
Vivendi Univeral SA	x	x		x	x	x		x	x	**31,2**
Viacom	X	X			x	x	X	x	x	**25,2**
Walt Disney	X	X	x	x	x	x	X	x	x	**20,6**
Bertelsmann	x	x	x	x	X	x	x	x		**16,6**
News Corporation	X	x	x	x	X	x	x	x		**16,5**

X being one of the top three in the respective business sector.
Sources: European Audiovisual Observatory, Yearbook 2004, p. 26 and adAge 2004.

Table 1. The business segments of the six media groups with the highest business volume.

different fields of media business, tries to improve its position in the USA. The German group Bertelsmann attains about one forth of its turnover in the USA, mostly as one of the leading book providers.

The American media groups Time Warner, Viacom, Disney and newly formed News Corporation belong to the market leaders within two to four sectors. Considering only the turnover of the audio-visual sector, Disney (74%), Viacom (83%), Vivendi Universal (65%), Time Warner (53%) and News Corporation (67%) rank among the most important producers – they generate more than half of their sales volume within the audio-visual sector. Only the Bertelsmann group with 42% and Lagardère with 10% respectively earn considerably less than the American competitors within that sector. Noteworthy is that the increase of the groups has seldom happened by 'natural' rates of growths but by acquisitions and/or tie-ups. Considering the most important fusions in the past ten years, one can deduct that all leading media groups have been involved. (Cf. Gershon 2001, p. 59; Con et al. 2003, p. 151.) However, if one compares media companies to the companies with the highest turnover in other branches of the economy, Time Warner only achieves 80th place in the Fortune 500 list, Walt Disney is at 165, Viacom at 171, Bertelsmann at 273, News Corporation at 326 and Lagardère at 405 (Fortune 2003: F8–F10).

Of the 50 media groups with the highest business volume in Europe, 13 stem from Great Britain and 12 from Germany (including the RTL group domiciled in Luxembourg). London can therefore be regarded as the media metropolis of Europe. (See tables on http: //www.mediapolicy.unizh.ch/publications/downloads/mediaconcentration.pdf.) Six other media groups are French, whereas Portugal, Belgium, Austria and Switzerland are not represented in the league of giant media groups. The Bertelsmann group – together with the RTL group – is one of the leading European media producers in a total of five media markets (TV, radio, magazines, music and books). Only Lagardère, having a leading market position in the magazine segment with 245 titles in 36 countries, possesses two leading positions, whereas all the remaining suppliers appear as prominent actors in one field at most.

Diversification and internationalization strategies of leading media conglomerates

The leading media companies in North America and Europe have pursued a strategy of diversification in terms of products, markets and geographical coverage firstly because of deregulation and privatization of television markets in many regions of the world, secondly because of market saturation in many west European and North American countries and thirdly because of the digitalization of respective infrastructures (Chan-Olmsted & Chang 2003, p. 214). Deregulation, however, has not just provided the leading national media companies with more favourable conditions for development, but has also made it easier for the giants in the branch to penetrate foreign markets. Thus, Time Warner's operations have grown to take in over 60 countries worldwide. Apart from this, in many markets the leading global media corporations don't simply operate in competition with each other but form a disproportionately large number of strategic alliances – for example, in the form of Joint Ventures – and thereby reciprocally strengthen each others' boards of directors.

The combination of a small number of key economic characteristics would seem to play an important role in the diversification and internationalization of the media.

> First, media conglomerates offer dual, complementary media products of content and distribution. Second, media conglomerates rely on dual revenue sources from consumers and advertisers media conglomerates. Third, most media content products are nonexcludable and nondepletable public goods whose consumption by one individual does not interfere with its availability to another but adds to the scale economies in production. Fourth, many media content products are marketed under a window process in which a content such as a theatrical film is delivered to consumers via multiple outlets sequentially in different time periods (e.g., pay per view, pay cable network, and broadcast network). Finally, media products are highly subjective to the cultural preferences and existing communication infrastructure of each geographic market/country and are often subject to more regulatory control from the host country because of their pervasive impacts on individual societies (Chan-Olmsted & Chang 2003, p. 217).

As far as Europe is concerned, the last point would seem to be the most important. It is only in linguistically and culturally homogeneous markets that companies can supply customers from the domestic market via exports. The more different the markets are the more likely it is that specific product variants are developed in order to achieve higher returns. In the print media segment a 'global' strategy is pursued, i.e. a global corporate strategy is developed together with a locally determined product strategy (Sjurts 2004, p. 23). In the process, the advantages of economies of scale and globalization are employed while the advantages of localization are also fully exploited. The preference of European media corporations for a strategy of targeted marketing, which takes regional and local particularities strongly into consideration, can be explained by the cultural embeddedness of the media products. The need to adapt is strongest in those media products that are textually based, as a rule in the information media – and, therefore, most pronounced in daily newspapers. As a result, it is only those media companies with the appropriate financial resources that are in a position to make inroads into foreign markets by establishing subsidiaries or by taking over local companies. While this reciprocal penetration may not necessarily lead to greater concentration in the major European markets such as Germany, France, Britain, Italy and Spain, foreign media companies very rapidly build up a dominant position in smaller markets. This applies above all to transformation countries in central and eastern Europe, where the dominance of foreign media corporations is most obviously apparent (see tables on http: //www.mediapolicy.unizh.ch/publications/downloads/mediaconcentration.pdf). For example, Austrian, German, French and British conglomerates have been able to penetrate the Hungarian newspaper market through complete or partial takeovers of former party newspapers; 75% of overall circulation is in German hands alone. In the Czech Republic, German media companies control 82% of the press. Moreover, the leading Swiss publisher, Ringier, rapidly became the biggest supplier of magazines. In Poland, the Axel Springer publishing corporation had become the biggest political daily within a year with its tabloid *Fakt*. Overall, foreign investors control 85% of the newspaper market (European Media Ownership 2003).

The impact of media concentration on media organizations, media markets, politics and culture

Even if horizontal, vertical, diagonal and conglomerate concentration produces different results, it is assumed here for the purposes of analysis that the barriers to market entry for new companies are already raised by a reduction in the number of economically independent media companies. For existing providers as well, the room for manoeuvre and market niches is reduced, as the costs of a sustainable presence in the market rise, making the launching of new products more difficult. As a rule, the decline in the number of autonomous media companies does not simply hinder the generation of new jobs in journalism: the reduction in the number of editorial boards also means that jobs are increasingly lost. The flexibility of the media producers, which is commercially driven, also leads to a homogenization of the norms and working practices within journalism.

In addition, as a result of the oligopolization of enterprises, the internal and external pressure to compete in terms of publishing quality and innovation drops. At the same time, critical monitoring declines, hitherto a central instrument of self-regulation in the sector. Media concentration eliminates self-reflection; the incentive to produce better journalism than competitors becomes less.

The declining number of economically independent media, together with simultaneous growth in the size of companies, nevertheless increases the opportunity for owners and shareholders to exert influence. The crucial question is: What impacts on journalism have different forms of ownership? Ownership in the media sector is seductive, since it suggests power, influence and prestige, and can represent a successful means of intervening in social discourse. Although news companies are not always run by old-style press barons, media moguls are characterized by the tendency to push their own, largely particular economic and socio-political conservative, aims into the foreground, creating business structures which – both internally and externally – render the development of a plurality of media outlets and opinions more difficult. The selective choice of the top management and the enforcing of loyalty in the everyday workings of the company produce a freedom of the press that is steered by media ownership, a situation that inflicts massive damage on modern democracy. Even if the typical CEO is most likely to be a professional manager and has not very much in common with Rupert Murdoch, almost all journalism takes place within a corporate setting, which limits and influences what journalists do (Hargreaves 2003, 140). Most journalists work for someone and usually for a media organization. Tom Johnson, former publisher of the *LA Times* and later president of CNN has observed:

Is is not reporters or editors, but the owners of the media who decide the quality of the news ... It is they who most often select, hire, fire, and promote the editors and publishers, top general managers, news directors, and managing editors – the journalists – who run the newsrooms ... Owners determine newsroom budgets, and the tiny amount of time and space allotted to news versus advertising. They set the standard of quality by the quality of the people they choose and the news policy they embrace. Owners decide how much profit should be produced from their media properties. Owners decide what quality levels they are willing to support by how well or how poorly they pay their journalists (Alterman 2004, p. 27).

The more that media corporations grow as a result of takeovers and mergers, the more attractive they become to potential investors and the more they are, in turn, subject to takeovers. Trade in media products and media companies with the aim of short-term profits via the stock exchange is increasing. In addition, industrial companies are increasingly taking control of the media in order to ensure against commercial risks within their own branch. The appearance of investor groups, which are alien to the media sector, not only leads to a new enterprise culture that is orientated towards predominantly commercial goals, conglomerate interpenetration also produces restrictions on editorial decision-making, largely through commercial pre- and self-censorship of editorial copy. The greater the number of enterprises within complicated holding structures, the more difficult it becomes for outsiders to identify the interests of the investors. In the process there is an increased risk of economic reporting becoming imbued with the spirit of corporate journalism.

The continuous interpenetration and enmeshing of the media sector leads to a reduction in the economic competition between different media. Control via market forces is declining constantly. The individual interests and influence of corporate owners are easier to realize. A primary objective, on the one hand, is the growth of profitability, to be achieved by imitation, duplication, standardization and internal company advertising for the various media products. On the other hand the orientation towards advertising customers and the end-users is increasing within conglomerate companies.

In highly integrated media corporations it is not just the production processes that are cheaper; internal marketing also generates advantages for smaller suppliers. The systematic preference for the company's own products and services in both advertising and editorial sections makes commercial sense; at the same time it also worsens the situation of those competitors that are not part of conglomerates.

As a rule processes of concentration reinforce publishing failures, but they are not necessarily the cause. Thus, both an increased pressure to raise profitability and special commercialization drives can also emerge under highly competitive conditions and create negative publishing results, not just in monopolized markets. If one looks at criticism of the media in the USA, a link is only made between oligopolistic ownership structures and the hostility of very conservative publishers to trade unionism and journalism with media concentration (Fengler 2002). Nevertheless, as companies grow and conglomerate linkages increase, so also do the opportunities for owners, investors and managers and associated social groups increase to realize not just economic but also political interests. Media tycoons like Robert Maxwell, Rupert Murdoch, Conrad Black, Robert Hersant or Silvio Berlusconi have repeatedly played out their power roles as media owners in a more or less subtle manner. Maxwell's justification for his editorial influence was revealing: '[Owning newspapers] gives me the power to raise issues effectively. In simple terms, it's a megaphone' (cited in Murdock 1994, p. 5).

The systematic marginalization of counter-opinions, which succeeds best in smaller communication spaces, is less rigorous but no less problematic. Monopolized media are not, in general, in danger of incurring financial losses or a declining reputation if they pursue particular political objectives or *de facto* keep certain points of view outside social discourse.

The conduct and shaping of media policy is also conducted increasingly in the interests of dominant media companies and less in terms of the interests of the general public or a democratic society. In contrast to other branches of the economy, media companies can constantly produce publicity, which is driven by self-interest, via trade associations or their membership. Branch members succeed repeatedly in influencing the statutory framework, as well as state measures within the media sector, through concerted pressure in the field of media policy.

Media Accountability as form of 'Media Governance'
The governance of the media 'covers all means by which the mass media are limited, directed, encouraged, managed, or called into account, ranging from the most binding law to the most resistible of pressures and self-chosen disciplines' (McQuail 2003, p. 91). Media Governance, however, is not simply an analytical concept, but also a normative concept which can be derived on the one hand from Corporate Governance and, on the other hand, from Public Governance.

Corporate Governance (CG) means deliberate but also responsible structures of management and control for private companies quoted on the stock exchange. CG is an answer to management failure. More precisely: an answer to the frequent disparity between the interests of the providers of capital and those of the company is management (board of directors, top management). Even if CG primarily involves an adequate consideration of shareholders' interests, two of the five OECD principles of Corporate Governance include the relationship of a company to its target groups – for example to the general public. The third principle of CG seeks to promote active cooperation between enterprises and stakeholders. The fourth principle of CG is supposed to ensure that all essential issues concerning the enterprise are published in good time, correctly and thoroughly.

Possible Consequences of Media Concentration for:

Media Organizations and Journalism	Media Market and Media Sector	Politics	Culture
■ Orientation towards advertising customers and end-users, accompanied by a devaluation of news with in the overall programming of the media ■ Homogenization of the content through editorial cooperation ■ Consideration of the interests of the owners and advertising companies ■ Self- or pre-censorship ■ Uncritical reporting, declining levels of self-reflection as well as partisan company journalism ■ Systematic marginalization/ignoring of opposing views ■ Raising productivity via imitation, duplication and the standardization of media products ■ Homogenization of journalistic norms and methods of work ■ Reduction of internal and external competition within the publishing sector and thus the scope for improving product quality and levels of innovation ■ Cross-subsidy and cross-promotion within individual corporations ■ Reduction in journalist posts and loss of alternative jobs for journalists (both male and female)	■ Reduction of economic competition between different media ■ Blurring of the distinction between the roles of PR and journalism: mixing of reporting, advertising and public relations ■ Higher barriers for market entry and reduction in niche markets and the latitude for new media companies ■ Decline in the number of qualified journalist posts through the repeated deployment of journalistic copy ■ Higher costs for debut market appearances and the launching of new products ■ Internal advertising for the corporation's various media products ■ Decline in diversity, including in supplier markets, since media corporations can negotiate favourable conditions from their suppliers by means of their purchasing (monopsony) power ■ Limited choice for advertisers to reach consumers and declining negotiating power of commercial customers	■ Thematization and realization of particular interests: influence on public discourse ■ Loss of alternatives for producing a public political forum for debate: impoverishment of political discourse ■ Increase in the risk potential: extended (economic and/ or political) sphere of influence for owners and shareholders ■ Blockade by media corporations of attempts to shape media developments via media policy: media policy is informed increasingly by the interests of dominant media companies and less by the interests of the general public/ civil society ■ Increased leverage for media corporations to influence state location and taxation policy as well as to attract direct subsidies, thereby increasing prospects of commercial success. This can have a spiralling negative effect on smaller competitors	■ Increasing influence on opinion-formation, since horizontal concentration reduces the number of media agencies shaping opinion and increases the importance of the remaining media ■ Declining opportunities for different forms of cultural expression, because of the reduced availability of appropriate platforms ■ Evolution of media systems of reference for children and young people through the disproportionate influence of the media corporations in the area of children's and young people's entertainment programmes ■ Increasing dominance of criteria of relevance which are alien (antipathetic) to culture

If one applies the CG-concept to the level of the national economy and social policy, then the focus shifts to Public Governance (PG). It is no longer the interests of the shareholders but the public interest that is at the centre of consideration. PG seeks answers to the central question about how the general public can ensure that commercial and public institutions and organizations provide a reciprocal service for the means and privileges that are placed at their disposal. It is not just enterprises and, in certain cases, the state that should have the means and the opportunity to influence commercial behaviour, but civil society as well. With an efficient system of checks and balances, the existing inequality of power between enterprises, state and civil society should be reduced, without damaging the commercial capabilities of the company. It is primarily accountability and transparency that are demanded here in a normative sense, which should facilitate a certain degree of control over power by civil society.

The so-called 'Media Governance Concept' envisages a comprehensive accountability of the media towards society. It involves a critical engagement with the commercial and journalistic risks that necessarily emerge as a result of media power (Trappel, Meier, Schrape, and Wölk 2002). By means of new models, audits involving the social environment, or ethical codes specific to the media, leading companies would be expected to render their commercial and publishing behaviour transparent and prove that they were fulfilling their increasing responsibility for democratic politics (regulated self-evaluation). At the same time they would be expected to justify effects of commercial strategies and behaviour that were detrimental to democracy through the medium of public hearings. If it were shown that they had ignored professional and editorial rules, all affected groups would have the right to invoke the company's legal liability. The territorially comprehensive implementation of this kind of 'Media Governance Concept' would force owners, management and media producers to address issues of commercial and journalistic risk on a regular basis. Through the regular presentation of a 'Media Governance Report', the societal process of self-explanation – which is so vital to democratic politics – would be maintained. The control of concentration in the sense of 'Media Governance' could help to hinder the extension of the dominant power to influence opinion of one or several media companies.

Media Governance as a system for the evaluation and treatment of commercial risks – in the shape of media concentration and media power – is rooted in a comprehensive entrepreneurial concept, which is practised, above all in Anglo-Saxon countries, as 'Corporate Social Responsibility' (CSR). The enterprise seeks to establish communicative relations with all affected groups in order to demonstrate their social responsibility, their rootedness in the specific spatial location and in civil society. The enterprise is concerned with creating transparency about how its commercial activities are pursued (transparency of behaviour). The central question, according to the communications scientist Stanley Deetz, is: 'What are the conditions that increase the likelihood of corporate responsiveness (answering to) the social?' (Deetz 2003, p. 607). It implies a challenge to the media corporations to engage in a debate about values that goes beyond the search for profit. Media Governance begins where Deetz locates the key deficiencies: 'The problem is that the processes of organization decision making, although heavily value laden, do not include a sufficiently representative set of values. Social irresponsibility (the inability to respond to the social) arises from the inclusion of only certain values in the decisional chain' (Deetz 2003, p. 609).

Media Governance obliges the companies not just to engage in a discussion about social expectations of the media, but also with the risk-laden negative consequences of their action: 'Ideally, then, the corporation should acknowledge that certain actions might have destructive effects on stakeholders, even if conclusive cause-effect relations cannot yet be established. Moreover, the corporation should reflect on how the sum of various actions might combine to produce effects that exceed the effect of each individual action in isolation' (Haas 2003, p. 615).

With the application of Media Governance, a company commits itself to address and to evaluate regularly the potential for risk and abuse in society and in publishing, which is created by media concentration and media power. At the same time the media company makes transparent the measures it has taken to reduce risks. Through the system of commercial and editorial reports, the media company has the opportunity to demonstrate its responsibility in a sensitive field, both internally and to the outside world by means of an enlightened discourse concerning risk.

Media companies and the increasingly homogeneous media sector are less and less transparent, both internally and to the outside world, because new actors are continually entering the media business. Competition and concentration are increasing, and with it the risk potential for 'publishing', i.e. for the variety and quality of media content. The question about how media companies deal with publishing mistakes or the question of whether media companies should accept a kind of product liability, point to the need for a discourse about risk which is particular to the media sector. This seems to be all the more urgent, because the professional methods of self-regulation within media companies are not yet very advanced. Any reflection that is promoted institutionally or within individual organizations happens by chance or in response to particular events. In this context, the ability to organize one's own regulation, rooted in media governance, would pre-empt state attempts at regulation and simultaneously strengthen the acceptance of the media within civil society, in a social culture which is increasingly influenced by the media.

In the framework of a Media Governance Initiative, parliament could supplement existing legal provisions by committing media companies to demonstrate the proposed measures for avoiding the unwanted effects of media concentration and media power publicly and on a regular basis. In this context, two different kinds of media company, affected by the results of media power to a very different degree, have to be distinguished. Participation in the Media Governance Initiative would involve the publishing/media companies on the one hand and the media producers themselves on the other, where the latter are confronted by media power from another perspective.

The involvement of media producers is aimed at establishing a discussion forum within the company or corporation, which regularly and institutionally thematizes the problematic aspects of concentrated and concerted media power.

A common orientation model could be developed as a basis for this kind of Media Governance Initiative that firmly establishes the basic features of a contractual and sustainable media order that considers the interests of both society and the enterprise. The realization of this model would then need to be demonstrated by the media companies in their annual reports. The media companies would thus be committed to justify their socially relevant action but, at the same time and in the framework of a regulated process, would be able to prove that they were not abusing the media power that they had acquired through concentration. For example, this kind of Media Governance Report could include statements concerning the following questions:

What does a leading media corporation do in order to

- preserve the journalistic independence of the individual editorial boards?
- offer a forum to various different voices within the region?
- minimize the influence of advertisers on editorial content?
- resist the substantive homogenization that emerges when several media are operating in the same market?
- prevent reporting being dominated by the interests of owners in the case of conglomerate concentration?
- consider differing points of view despite having a centralized editorial structure?
- maintain innovative projects, even if there is no direct competitive incentive to do this?
- not discriminate against the products and services of competitors from other media corporations within the corporations own media?
- resist the attempts of political or economic actors to influence editorial policy?
- ensure that smaller or opposition groups have the opportunity of presenting their views?
- accord news broadcasts the appropriate level of social importance within overall programming policy?
- reduce partisan corporation journalism to a minimum?
- maintain a high degree of high-quality posts for journalists?

This list of questions is deliberately incomplete and needs supplementing against the background of contextually specific problems. Above all, it contains a challenge to the companies and media producers affected to identify the problematic issues from a professional and commercial perspective. In the course of this process of self-explanation within the associated groups of addressees, a register of relevant and significant issues would arise, whose origins are to be found in constellations of media power and processes of concentration and where strategic responses can involve the most diverse means. The documentation of the Media Governance Initiative could be employed to generate an exchange of experience between the actors in the field.

This kind of Media Governance Report would not simply generate a high degree of transparency but would set in motion a debate about the role of the media in society as well as the consequences of media power and media concentration for society. Needless to say, this kind of initiative cannot answer all the open questions raised. Above all, it is impossible to depict economic mechanisms with this kind of discursive instrument. Thus, it would be almost impossible to give a meaningful answer to the question as to what a media company does to lower the barriers to market entry.

In conclusion, a Media Governance Initiative could reverse the burden of proof for suspected or denied consequences of media power and concentration, could offer media companies an appropriate – regulated – forum for presenting perceptions of their responsibilities and could provide the various media stakeholder groups with a constant and enlightened debate about the power and influence of media corporations. However, whether the media companies and the state are yet ready to take this step is more than doubtful.

Conclusion

If predictions are correct, that we are heading towards a global information and media society in which the media play a dominant role, then it is necessary to focus more intently on changes in the global media, both in terms of communications science and in terms of media policy. Media concentration is the expression of the economic and political power of the media and, accordingly, has to be analysed scientifically and treated politically. There is still a lack of empirical evidence from independent scientific research bodies: 'One of the worrying conclusions that emerges from studying recent changes in media ownership policy in the UK and across Europe is that relatively little independent investigation or systematic analysis of the consequences of these changes has been carried out by policy-makers' (Doyle 2002, p. 172). The giant media owners are themselves an important subject for research as a means of assessing what they do with their acquired financial power with the help of their media outlets and content platforms (Cranberg et al. 2001). Since the government's role as regulator has declined substantially over the years in Europe and the US, we need to analyse the changing power relations between government, regulatory bodies and a converging and booming media industry. An overview of a converging field is essential to assess how interlocking contracts and ownership agreements influence the content of the media. It remains incontrovertible in any case that both the scientific analysis of media concentration as well as the efforts to combat media concentration leaves much to be desired. Quite apart from this rather desolate situation, and in addition to traditional media and competition law, we do need to create – between state/government, the media industry and civil society – new models of media governance at national as well as European Union level. As long as the EU is still rather unwilling to take action in the field of media concentration/media pluralism and diversity – due to the high sensitivity, complexity and conflictual nature of the issue – the national states have the duty to come up with an array of 'soft laws and instruments' in order to ensure media pluralism and diversity. This is a matter of particular urgency because 'it seems obvious that regulation in Europe is shifting from ex ante to ex post control of economic developments and from ownership and control-based policies *vis-à-vis* all possible bottlenecks ("gateway monopolies") in all ICT-related sectors' (Van Loon 2001, p.74).

For all the reasons cited above we therefore propose an elaborate system of monitoring which, on the one hand, secures the means for both recording and accessing current data on media concentration and, on the other, establishes a system involving an annual media governance report in which all the leading media corporations in the most diverse of communications fields seek to demonstrate the compatibility of their operations with society and democracy. This would allow the authorities, the media companies and representatives of civil society to conduct an enlightened discourse on the power and influence of the media in democratic societies which also helped the institutions involved to be better understood.

References

Albarran, Alan B. (2002), Media economics: Understanding markets, industries and concepts, 2nd ed., Ames IA.

Albarran, Alan B. (1996), Economies of multiformity and concentration in the communication industries. Journal of Media Economics 9, 41–49.

Albarran, Alan B. / Mierzejewska, Bozena I. (2004), Media Concentration in the U.S. and European Union: A Comparative Analysis. Paper presented at the 6th World Media Economics Conference in Montréal, Canada, May 12–15.

Albarran, Alan B. / Dimmick, John (1996), Concentration and Economies of Multiformity in the Communication Industries. In: The Journal of Media Economics, 9/4, 41–50.

Alterman, Eric (2004), What Liberal Media? The Truth about Bias and the News. New York.

Bagdikian, Ben H. (2004), The New Media Monopoly, Boston.

Bettig, Ronald V./Hall, Jeanne Lynn (2003), Big Media, Big Money. Lanham.

Chan-Olmsted, Sylvia M / Chang, Byeng-Hee (2003), Diversification strategy of global media conglomerates: examining its patterns and determinants. Journal of Media Economics, 16(4), 213–234.

Chon, Bum Soo et al. (2003), A Structural Analysis of Media Convergence: Cross-Industry Mergers and Acquisitions in the Information Industries. In: Journal of Media Economics 16(3), pp. 141–157.

Compaine, Benjamin M./Gomery, Douglas (2000), Who Owns the Media? Competition and Concentration in the Mass Media Industry, Third Edition. Mahwah, New Jersey.

Council of Europe (2004), Concentration of Media Ownership and Its Impact on Media Freedom and Pluralism. http://www.mirovni-institut.si/media_ownership/conference/conclusions.htm, (6.10.2004).

Cranberg, Gilbert et al. (2001), Taking Stock: Journalism and the Publicly Traded Newspaper Company, Ames, Iowa.

Curran, James (2002), Global media concentration: shifting the argument. Manuscript, May 23.

Curran, James/Seaton, Jean (1997), Power without Responsibility. The Press and Broadcasting in Britain, 5th Edition, London.

Deetz, Stanley (2003), Corporate Governance, Communication and Getting Social Values into the Decisional Chain. In: Management Communication Quarterly, vol. 16, no. 4, May, 606–611.

Doyle, Gillian (2002), Media Ownership. London.

Eastern Empires (2003), European Media Ownership in Central and Eastern European Media. European Federation of Journalists. Ownership, Policy Issues and Strategies with the support of the European Initiative for Democracy and Human Rights, Brussels, June.

European Media Ownership (2003), Threats on the landscape, updated January 2003. A survey of who owns what in Europe. Published by the European Federation of Journalists, Brussels.

Fengler, Susanne (2002), Medienjournalismus in den USA (Media journalism in the USA). Konstanz.

Fortune (2003), Global 500. The world's largest corporations. July.

Frank, Thomas (2001), Das falsche Versprechen der New Economy (The false promise of the New Economy). Frankfurt/New York.

Gershon, Richard A. (2001), The Transnational Media Corporations and the Economics of Global Competition. Global Communication Edited by Yahya. R. Kamalipour, Belmont, Calif., 51–72.

Gershon, Richard A./Alhassan, Abubakar D. (2004), AOL Time Warner & WorldCom Inc. Corporate Governance and Diffusion of Authority. Paper presented at the 6th World Media Economics Conference in Montreal, Canada, May 12–15.

Giddens, Anthony (2001), Entfesselte Welt (`Runaway World`), Frankfurt.

Haas, Tanni (2003), Toward an 'Ethic of Futurity'. Corporate Social Responsibility in the Age of the Risk Society, Management Communication Quarterly, vol. 16, no. 4, May, pp. 612–617.

Hachmeister, Lutz/Rager, Günther (eds) (2003), Jahrbuch 2002. Die 50 größten Medienkonzerne der Welt (Yearbook 2002. The 50 biggest media corporations in the world). München.

Hale, Dennis F. (2003), Political Discourse Remains Vigorous Despite Media Ownership. In: Harper, Joseph / Yantek, Thom (eds.): Media, profit, and politics. Competing priorities in an open society, Kent/Ohio, 142–156.

Hargreaves, Jan (2003), Journalism. Truth or Dare? New York.

Kelly, M./Mazzoleni, G. and McQuail, D. (eds.) (2004), The Media in Europe. The Euromedia Handbook. Third Edition, London.

McChesney, Robert W. (2003), Corporate Media, Global Capitalism. In: Simon Cottle (ed.) Media Organization and Production, London, 27–39.

McQuail, Denis (1992), Media Performance. Mass Communication and the Public Interest. London.

McQuail, Denis (2003), Media Accountability and Freedom of Publication. New York.

Meier, Werner A / Trappel, Josef (1998), Media Concentration and the Public Interest. In: McQuail, Denis/Siune, Karen (eds.): Media Policy. Convergence, Concentration & Commerce. London, 38–59.

Murdock, Graham (1994), The new Mogul empires. Media concentration and the control in the age of convergence, Media Development 4, 410–419.

Noam, Eli (2004), Local Media Concentration in America. Paper presented at the 6th World Media Economics Conference in Montréal/Canada, May 12–15.

Picard, Robert G. (2001), Relations among Media Economics, Content and Diversity, Nordicom Review, vol. 22/1, June, 65–69.

Report on Media diversity in Europe (2002), Media Division, Directorate General of Human Rights, Strasbourg.

Sjurts, Insa (2004), Think global, act local – Internationalisierungsstrategien deutscher Medienkonzerne. Aus Politik und Zeitgeschichte. Beilage zur Wochenzeitung 'Das Parlament', B 12–13, 22–29.

Trappel, Josef et al. (2002), Die gesellschaftlichen Folgen der Medienkonzentration. Veränderungen in den demokratischen und kulturellen Grundlagen der Gesellschaft (The consequences of media concentration for society), Opladen.

Trappel, J., Meier, W. A., Schrape, K. & Wölk, M. (2002), Die gesellschaftlichen Folgen der Medienkonzentration. Opladen: Leske und Budrich.

Van Loon, Ad (2001), EU Involvement in National Television Ownership and Control Policies and Practices. In: Television and Media Concentration. Regulatory Models on the National and the European Level. Edited by the European Audiovisual Observatory, 63–74.

Telecom Liberalization: Distributive Challenges and National Differences

Tanja Storsul

Introduction[1]

Within the information and communications sectors we have witnessed substantial changes over the past decades. There have been considerable *technological* developments with digitalization and development of new services creating new challenges for market actors like public broadcasters (see Machill, this volume). *Politically*, the telecommunications monopolies have been abolished. *Economically*, telecommunications and other information and communications industries have grown to take larger shares of the economy with important impacts on the structure of media ownership (see Meier, this volume). *Socially*, we have received new channels for information, communication and participation regardless of time and space. For citizens, one consequence of this is that access to telecommunications networks and services are developing into increasingly important communicative resources relevant for social, cultural and political participation, economic activity, playing and fun. Thus, the distribution of such resources is one significant aspect of the allocation of power and welfare in society. For an Information Society to be an inclusive society, everyone should have access to important telecommunications networks and services.[2]

But, how can distributive justice of telecommunications be ensured in liberalized markets? In the monopoly era cross-subsidies between profitable and non-profitable areas could be used to ensure service provision to all parts of the country. A contemporary political challenge is how to ensure such inclusiveness in liberalized markets.

This chapter investigates and compares how issues of distributive justice have been handled in Norwegian, Danish and Irish telecommunications policy. We shall first see how these challenges have been met in national *policy*; what policy objectives are promoted, and what general mechanisms for market regulation have been established? Secondly, we shall take a closer look at the *implementation* of this policy and how the regulatory regimes are operating. Thirdly, the *outcomes* of this in terms of prices and service penetration will be reviewed. Finally, the telecommunications market is still developing and we shall also discuss some *future* challenges in promoting distributive justice of new networks and services and the role of national and local politics in this.

The three states investigated, Norway, Denmark and Ireland, provide an interesting comparison. Ireland and Denmark are members of the European Union (EU), whereas Norway is a non-member, but part of the EU single market through the agreement on the European Economic Area (EEA). Thus, these states all are subject to the EU regulations and must act within an international framework with common EU regulations and global markets which constrain their degrees of freedom for policy-making. Some argue that such constraints are especially important in small states that are highly dependent on world markets (Katzenstein 1985). Thus, this situation may lead to a political convergence where national differences diminish.

However, as this chapter will show, in spite of technological driving forces, market integration and a common EU framework, there are still differences in the state's approaches to telecommunications policy and regulation. Important factors in explaining this are variations between them regarding their national characteristics, institutional legacies, welfare systems and political cultures. Norway, Denmark and Ireland were all concerned with how to ensure distributive justice in liberalized telecommunications markets, but they approached the issue with different legacies and political priorities.

Re-regulation of liberalized markets

In the three states investigated telecommunications were regulated as monopolies for almost a century. In Norway and Ireland, these monopolies were national, whereas in Denmark they were regional. In the 1980s a step-by-step process of market liberalization started, and in 1998 the markets were fully liberalized in all three states.[3] Liberalization did not, however, mean de-regulation. Parallel to the de-monopolization of the telecommunications sector, a new regulatory regime was established. There were three main reasons for this (Hills 1986; Storsul 2002). Firstly, there was a need to ensure *common standards* and compatible networks. Secondly, re-regulation was seen as necessary in order to promote *competition*. Without regulations, the market would most likely not be competitive as dominant actors could use their market power to hinder smaller actors from entering the market, or in performing in the market. The third reason was to ensure *universal provision of services*. In the monopoly era, the companies were given obligations to provide services nationwide in exchange for their monopoly privileges and could cross-subsidise between profitable and non-profitable areas. In a liberalised market, this was no longer possible. Consequently, the question of how to ensure nationwide access to telecommunications services became politicized.

Robin Mansell (1993; 1997) has identified two dominant views on the need for regulation in this area. The first is what she calls the *Idealist* model of telecommunications development. This model assumes that technical innovation and competition will create an ideal market in which services and resources will be allocated as other commercial goods through free and fair competition. According to such a view, universal service regulations will not be necessary. On the contrary, instead of promoting equality, many argue that universal service obligations imposed on telecommunications carriers, especially if funded through fees or funds that all market players have to contribute to, can create barriers to market entrance, and thereby distort competition (Noam 1994; KPMG Consulting 1996).

The second model is called the *Strategic* model and argues that full competition is not a likely outcome of market liberalization. Instead, we may expect tendencies towards the monopolization and oligopolization of markets in which market imperfections leads to an 'uneven development of the terms and conditions of network access' (Mansell 1993: 9). Consequently, according to this model, provision of universal services will have to be secured by regulatory measures (Collings 1994; Garnham and Mansell 1991; Hills 1993; Mosco 1988, 1990).

These dominant views are easily recognizable in national debates. Market actors are in general sceptical towards regulation of the end-user market as these may cause the market as a whole to be less profitable. They have therefore argued against price regulation of end-user services, and pushed for a light regulation of universal services. Between the political parties, the faith in the market varies with the parties' more general position on market regulation. The majority has, however, been sceptical that the market alone will sustain distributive objectives. Both the EU and individual states have therefore concluded in accordance with a strategic model and regulated the market – also to ensure universal services (Skogerbø and Storsul 2000, 2003; Storsul 2002, 2003).

In the following we shall look at how questions and concerns for universal service provision have been met politically in the first period after the markets were liberalized, i.e. from the time of full liberalization in 1998, until 2002 when the EU adopted a new regulatory package.[4]

Universal service policies

When telecommunications markets were fully liberalized in 1998, the European Union not only formulated the criteria for de-monopolization and competition, but also established a quite detailed framework for universal service regulation. The EU's motivation for this was not only a general concern about the distributive consequences of market liberalization, but also a concern that divergent national approaches could hinder the establishment of a joint European telecom market. Therefore a common framework for universal service obligations (USO) was established. This framework defined universal services as:

> [...] a defined minimum set of services of specified quality which is available to all users independent of their geographical location and, in the light of specific national conditions, at an affordable price.[5]

The services which should be made universally available were: the provision of network connections and access to telephone services including national and international calls, speech, facsimile and/or data communications, directory services, public payphones, and measures for disabled users and users with special social needs. The member states could designate one or more operators to be responsible for the universal provision of these services. To ensure that these services were actually available to citizens, they had to be affordable for all and the states could 'implement price caps of geographical averaging or other similar schemes for some or all of the specified services until such time as competition provides effective price control.'[6]

If universal service obligations represented an unfair burden on an actor, the member states could establish a mechanism for sharing the net cost of the universal service obligation with other market actors through a fund or charge.[7]

Although the EU regulatory regime on universal services was quite detailed, it gave the member states a certain degree of freedom on where to set the level of affordability, whether or not to introduce price caps, and over the implementation of a financing mechanism. Further, the states could decide to extend the scope of universal services beyond the EU-defined minimum. However, the funding mechanism could only be used to finance universal provision of the services the EU had defined. This meant that if a state decided to impose obligations on a company to provide ISDN or broadband services nationwide with or without a maximum price, the extra cost could not be shared with other market players.

Norwegian USO policy

Before liberalization, Norwegian Telecom (later Telenor) enjoyed monopoly privileges and was in return obliged to provide the whole country with telecommunication services. These should be equally charged regardless of where people lived, i.e. between rural and urban areas. Entering the 1990s, the main objective in Norwegian telecommunications policy was to ensure 'nation-wide provision of services at *equal prices* in all parts of the country'.[8] When competition was introduced, these principles could no longer be pursued, but new distributive measures were established.[9]

Voice telephony, including special services for the disabled, should be available to all households, businesses and enterprises, whereas leased lines and data communications should be available for all businesses and enterprises. Moreover, all customers should be offered connections to digital networks, payphones should be widely available, and directory services should be available for all.

The obligation to provide these services universally was imposed on the state company Telenor. Although the principle of equal prices was abandoned, the Labour Government stressed that 'To counteract possible unfair regional differences, the Government will introduce maximum prices' on voice telephony and leased lines.[10] As with most European states, Norway did not establish a financing mechanism to compensate for the extra costs of the universal services obligations. The reason was simply that, as Telenor was the dominant actor in the telecommunications market, such an arrangement would basically mean that Telenor would pay for its own expenses.

In two respects, these Norwegian regulations went beyond the EU regime. One was that all customers should be offered connection to a digital network, and the second was the maximum price on leased lines. However, these provisions had little impact on the telecommunications market. The digitalization of the telecommunications network was almost finalized at the time the legislation was decided, and thereby all customers would have this offer regardless of regulation. The prices of leased lines were originally very high and decreased beyond the relatively light price caps throughout the period. Hence, in effect, and definitely for the service provision to households, Norwegian regulations of universal services were in accordance with the EU minimum, leaving the provision and prices of ISDN and more advanced services to be determined by the market.

Danish USO policy

The Danish starting point was different from the Norwegian as the telecommunications sector until 1990 was organized with regional companies in addition to the state company. This structure meant that in Denmark there were considerable differences between the pricing structures of the regional companies. However, the state had measures to regulate the licensed regional companies, including their pricing policies (Thestrup 1992: 320). When the regional companies in 1990 were united into one corporation, Tele Danmark, it was specified that the Minister could impose obligations and supervise the company's compliance with them.[11] However, the obligations that were imposed on the company were rather vague, and as the liberalization process evolved, the need to formulate more specific conditions for universal service regulation became evident.

In the Universal Services Act of 1996[12] it was stated that all users should have the opportunity to access voice telephony and ISDN services. Leased lines should be provided to industry and special services to users with disabilities. Payphones and directory services were also part of the obligation. In order to ensure affordability of these services in all areas, price cap regulations were introduced.

Thus, the approaches in Norway and Denmark were rather similar. What differed was the Danish inclusion of ISDN as a universal service which should also be price regulated. The Danish Government had worked within the EU to gain acceptance for extending the scope of which services could be financed through a shared mechanism, but were not successful.[13] Nevertheless, Denmark used the degree of freedom within the EU framework and chose a broader scope of universal services. The extra costs of this price cap were imposed on Tele Danmark without compensation. A joint financing mechanism for the universal provision of the other services was not implemented in Denmark for the same reasons as in Norway.

Irish USO policy

In the monopoly era in Ireland Telecom Eireann had an obligation to provide services throughout the state 'so far as the company considers reasonably practicable'.[14] The focus on what the company considered practicable signified a different emphasis on the goal to ensure equal provision of services in all parts of the state compared to the Scandinavian countries. The penetration rate was also much lower in Ireland, and in 1984 fewer than half of the households had a telephone (Flynn 1998: 259). Tariffs were, however, equal in all parts of the country.

In 1996, the liberalization of telecommunications was planned.[15] The obligations imposed on Telecom Eireann were not changed, but provisions were made for price cap regulations. Considering that the market was not fully liberalized until December 1998, price caps were introduced relatively early in Ireland. This may be explained with reference to three factors. The first is that Telecom Eireann was partly privatized in 1996 and the Government needed to find new means of controlling prices. Secondly, there was considerable public discontent over the prices, especially after a steep increase in 1993. Thirdly, the price cap regulations in Ireland were not related to universal service provision as such but to the lack of competition.

In 1996, price cap regulations were specified to cover a relatively broad basket of services including regular telephony services, ISDN connections, directory services and payphone calls.[16] At this time, these services were monopoly services, and the price caps were a tool to prevent Telecom Eireann overpricing the services. After liberalisation Ireland retained the price cap on ISDN services.

Differences in USO strategies

As we have seen, there has been a considerable degree of policy convergence. The main regulatory measures chosen, the obligations to provide services and price caps, were all instruments within the EU framework. However, on a more detailed level, there were also variations. The main differences were that Norway and Denmark had a broader scope of universal service regulations than Ireland, and that Ireland and Denmark imposed price caps on ISDN services, whereas Norway did not.

At first glance, these differences were unexpected. We could have expected that the EU framework, which was also detailed on universal service regulations, would have eliminated differences to a greater degree. But, as we have also seen, the framework gave the states a certain degree of freedom, which the three states used differently.

With universal services, Norway and Denmark chose a somewhat broader scope than Ireland, as the two Scandinavian states also included leased lines and digital networks or ISDN as services, which should be provided universally. These differences may be explained with reference to continued differences between the states' welfare state legacies and political cultures, as redistribution of resources and egalitarian values were traditionally more important in the two Scandinavian states than in Ireland. Moreover, the level of network development varied between the states, the Irish network being less developed than those of the two other states. Consequently, the narrower scope of the Irish regulations may be an expression of the priority of ensuring universal provision of voice telephony, which was still not accomplished by the mid-1990s.

The differences between the states' price-cap regulations, however, followed a different pattern. Denmark and Ireland chose to price cap, not only the services defined as basic by the EU, but also ISDN, whereas Norway did not. It may seem surprising that Norway, which was the least integrated state in the EU with a strong political culture for egalitarian solutions, did not choose as extensive regulations as those adopted by Denmark. Furthermore, Ireland, with the least egalitarian political culture, could have been expected to have the least extensive regulations. However, when we take a closer look, the fact that Norway chose to regulate in closer accordance with the EU framework than Denmark and Ireland, may not be so paradoxical after all. One reason for this is that Denmark and Ireland had many years of experience identifying national approaches within the EU framework, promoting their own solutions to EU initiatives, and identifying the degrees of freedom they had, and how to manoeuvre within these, in accordance with their national interests. In Norway the situation was different. The EU was highly controversial in Norwegian politics after two referendums in which the majority of the votes were against EU membership. The EEA agreement was regarded as a national compromise, which few political parties wanted to question. Hence, the desire of most politicians to avoid conflict around EU issues became an incentive to accept EU guidelines and implement them directly into Norwegian politics (Skogerbø and Storsul 2000: 141).

When Ireland chose a more extensive price cap regime than the EU, the main reason was the lack of competition in the ISDN market and the need to prevent the company from exploiting its market power in relation to its customers. For Denmark, the price regulation of ISDN services may be explained with reference to the fact that there was already a tradition in the Danish telecommunication system for market regulation, as the regional companies had been regulated to avoid abuse of monopoly power. Thus, the institutional legacy made price regulations a more obvious alternative in Denmark.

Universal service implementation

The above discussions indicate how differences in the relation to the EU, as well as different institutional legacies and national characteristics, may contribute to explaining the three states' different approaches to universal service regulations. Nevertheless, the states all complied with the EU framework and universal service regulations were the basic political instrument for ensuring that all citizens would have access to basic services in liberalized markets. However, without effective implementation, the aim to ensure universal access to important services would be of symbolic value only. This section analyses the mechanisms the states employed in their implementation of their universal services policies.

Implementation in Norway

In Norway, universal service obligations were imposed on Telenor through the company's licence[17] issued by the Ministry of Transport and Communications. The license stated that Telenor had an obligation to provide a public telecommunications network and telephone services to all locations in the state with permanent residents or businesses. This obligation could be fulfilled with different technological solutions, but if Telenor chose to use mobile access, the cost for the customer should not exceed the joint costs for subscription and similar services in the fixed network. The Norwegian Post and Telecommunications Authority (PT) was responsible for monitoring compliance with the license requirements. They did not gather information about this in any systematic way, but depended on the individual customer's complaints. The PT assumed that, as long as there were not many complaints, Telenor met its requirements.

The license also provided for price caps which were imposed through letters from the Ministry to Telenor.[18] These prescribed price reductions calculated in percent related to the consumption price index (CPI). The price caps applied to a basket of services with both subscription rates and charges for national and international calls.[19] It was the total price of the basket that had price-cap restrictions. Hence, the price cap allowed increased prices for individual products if the price of the total basket decreased in accordance with the price cap. The arrangement therefore allowed for price rebalancing. This was an important reform in most European states and meant that subscription charges increased whereas the charges for the use of telecommunications services decreased.

The Ministry was responsible for monitoring compliance with the requirements and did this by reviewing reports from Telenor annually. Thus, the Ministry took part not only in formulating the rules, but also in imposing price caps and in monitoring Telenor's compliance with these criteria. The general monitoring of the market was, however, PT's responsibility, but the main focus of the PT was on the conditions for competition in the market and not on specific universal service obligations.

Implementation in Denmark

The Danish implementation of the universal service obligations differed from the Norwegian approach. In Denmark, there was no license requirement for operators in the fixed network. Consequently, the Danish universal service policy was implemented through other legal mechanisms such as acts[20] and executive orders. The requirements for service provision, price capping and the procedures for appointing the universal service provider, were settled by the Ministry through an executive order on universal services.[21] This order, which was very detailed, authorized the Danish regulatory authority, the National Telecommunications Authority (NTA), to develop even more specific criteria for compliance with the obligations. Tele Danmark was formally appointed in 1998 as the universal service provider with the obligation to provide services nationwide.[22]

Price caps were imposed in order to ensure developments in real prices that satisfied two criteria. The first was that the average private user's telephone bill should fall by at least a certain percent each year in relation to the CPI, and the second was that the average small-user's bill should also fall with at least a certain percent annually. This division into average and small users was intended to protect small users from unwanted effects of price rebalancing. Such rebalancing towards higher subscription charges and lower prices for use of telecommunications services implied that, even if there were substantial decreases in the average user's bills, the small users could experience price increases in their total bill, as subscription charges were the major part of their total expenses.

Another special feature of the Danish regulatory frameworks was that, when price-structures were changed, no private customer should experience an increase in his or her quarterly bill of more than 50 DKK.[23] This rule was an additional insurance for small users against increased bills as a result of price rebalancing. However, this rule was strongly criticized for hindering necessary price rebalancing and was removed in 2000.[24]

Until 2000, the Ministry set the price caps. In 2000, new regulations transferred this responsibility to the regulatory authority, the NTA. Thus, compared to Norway where the Ministry still played an active role in policy implementation, more responsibilities were given to the Danish regulator.

Implementation in Ireland

In Ireland, all operators needed a license and they all received standard licenses. Licensing therefore was not an instrument for regulating universal services. The Irish universal service obligations were specified in 1999 through a Statutory Instrument.[25] The Office of the Director of Telecommunications Regulation (ODTR)[26] was responsible for designating one or more operators as having an obligation to provide universal services and designated Telecom Eireann.[27]

A difference from the Norwegian and Danish regulations was that price-cap regulations were not part of the universal service regulations in Ireland. However, as discussed earlier, Ireland did have regulations, even if these were not grounded in the concern for distributive justice. The basic structure of the Irish price-cap arrangements[28] was that a price cap was introduced for a basket of services, which implied, as in Norway and Denmark that the tariffs of these services in total should fall by a certain percentage in relation to the consumption price index. The basket arrangement was meant to allow for price rebalancing as the prices on one of the services in the basket might decrease less than the total price cap if the total decreased according to the cap. In addition, two sub caps were introduced. The first was a sub cap for individual services and this was supposed to ensure against increased prices for any of the services within the basket. The second was a price cap for the lower quartile bills, which was an arrangement similar to the Danish price cap on small-user bills, and was supposed to ensure that small users (the lower quartile) also experienced decreasing prices. Thus, the distributive concern seems to have played a role after all.

Once a year, ODTR controlled eircom's prices for the previous year.[29] The obligation to provide services universally was, however, not monitored systematically, but, as in Norway, through individual complaints.

Variations in implementation
As we have seen, the basic procedures for implementation of the three states' universal service policies were similar. They all imposed obligations on the largest operator to provide certain services, and they implemented price-cap regulations. Still, the differences were significant and not only related to the scope of the universal service obligations as discussed earlier. Two additional sets of differences between the states were also significant.

One set of differences was *institutional* and involved the division of tasks between the national ministries and the regulatory authorities. In implementing universal services, the Norwegian Ministry was the most active. It was involved not only in developing regulations, but also in implementing obligations and price caps through its licensing. Further, it was the Norwegian Ministry's responsibility to monitor compliance with the price cap. In contrast, the Danish Ministry had delegated more responsibilities to the regulatory authority, the NTA, which was responsible for designating the universal service provider and, after 2000, for both imposing and monitoring the price caps. The Irish Ministry also had a less active role than the Norwegian, as important functions both in specifying the universal service provision and in designating the universal service provider had been transferred to the Irish regulator, the ODTR.

A second set of variations was between the states' *price-capping* arrangements. These were similar in that the states all employed a basket of services for calculating prices and related the price cap to the consumption price index. The main differences between the price-cap regimes were which services were price capped, and whether or not there was a special cap for small-users' bills. Ireland and Denmark had included ISDN-connection and services in their price-cap arrangements, whereas Norway had not. Moreover, both Denmark and Ireland had imposed a special cap for small users in order to ensure these user groups against rising prices as a result of price rebalancing. Hence, Ireland and Denmark had more extensive price-cap regulations than Norway. How can this be explained?

The role of the EU in national politics has already been considered as one important factor that contributed to the different scopes of the three states' universal services regulations. This review of the implementation processes might indicate some additional explanations. One of these may be the level of politicisation in the implementation process. In Denmark and Ireland, where the ministries' involvement in implementation was lower, the regulations themselves needed to be explicit to allow transparent implementation. Extensive price capping could be regarded as part of this. In Norway the legislation was less explicit,[30] which may be an indication that politicians perceived that they also had other means of political interference, such as the role of the Ministry in the implementation processes suggests. Furthermore, the Norwegian state still held a majority of shares in Telenor, and there might have been a political concern not to put too large a burden on the company. A final explanation might be that there was a stronger need for price-cap regulations in Ireland and Denmark than in Norway. If, in general, prices had been higher in these countries, this may explain why a more extensive price-cap regulation was regarded as necessary in these states than in Norway. But what were the outcomes of the three regulatory regimes' in terms of service penetration and prices?

Policy outcomes

A comparison of network development and price levels in the period investigated, 1998–2002, might help illuminate any differences between the outcomes in the three states. This will also give some indications to what degree these outcomes relate to differences in the policies and regulatory measures discussed above.

Table 1 shows that during the 1990s the number of telephone main lines per 100 inhabitants increased rapidly in all three states. In 2002, Norway and Denmark both

Table 1. Telephone main lines per 100 inhabitants 1990–2001.

	Norway	Denmark	Ireland
1990	50.3	56.7	28
1995	56.8	61.2	36.3
1998	66.0	66.0	44.1
2002	73.4	68,9	50,2

Source: ITU (2001; 2002, http://www.itu.int/ITU-D/ict/statistics [15.06.04])

had about 70 lines per 100 inhabitants, among the highest penetration rates in the world. Ireland was lagging behind with only 50 lines per 100 inhabitants. Hence, the situation in 2002 confirmed that the Irish network was still less pervasive than the Norwegian and the Danish.

Furthermore, the price levels of telephony in 2000 reinforced this general pattern of divergence between the two Scandinavian states and Ireland as telephone charges in Norway and Denmark were considerably lower than in Ireland. As the figures in Table 2 are adjusted for purchasing power, they illustrate that both telephone subscription and usage were more costly for Irish citizens than for Norwegian and Danish citizens. The Irish price level was also above both the OECD and the EU averages.[31] Hence, the Irish telephone market was characterized by fewer main lines at a higher price level than in the Scandinavian states. This was a continuation of traditional differences in network developments and price levels between the states. Further, it underlined the Irish need for price-cap regulations, simply because telephony was more expensive. The fact that the Irish price caps prescribed higher percentage decrease in price levels than the Norwegian and Danish price caps is in line with this.[32] Towards 2002, the Irish prices fell and the Scandinavian increased, reducing, but not eliminating, the differences.[33]

But, what kinds of network did people use? Was the standard telephone line still the most important, or did other services like ISDN or broadband start playing an important role?

Table 3 shows the types of networks that were used for Internet access in the homes in 2001 and shows quite divergent levels of diffusion of the different networks between the states. In Norway, a majority of the Internet users used other means of access than the standard telephone line. The most frequent kind of access was ISDN, which was used by 54% of the Internet users. In Denmark, the situation was different. Here, the majority of Internet users still accessed Internet through the standard telephone line. ISDN had not diffused as widely as in Norway and less than 20% accessed Internet through ISDN lines. 18% used ADSL or Cable modem connections. In contrast to these figures, 91% of Irish Internet users used the standard telephone line for their Internet access.

Table 2. Prices. OECD basket of residential telephone charges, August 2000 (excludes international calls and calls to mobile networks). USD PPP (US dollars adjusted for purchasing power).

	Norway	Denmark	Ireland	OECD
Fixed	186.55	173.90	230.13	195.55
Usage	119.63	119.31	216.23	207.13
Total	306.19	293.21	446.36	402.68

Source: OECD 2001: table 7.8.

Table 3. Type of Internet access in homes (multiple answers possible). Nov. 2001. % of Internet users.

	Norway	Denmark	Ireland	EU15
Standard telephone line	38	61.4	91.1	71.8
ISDN line	54.2	19.2	5.1	16.0
ADSL line	3.0	11	0.3	6.3
Cable modem	3.2	7.2	3.6	9.1

Source: EOS Gallup Europe (2001)

How can these differences be explained? The high degree of Irish reliance on the standard telephone line for Internet access, followed the general pattern of a less developed Irish network. But also the Norwegian and Danish patterns differed. In spite of the Danish ISDN price cap, fewer Danish Internet users accessed the Internet through ISDN lines. One possible explanation for this could be that the Danish price caps were introduced because their ISDN prices were particularly high. However, a comparison of the ISDN price levels in 2002 indicates that this was not the case.

As Table 4 shows, the Danish price levels were considerably below the Norwegian on subscription rates and initial prices, whereas prices per minute were slightly higher.[34] The reason for the different ISDN diffusions in Denmark and Norway must therefore lie elsewhere. The Danish regulatory authority, the NTA, suggested that the main explanation for the low Danish take-up was not to be found in the regulatory framework, but in the business strategy of Tele Danmark, which did not emphasize the ISDN market as much as Telenor did in Norway.[35] Although the regulatory framework was developed in order to promote ISDN development in Denmark, ISDN was more widely used in Norway where it had been an important part of Telenor's national marketing strategy for many years.

Table 4. ISDN prices. May 2002. Norwegian kroner (NOK).

	Norway (Telenor)	Denmark (TDC)	Ireland (eircom)
Subscription, month	239 NOK	167.68 NOK	281.43 NOK
Connection charge	0.59 NOK	0.25 NOK	*
Price per minute	0.21 NOK	0.25 NOK	0.09 NOK

* Not available in eircom's price list
Sources: www.telenor.no, www.tdc.dk, www.eircom.ie, all accessed in May 2002

These differences in the diffusion of ISDN may also contribute to explaining the differences in ADSL development. In Norway, where ISDN was widely used, few seemed to upgrade their access to ADSL in the early phase.[36] In Denmark, ISDN had not diffused equally widely and, consequently, ADSL had a larger potential market when this service was first introduced. This might indicate that users in Denmark leapfrogged the ISDN stage and went directly onto ADSL. A supplementary explanation could be that the companies' strategies varied, not only concerning ISDN, but also concerning ADSL, and that Telenor wanted to harvest the ISDN monopoly market as much as possible before its customers upgraded to ADSL. Further, geography makes ADSL development more costly in Norway than in Denmark and in January 2003 about 40% of the Norwegian households still did not have an ADSL provider that served their area. This illustrates one of the great challenges for future telecommunications policy.

Future challenges
As we have seen, the universal service regulations have basically focussed on ensuring access to the standard telephone line. In 1998, when the telecom markets were liberalised, broadband services had not diffused widely. As several European states also had a low penetration rate of telephony, the narrow focus of the EU universal service regulation was a logical choice. Some countries, like Denmark and Norway, were, however, concerned that all should also have access to ISDN or digital networks, and made provisions for this in their universal service regulations. The political interference in ADSL and broadband markets has been very limited. In Norway and Denmark governments have decided that the only role of the state in this market will be to regulate for competition and to stimulate the market through service demand from public schools, offices etc. In Ireland, there has been some state and EU funding of broadband rollout between regions, but not to households (Storsul 2002). Consequently, the distribution of ADSL and broadband services to private households is basically left to the market.

Over the last years, network developments have made ADSL and broadband services accessible to many households and businesses, and the actual take up of such services is increasing. However, many still cannot access such services, and none of the operators are prepared to provide ADSL or more advanced services to unprofitable areas in the foreseeable future. Network development is expensive, and remote or scarcely populated areas will obviously be less profitable than densely populated areas. Some areas might even be unprofitable for network development. What consequences this could have for access to high-speed networks and services is uncertain. In Norway, Telenor has estimated that 10% of the households will remain unserved by ADSL services. Broadband distribution will probably be lower. Thus, leaving network development solely to the market may cause new differences between geographical areas in countries like Norway, which is mountainous and with a scattered population. In countries like the flat and densely populated Denmark, these problems might be smaller, but even this remains to be seen.

Thus, questions about ADSL or broadband developments are becoming increasingly important social and political issues. Many households want broadband to access new services or to reduce the price of being online, but still quite a few cannot get such services as there are no operators serving their area. Today, this is a matter of irritation for those concerned. In the future, if broadband services become important for social or political participation, inequalities in network access could have more severe implications for welfare and democratic equity in society. Of more immediate concern is the situation for businesses and other organizations. These are heavy users of telecommunications services and very many regard broadband access as crucial for their ability to perform and compete and are not satisfied with a situation in which they are left behind (Skogerbø and Storsul 2003).

Governments and politicians are also concerned about broadband development as they see this as one of the cornerstones in the development of future 'information societies' at which they all aim.[37] The contested questions are whether large inequalities in access should be tolerated, and to what degree the state should interfere in the market to promote distributive justice of high-speed services.

The views that different actors have on such questions depend to a large extent on their position in the marketplace. Users of telecommunications services are more likely to be concerned about the distributive consequences of leaving this to the market, whereas the telecommunication industry is highly sceptical towards any regulation of the end user market (Skogerbø and Storsul 2000, 2003; Storsul 2003). The telecom industry has accepted current USO regulations as these are quite limited in scope and cause little disturbance of the market. They do, however, strongly oppose any extension of the current regulations and price caps, as this would make the market less profitable (Storsul 2003).

So far, the telecom industry seems to have had the greatest success in pursuing their interests for the future. In the new EU framework for telecommunications implemented from 2003,[38] the scope of universal service is not changed.[39] It is, however, stated – as it was in 1998 – that the scope of the regulations should be reviewed. But it is not very likely that this will happen. One reason is the strong pressure from the industry which, in contrast to consumer and citizen interests, is well networked (Skogerbø and Storsul, 1999; 2000; 2003). Another reason is that the member states have diverging interests. Some countries have highly developed networks and are concerned about high-speed services, whereas others still lack full penetration of basic telephony and would perceive an extension of USO to high-speed access as too expensive.[40] Therefore, in the foreseeable future, it is probable that the universal service regulations will be quite stable on the EU level.

But, this does not necessarily imply a status quo on the national level. As we have seen, in the first post-liberalization years, the states used their degree of freedom within the EU framework to formulate and institutionalize their universal service regulations in accordance with their own priorities. This may well happen for broadband and high-speed access as well even if the EU framework limits the degree of freedom the states have. One such limitation is that if the states chose to extend their universal service regulations to include high-speed access, this cannot be financed by a USO financing mechanism. As such an obligation without compensation would be a heavy burden on any company, a policy that wishes to promote universal high-speed access would probably have to use measures other than the USO mechanisms. The choice of such measures would also be delimited by the general EU telecommunications regulations.[41] The basic ambition of this framework is to create and sustain competition in the telecommunications market. State initiatives could not, therefore, include giving one or a few companies special privileges.

What kinds of policy measures would, then, be available? The state and EU funding of fibre rollout in Ireland illustrates one option. The Norwegian experience with local industries and municipalities, that form alliances to make the operator provide broadband services in their area, indicates another. Swedish tax policies, where broadband subscription gives tax reductions, is a third possibility. What is important is that such mechanisms of public funding or tax reductions do not favour specific companies or technologies.

Such initiatives may have different shapes and be taken on different levels – local, regional or national – in order to meet local, regional or national challenges and priorities. In some countries, the market may provide high-speed access to almost everyone, whereas in other countries, geographical, economic or other factors may cause greater challenges to an inclusive broadband development, so that market interference would be necessary in order to achieve such an ambition. While the EU will probably not provide common measures for such market interference, it is important that it does not create a framework that restricts the degree of freedom of the member states or local communities so much that they cannot respond to national or local challenges and priorities in network development.

Concluding remarks
As we have seen, there was a significant tendency of convergence between the telecommunications policies in Norway, Denmark and Ireland. However, national concerns still mattered and the more that policy was put into concrete terms, the greater degree of freedom the states had within the EU framework, and the stronger differences there were between the states' approaches. These differences were not accidental but were linked to persistent variations in the states' institutional legacies, political cultures and other national characteristics.

In the three states the regulation of universal services has focused on basic telephony, and to a varying degree, on ISDN. The differences in regulatory mechanisms chosen illustrate that the states had different strategies on how to solve the tension between distributive justice and liberalized markets. In the broadband markets, where the markets are less developed and network development faces different challenges in different circumstances, we expect to see even stronger divergence in political approaches in the future.

So far (2004), the provision and distribution of broadband networks and services have, with some exceptions, been left to the market. As broadband networks and services become more widespread and the use increases, access to these services will probably become more significant for citizens, businesses and the public sector. In such a situation, the political concern for the distributive aspects of this may increase as the market is likely to leave unprofitable areas unserved. The concern for distributive justice and the trust in the market, will, however, probably still vary between countries. Some will want to leave the development completely to the market, whereas some will want to interfere politically through funding, tax reduction, local or regional development initiatives etc. But, even if the ambition is to promote broadband development throughout the EU/EEA area, such a lack of convergence between the individual states should not be seen as a problem.

The paradoxical situation is that, taken seriously, an inclusive European Information Society, calls for flexibility on the EU level on how to approach broadband development. The reason is that, if the states all wait for the EU to act on network development, the whole area may risk a slow development because the EU might not act, and that might leave large areas without such services. Further, the states' challenges and starting points vary, and one solution might not fit all. Therefore, the EU should not delimit, but encourage multiple responses to the challenges of ensuring inclusive network development. The EU may discuss and promote goals that all states should work towards, but not in a way that restricts the states' possibilities to achieve these goals through different means.

Notes

1. This contribution builds partly on my earlier work (Storsul 2002).
2. However, as pointed out by Maier-Rabler (this volume), access itself is not sufficient in order to achieve such inclusivity, but it is a necessary precondition.
3. The remaining parts of the monopoly privileges were removed in 1997 in Denmark, 1.1.1998 in Norway and 1.12.1998 in Ireland.
4. This regulatory package was effectuated into the national telecom regimes in July 2003.
5. 98/10/EC *Directive on the application of Open Network Provision to voice telephony and on universal service for telecommunications in a competitive environment (Directive on Voice Telephony)*. Article 2f.
6. 98/10/EC. *Directive on Voice Telephony*. Article 3.
7. 97/33/EC *Directive on interconnection in telecommunications with regard to ensuring universal service and interoperability through application of Open Network Provision (Directive on Interconnection)*.
8. St. meld nr 8 (1991–92) *Om televerksemda i Noreg og om fullmakter på statsbudsjettet for 1992 vedkomande telekommunikasjoner*. My translation and emphasis.
9. St. prp nr 70 (1995–96) *Om avvikling av resterende eneretter i telesektoren*.

10. St prp nr 70 (1995–96) *Om avvikling av resterende eneretter i telesektoren.* My translation.
11. Act no 743, 14 November 1990. *Lov om visse forhold på telekommunikationsområdet.*
12. Act no 446, 12 June 1996. *Lov om forsyningspligt og visse forbrukerforhold inden for telesektoren.*
13. L 241 (1995–96). *Forslag til Lov om forsyningspligt og visse forbrukerforhold inden for telesektoren.*
14. Act No 24 of 1983, *Postal and telecommunications services Act,* Section 14.
15. Act No 34 of 1996. *Telecommunications (miscellaneous provisions) Act,* §7 Section 2.
16. ODTR 99/19. *Review of the Price Cap on Telecom Eireann.*
17. *Konsesjon for Telenor AS.* The analysed version was set by the Ministry 2 March 1999 and changed 2 August 2001.
18. Letters from the Ministry to Telenor of 20.12.1996, 03.07.1997, 26.06.1998 and 30.06.2000.
19. Letter from the Ministry to Telenor of 20.12.1996.
20. Act no 466,12 June 1996. *Lov om forsyningspligt og visse forbrukerforhold inden for telesektoren,* and Act no 418, 31 May 2000. *Lov om konkurrence- og forbrugerforhold på telemarkedet.*
21. Executive Order no. 1010 of 6 November 2000. *Executive Order on USO Services.* Although there have been several versions of this order, but the basic provisions have been stable.
22. National Telecommunications Agency. *Vilkår for Tele Danmark AS varetagelse af visse forsyningspligtydelser på telekommunikationsområdet.* 23. February 1999.
23. Executive Order no 705 of 9.1999, *Executive Order on USO Services* §15 -3.
24. Ministry of Information Technology and Research (1999) *Sund konkurrence og ægte valgfrihed. Danskernes adgangsbillet til netværkssamfundet. Status og visioner for telepolitiken.*
25. S.I. No 71 of 1999. *European Communities (Voice Telephony and Universal Service) Regulation.*
26. The ODTR was the regulatory body in the period investigated in this article and will be referred to in the following. From 1.12.2002 the ODTR was, however, replaced by the Commission for Communication Regulation.
27. ODTR D/99. *Designation of Universal Service Provider.*
28. SI No 393 of 1996. *Telecommunications Tariff Regulation Order* and SI 438 of 1999. *Telecommunications Tariff Regulation (Modification) Order.*
29. See, for example, ODTR 99/33, ODTR 00/35 and ODTR 01/20, all Compliance Statements on the Price Caps on Telecom Eireann/eircom.
30. Although the Norwegian legislation of the liberalized telecommunications market was more detailed than the legislation in the monopoly era, it was not as detailed and explicit as the Danish and Irish legislation. In the Norwegian regime, the legislation called for further interpretation by the Ministry on, for example, how to calculate and monitor the price-cap regulations (see Storsul 2002 chap. 6 for a closer analysis of this).
31. Calculated from OECD 2001, table 7.8, the average EU total basket accounted for 379,23 USD PPP.
32. Examples are: The Norwegian price cap for 1998–2000 was CPI-3%, the Danish for 2000 was CPI-4% for average bills and the Irish was CPI-8% for average bills (Storsul 2002: 189–196).
33. See OECD 2002 table 6.9.
34. Although these prices are from 2002 and do not show the *development* of prices, the Danish price caps for ISDN indicate that there have not been any sudden price decreases on ISDN

in Denmark. We may therefore assume that even if the level of price differences may have changed, the basic pattern was relatively consistent.

35. National Telecommunications Agency *Danskernes adgang til Netværksssamfundet. Telestyrelsens utredning om nye hurtige adgangsveje til Netværkssamfundet.* 31. October 2000.

36. After 2001, the number of ADSL subscribers have increased rapidly in the Norwegian cities, and by 2003, 18% of Internet users accessed the Internet by ADSL (Post og teletilsynet 2004).

37. Throughout Europe, governments have adapted policies to promote the development of what they describe as Information Societies. This set of Information Society policies is highly value laden and part of the liberalization project itself.

38. Directive 2002/22/EC of the European Parliament and of the council of 7 March 2002 on universal service and users' rights relating to electronic communications networks and services.

39. The speed of access is not specified, but it is stated that everyone should have the opportunity to access a network capable of Internet access.

40. The number of states with poorer developed networks is growing with the 2004 EU enlargement.

41. Especially relevant is the Framework directive (Directive 2002/21/EC of the European Parliament and of the council of 7 March 2002 on a common regulatory framework for electronic communications networks and services) and the Interconnection directive (Directive 2002/19/EC of the European Parliament and of the Council of 7 March 2002 on access to, and interconnection of, electronic communications networks and associated facilities).

References

Collings, J. J. (1994), 'Managing the Process of Sector Reform', in Wellenius, B. and Stern, P. A. (eds.) *Implementing reforms In the telecommunications sector. Lessons from experience* (Washington DC, The World Bank), pp. 567–580.

EOS Gallup Europe (2001), *Flash Eurobarometer 112 Internet and the Public at Large,* Gallup Europe.

Flynn, R. (1998), *POTs and USO in Ireland: 1880–1998,* Presentation to IAMCR CTP Session 30 July 1998.

Garnham, N. and Mansell, R. (eds.) (1991), *Universal service and rate restructuring in telecommunications,* Information Computer Communications Policy Series, 23. Paris, OECD.

Hills, J. (1986), *Deregulating Telecoms. Competition and Control in the United States, Japan and Britain,* London, Frances Pinter Publishers.

Hills, J. (1993), 'Universal service: Connectivity and consumer rights', in Christoffersen, M. and Henten, A. (eds.) *Telecommunications: Limits to Deregulation,* (Amsterdam, IOS Press), pp. 131–148.

ITU (2001), *World Telecommunications Indicators Database,* International Telecommunications Union.

ITU (2002), *World Telecommunications Indicators Database,* International Telecommunications Union.

Katzenstein, P. J. (1985), *Small States in World Markets. Industrial Policy in Europe,* Ithaca, Cornell University Press.

KPMG Consulting (1996), *Public policy issues arising from telecommunications and audiovisual convergence,* Report for the European Commission.

Mansell, R. (1993), *The New Telecommunications. A Political Economy of Network Evolution*, London, Sage Publications.

Mansell, R. (1997), 'Designing Networks to Capture Customers: Policy and Regulation Issues for the New Telecom Environment', in Melody, W. (ed.) *Telecom Reform. Principles, Policies and Regulatory Practices*, (Lyngby, Den Private Ingeniørfond, Technical University of Denmark), pp. 77–89.

Mosco, V. (1988), 'Toward a Theory of the State and Telecommunications Policy', in *Journal of Communication*, 38, winter, pp. 107–124.

Mosco, V. (1990), 'The Mythology of Telecommunications Deregulation', in *Journal of Communication*, 40, winter, pp. 36–49.

Noam, E. (1994), 'Beyond Liberalization III. Reforming Universal Service', in *Telecommunications Policy*, 18: 9, pp. 687–704.

OECD (2001), *Communications Outlook 2001*, Paris, OECD.

OECD (2002), *Communications Outlook 2002*, Paris, OECD.

Post og teletilsynet (2004), *Det norske telemarkedet 2003*, Oslo.

Skogerbø, E. and Storsul, T. (1999), 'Telepolitikk - fra trendsetting til tilpasning' in Claes, D. H. and Tranøy, B. S. (eds.) *Utenfor, annerledes og suveren? Norge under EØS-avtalen* (Bergen, Fagbokforlaget), pp. 193–208.

Skogerbø, E. and Storsul, T. (2000), 'Prospects for Expanded Universal Service in Europe: The Cases of Denmark, the Netherlands, and Norway', in *The Information Society*, 16: 2, pp. 135–146.

Skogerbø, E. and Storsul, T. (2003), *Telesektoren i endring. Mål, midler og marked*, Oslo, Unipub.

Storsul, T. (2002), *Transforming Telecommunications. Democratising Potential, Distributive Challenges and Political Change*. Dr. polit thesis, University of Oslo. [http://wo.uio.no/as/WebObjects/theses.woa/wa/these?WORKID=9248].

Storsul, T. (2003), 'Norsk telepolitikk – Ambisjoner og interesser på kryss og tvers?', in God, H. (ed.) *IKT etter dotcom-boblen* (Oslo, Gyldendal Akademisk), pp. 141–159.

Thestrup, P. (1992), *P&Ts Historie 1850–1927. Vogn og tog - prik og streg*, Copenhagen, Generaldirektoratet for Post- og Telegrafvæsenet.

Tranøy, B. S. and Østerud Ø., (eds.) (2001), *Mot et globalisert Norge? Rettslige bindinger, økonomiske føringer og politisk handlingsrom.*

Public Service Television's Mission in France: An Analysis of Media-Policy Instruments – Including the Use of the Internet as a New Distribution Channel

Marcel Machill

Introduction[1]

While French media policy in the 1980s and 1990s was characterized by numerous inconsistencies and discontinuities, particularly during the period between 2000 and 2002 the then socialist French government took decisions by offering public service television new development opportunities in an age of digital and converging technologies and by providing its mission with an accentuated profile. Whereas these political decisions have had limited effects on the television landscape in France itself, they provide interesting material for a policy analysis within the European context: The challenges for public service television (and its online branches) are similar in most European countries. The French case study might help other countries' political decision-makers to find a balance for their public service in the era of technological convergence.

While not replacing the protectionist impulse that has traditionally exerted influence on French cultural policy, the 'new' media policy approach does, however, introduce elements into television policy that put public television on a sound footing, even by international comparison. The catalogue of measures aimed at achieving this objective includes the use of new technology in the creation of public regional and specialist channels; the conclusion of an agreement on specific objectives; the limitation of air time for commercials, and an increase in public funding; the decoupling of public service television from viewer ratings as the dominant gauge of success for a particular programme; and last, but not least, medium-term financial planning instead of a broadcasting tax that has to be determined on a yearly basis.

The development of the French television landscape, in particular that of public service television, has for decades been characterised by two constants: first, by cultural protectionism and second, by a particular desire on the part of the rapidly changing political majorities to shape the landscape. However, the media-policy development process exhibits a variety of contradictions. In the 1980s a particular objective of French media policy was the creation of an internationally competitive media industry. The dilemma was and still is, however, that this objective is to a large extent incompatible with a different objective pursued by *all* political forces: cultivation of the State, the protection of national culture, contents, language. These dilemmas (for example, the rapid increase in US American contents in the wake of the commercialization of the television landscape) were combated by new media policy protectionist measures (for example, TV quotas for French productions). The French State – represented by a leading elite that is homogeneous in comparison with the elites found in other countries – has rarely limited its reach with regard to (public service) television. Since every political leadership of the Fifth Republic has thus far drawn attention to the advanced French culture and the French language for the purpose of endowing acts with meaning, ensuring the cohesion of the nation internally and delimiting it from other states externally and for the purpose of its own legitimation and, as the media are organized in a manner characterized by their relatively close proximity to the State, they are predestined for such instrumentalization. In this regard Brun-Buisson (2001: 21) points to the difference in meaning between the terms *intérêt public* in French usage and *public interest* in Anglo-Saxon usage. Whereas in the case of public interest broadcasting it is possible, in an ideal scenario, to assume a channel that is oriented towards the communication needs of the population – definitely not a channel defined by the State – according to Brun-Buisson there is the tendency in France to confuse *intérêt public* with *intérêt général*: i.e. with what the public authorities translate into practice and the public representatives define. 'Le service public de l'audiovisuel est manifestement assuré par des entreprises publiques, possédées par l'Etat et instrumentalisées par lui' (Brun-Buisson 2001: 21).

Public service television finds itself at the centre of numerous media-policy and general policy endeavours. For example, the quota principle for programme contents has been a well-known feature since the mid-70s, long before the European Directive 'Television without Frontiers' (European Council 1989) with whose framework the French government also ensured the implementation of the quota policy at a European level. In Article 15, the 1974 Media Law (cf. Loi 74–696) introduced the specification booklets (*cahiers des charges*) for the public service television stations. These booklets laid down for the first time the objectives of state television, 'in particular (...) the minimum programme offering' (Art. 15 Loi 74–696).

The specification booklets have since been amended on a number of occasions. Whereas critics reproach the booklets for their declamatory function, for de Broglie (2001: 23) they are a manifestation of the fulfilment of public service television's mission. In its current mission the public service television stations are to offer specific programmes based on four primary characteristics (cf. Décret 94–813: 13378ff.). The programmes are to

■ Fulfil the cultural, educational and social mission that is laid down in law. The television stations shall be the purveyors of information, cultural enrichment and entertainment. They shall convey as values the principles of integration, solidarity and civil responsibility;
■ They shall safeguard pluralism by availing themselves of all genres and reaching out to all public sub-groups while at the same time respecting their cultural diversity;
■ In particular, they shall have a rich offering of cultural and youth programmes;
■ They shall make significant efforts to create audio-visual works. These shall involve the search for innovative forms. Support shall be given to the creation of contents/film scripts and new productions are favoured. In the case of the new productions, the French nation shall take centre stage.

It may be symbolic: from a content-related point of view, these four aspects are bracketed together initially by the specific cultural mission (*mission culturelle*) and finally by the emphasis on the French heritage (*le patrimoine français*). The reference to the cultivation of the State, national culture and language as mentioned at the start of this chapter therefore remains dominant. The imparting of the values of 'integration (of foreigners), solidarity and awareness of civil duty' (first bullet point) as well as 'respect for cultural diversity' (second bullet point) was not added until 2001. Bearing the hallmark of Jospin's socialist government, these aspects serve as an example of the living nature of the specification booklets and the inclusion of public service television in comprehensive socio-political strategies.

The use of public service television for such socio-political objectives becomes particularly apparent as a result of a further change to the specification booklets which was implemented by decree in 2001[2]: a clear programming demand was introduced into Article 3 'Elle [the television company] contribue, à travers ses programmes [...] à la lutte contre les discriminations et les exclusions de toutes sortes.'

It is necessary to emphasize at this juncture that the analysis of the French situation *by no means* aims to point accusingly at it. This chapter, in which France is the focus of research interest, can only develop to the full within the framework of the consciously comparative structure of this publication. In the definition of a mission for its public service television, every country has its own 'particularities' and historical conditions for media policy. It is not possible for each individual contribution that is devoted to a case study to make reference to these particularities and conditions in the sense of political correctness. In this chapter the author therefore dispenses with too many international references and is sure that these nevertheless become clear in the context of the publication as a whole.

In addition to the four generally stated main characteristics, in particular with regard to the cultural programmes, the specification booklets lay out in detail – right down to stating the minimum numbers of programmes per year – which type of content must be broadcast and how often. It is not possible to talk here about programme autonomy. The State also defines the mission numerically.[3] Table 1 provides an overview of the programme demands that result directly from the specification booklet for France 2,[4] in particular from the Articles 24–27 (cultural programmes), 16–18 (specific information programmes) and 19–20 (educational and social programmes). A further comprehensive overview of the demands made on programmes that includes the quotas can be found in Machet, Pertzinidou and Ward (2002: 35ff.).

Against the background of the French 'particularities', this chapter will discuss the mission of public service television in the course of technical and political development. After summarizing the political background of French media policy for public service TV, I will show recent developments at the beginning of the twenty-first century and discuss how the Internet is used to support the public service mission. Again, it is not

Table 1. Demands made on the function of France 2 according to the specification booklet (selection).

Content	Demand
Government declarations or announcements by the government	At all times, without a time limit, free of charge
Religious programmes	Sundays
Consumer protection information	10 minutes per week
Programmes for the integration of foreigners	Generally
Poetry, choreography, drama	At least 15 transmissions per year
Literature, history, cinema, plastic art	Regularly
Music (in particular, new talents)	At least 2 hours per month
Classical music	At least 16 hours per year
Young people	At times when young people watch TV (consideration taken of the school holidays)
Sciences, technology, economics and the arts	Regularly
Game Shows	They shall convey historical, cultural, economic and scientific knowledge.
Sport	Covering as many types of sport as possible. The station is called upon to conclude transmission agreements with all sports associations.

Source: Decree 94–813 of the 16th of September 1994

the objective of this chapter to analyse the effectiveness of measures taken within France. The objective is to show particular media policy instruments to a European readership. Within Europe, France has proven to be a particularly useful case study because new and courageous political measures, such as the decoupling of the viewer rates, have been taken.

Socio-political background of French media policy

Language policy: French as the 'Langue de la Liberté'

Some historical background information is required to fully appreciate France's current media and language policy (and consequently the relevant passages in the mission for public service broadcasting). In France, language policy was always also a means of cementing Parisian central power. As early as the sixteenth century the (linguistic) centralization promoted by the royal court laid the foundation for a principle which even today enables social advancement: 'The French language is the means that enables access to the jobs in public administration' (de Certeau, Julia and Revel 1975: 30). It was Malherbe (1555–1628) who, at the court of Henry IV and later Louis XIII, drove linguistic standardization forward. Seven years after his death linguistic standardization was institutionalized with the foundation of the Académie Française (1635).

With the French Revolution the French language acquires an additional meaning: it becomes the vehicle of a political concept, the Langue de la Liberté. Ideals of the Revolution, such as a comprehensive educational policy, are linked to the spread of the French language. The country of the French Revolution was by no means a French-speaking nation: 'In the French Revolution, for the first time, large numbers of the French came to draw the common modern equation between the legal category of nationality and the cultural fact of language' (Bell 1995: 1405f.). Some characteristics influencing in particular modern media policy have survived from the concept of revolutionary language, culture and education policy as described above.

Effects of the Loi Toubon on public service television

A particularly prominent example of this form of language policy (one directly impacting on media policy) is the Loi Toubon (cf. Loi 94–665). Known beyond France's borders, this 1994 law, named after the Minister of Culture Jacques Toubon, was essentially designed to prevent the use of foreign-language – above all English – synonyms if a French expression exists for the word in question. Numerous statutory orders designed to also stop the influence of English in broadcasting were enacted as early as the 1960s.

The crucial question that arises in connection with the mission of public service television (and radio) is whether, by means of a law such as the Loi Toubon, the state-defined 'correct' use of language can be prescribed for the audio-visual media. After the passage of the law in the National Assembly on the 1st of July 1994, sixty – mainly socialist – members of parliament submitted a constitutional complaint. This proved successful, in particular in relation to the passages of the law devoted to the media. According to the original version of the law, journalists could have been prosecuted for using 'incorrect' foreign terms in the media. However, the Constitutional Council (*conseil constitutionnel*) found that although, on the one hand, the legislator must be allowed the right to prescribe the use of a codified French to institutions and persons during the performance of a public task, this right on the part of the legislator does not extend to limitation of the language used by broadcasting companies. The crucial section of the Constitutional Council's judgment reads as follows: '[The legislator/M.M.] ne pouvait imposer, sous peine de sanctions, pareille obligation aux organismes et services de radiodiffusion sonore ou télévisuelle, qu'ils soient publics ou privés' (Décision 94–345 DC).

Although this decision on the part of the Constitutional Council meant that the statutory rule prescribing the introduction of a codified French no longer applied, shortly afterwards the legislator again searched – at the lower level of a decree – for a way to integrate the reinforcement of the French language and the avoidance of foreign words into public broadcasting's mission statement. With the decree 94–813 (cf. Décret 94–813) new *cahiers des charges* were laid down for France 2 and France 3. In Article 4 of the decree the television companies are obliged to 'watch over' the personnel that appear on the television screen. Personnel are obliged to 'use and respect the French language'. The television companies in particular are to avoid foreign terms in cases where a French equivalent exists. This wording means that presenters, journalists etc. can no longer be directly 'taken into custody' as a result of the provisions contained in the Loi Toubon. In addition, the reference to the words laid down by a *commission de terminologie* is also missing from the decree. Account is taken of the Constitutional Council's decision by the fact that TV personnel can no longer be directly prosecuted for an incorrect use of language. However, the spirit of the Loi Toubon finds its way – through the back door, as it were – into the mission of public service television: although a legal obligation cannot be imposed on those involved in media creation, the television companies are now obliged to 'watch over' their personnel.

Francophony: The television as a means of disseminating language and political concept

In addition to the decree 94–813, through its Article 13, the Loi Toubon impacts directly on television's mission. In its essential provisions, Article 13 was regarded by the Constitutional Council as conforming to the Constitution. The obligation placed on the television stations '*le respect de langue française et le rayonnement de la francophonie.*'[5]

The degree to which a political concept is closely associated with the concept of francophony[6] is not only apparent in an historical dimension in connection with the era of the French Revolution, it also becomes clear from the more recent past. For example, for Guillon (1993: 7), quoted on behalf of many others, what is involved here is a '*réelle chance historique pour la France d'être encore présente dans le monde, d'y être écoutée, d'avoir un rôle unique à y jouer.'* As in the period of the French Revolution, the French language is the medium of a political 'idea' and, in its mission, television is obliged to participate in the dissemination of this idea. The rejection of another language – Toubon links this with the hyphenated word *anglo-marchand* – amounts to the rejection of a design for a particular social system.

It is important to emphasize that there is an historical foundation to the modern language and media policy and that French language policy has found a direct route into the mission of public service television. To the present day it is the will of the legislator to use television not only as a means of spreading the French language (purely linguistically) but also, in the sense of francophony, for the purpose of propagating a system of cultural and political values.

Measures for the support of French film and television production as a core function of (public service) television

A key function of public service and private television in France is to support French film production. The binding quotas in France are one of most prominent means of achieving this objective. There are broadcasting quotas (quotas de diffusion) and production quotas (quotas de production) that apply both to television films and to cinema films shown on television (feature films). In addition, numerous statutory orders and the *cahiers des charges* stipulate when and which type of film television stations may broadcast. The *Institut National de l'Audiovisuel* talks almost with self-irony about the fact that broadcasting a cinema film is a 'difficult act' to perform (INA 1995: 25). The background to this complex of rules is – as in many European countries – the expansion in the volume of programmes occurring in the wake of the commercialization of the television landscapes. For example, in France the number of cinema films shown on television doubled between 1983 (474 films) and 1993 (913 films) (CSA/CNC 1994: 10). The commercial stations met this need by showing increasing amounts of American productions. It was for this reason that in 1991 the *Centre National de la Cinématographie* (CNC), which is under the Ministry of Culture, demanded media-policy interventions for the purpose of 'harmonizing the relationships between television and the cinema' (CNC 1991: 1).

Broadcasting quotas

Relevant for an understanding of the mission is the fact that in France the passage in the EU Directive 'Television without Frontiers', according to which half of the film and television broadcast by a station shall be of European origin, is not only interpreted as a *political objective,* as is the case in Germany. Instead, it is implemented by decree: compliance by French television (public service and commercial) being controlled by the Media Supervisory Authority CSA. The legislator has laid down that 60 per cent of the film and television productions that are broadcast must be of European origin. What initially appears to be over-fulfilment of the European quota is made relative by the additional provision that 40 per cent of the productions must be of French origin. The 40% are counted towards the 60% so that effectively there is room for 40% French productions, 20% non-French but European productions and 40% non-European productions. The implementation, modification and control of compliance with these quotas have shaped wide areas of French television policy for a number of years. The principle is shared beyond the boundaries of the political parties (even though in questions concerning the detail of its application the opposition in each case has expressed differing views).[7] As described at the outset, the principle of laying down quotas for programme contents is not something that has only become known and recognized since the 1970s. In the 1980s the principle received statutory reinforcement as a result of the skeleton media law of the 30th September 1986 and numerous decrees, particularly at the start of the 1990s, in the form of the so-called *décrets Tasca* (cf. Décret 90–66; Décret 90–67) named after the Minister of Communication Cathérine Tasca.[8i] France did not succeed, however, in turning the programme quotas in the television directive into a legally enforceable instrument of media policy.

Party-political discontinuities in media policy

A reference to the numerous changes of government since the beginning of the 1980s and the associated inconsistent development of media policy is an essential feature of any discussion of the function of public service television in France. Hoffmann-Riem (1996: 159) correctly observes, 'French developments lacked a clear concept comprehensible to outsiders. Changing political majorities, moreover, have led to alterations in the broadcasting order, which has precluded the system from being able to mature [...].' The development of the French television landscape against the background of these inconsistencies has been well analysed in German and English-language research.[9] At this juncture it therefore suffices to draw attention to some historical facts that symbolize the difficulties encountered when trying to achieve continuous discussion – one that is oriented towards the communication needs of the population – about the function of public service television.

First is the creation of three different national media supervisory authorities, each of which came into existence after a change in the government majority in the 1980s. Each government created 'its' own authority. Minc (1993: 21) talks in this connection about the 'Nigerianisation of the media and French society'. Only today's supervisory authority, *Conseil Supérieur de l'Audiovisuel* (CSA), has since been able to emancipate itself to a certain degree from party politics.

Second is the continuously recurring discussion about the privatization of parts of public service television. These discussions are particularly heated in France because in 1987 Chirac's cohabitation government (under State President Mitterand) demonstrated, in a manner unique among European states, how the most popular public service television station in the country, TF1, was sold and transformed into a commercial station. This process took place after the new government majority had a short time earlier disbanded the 'old' media supervisory authority HACA[10] and had formed the CNCL.[11]

Third, it is essential to refer to the political system which readily enables the particular government majority to shape laws from maximum media-policy positions. This becomes possible due to Article 49 (3) of the French Constitution, according to which the vote on a bill can be linked to a vote of confidence: if there is not a successful vote of no confidence within 24 hours after the introduction of a law, the law is considered to have been adopted without the need for any further vote. It is indicative of this situation that not one but two comprehensive skeleton media laws – the laws of 1986 and 1989 – came into being in this way. Both the neo-Gaullist-centrist government and the socialist government therefore committed a 'crime' against a continuous media policy and gave precedence to party-politically motivated questions of power. Whereas, for example, in Germany such disjointedness in the debate about the function of public service television cannot occur for the reason alone of the competencies of the sixteen federal states in the area of media policy, a change of direction can take place in France within an extremely short space of time. Brun-Buisson (2001: 21) calls this 'la réforme permanente' of public service television with which the latter seems to be put into question. This is important background knowledge for section 4 where, in conclusion, we take a look at the situation at the beginning of the twenty-first century. At the same time this disjointedness is relativized by the consensus that exists beyond party boundaries about the need to protect French culture and language.

The situation at the beginning of the twenty-first century

Cultural protection also remains a dominant factor in French media policy at the beginning of the twenty-first century. The statement made on the 17th of December 2001 by Jean-Marie Messier, who was at the time the chairman of the board of Vivendi, about the demise of the *exception culturelle*, provoked heated debates in the feature pages. The claim was refuted beyond party political boundaries (cf. on behalf of many Bezat and Chombeau 2001 and Weber 2002). Likewise, at the beginning of the twenty-first century there continue to exist extremely state-centric definitions of the function of public service television that regard television as an instrument of the State. The senator Jean-Paul Hugot (2001) speaks for many when he says: 'Je considère, de mon côté, le service public comme *la réponse de l'Etat* à des besoins culturels, politiques et sociaux explicitement *identifiés par lui* [...].'[12]

However, new impulses have entered the debate about the function of public service television. These impulses have been triggered, for example, by technical development (digital television, the Internet), by restrictions on advertising times for public service television and by the will to 'solve' the constant question of finance. In the following I will employ five theses to analyse the main lines in this debate about the function of public service television and the media-policy instruments that are used to give this function contours.

Thesis 1: Technical development will not undermine the political objective of cultural protection even if its enforcement becomes more difficult.

The French television landscape at the beginning of the twenty-first century is much more diverse than at the time when the decision was taken to use programme quotas as a means of media policy. Cable television, satellite television and terrestrial digital television make the enforcement of a uniform quota policy more difficult: how is one to oblige stations that are based abroad to adhere to the broadcasting and production quotas? Nevertheless, the French legislator shows remarkable continuity with regard to this question: On the 28th of December 2001 several decrees (cf. Décret 2001–1329; Décret 2001–1330; Décret 2001–1333) were passed which also oblige the providers of digital television to adhere to quotas. A certain flexibility is, however, discernible. No-fee stations are, for example, treated differently from pay-TV stations.[13]

Thesis 2: Technical development, in particular terrestrial digital television, provides public service television with the opportunity to accentuate its function.

The question that arises in many countries is how public service television reacts to the opportunities for programme diversification as a result of an increase in the frequencies. In France, both topic-based channels and greater regionalization of public service television are in preparation. Chirot (2001) even talks of *'la dernière chance de la télévision publique'*. France 3 – responsible for regional reporting – has already presented a concept. In its concept, which provides for the creation of eight terrestrially broadcast regional digital stations, France 3 responds to an increased interest on the part of commercial providers to provide regional and local television (e.g. city television). These eight stations are in each case intended to provide catchment areas of six to eight million inhabitants with their own programme.[14]

The contents of the new public service regional stations shall have four foci of interest (cf. Garrigos and Roberts 2002): regional information programmes, magazine programmes and documentaries, regional interactive forums as well as regional culture and sport transmissions. In addition to producing their own programme, the regional editorial offices shall perform two further functions: they shall also improve the regional reporting for the sister station France 2 and feed the planned public service news channel. Technological development – digital editing technologies, opportunities for digital archiving and technologies for digital transmission between the regional editorial offices – accelerates this exchange of programmes. At the same time this technological convergence arouses fears among the journalists who expect a fundamental change in journalistic culture: the journalists' union *Syndicat national des journalistes* (SNJ) fears that, in view of the many thousands of digitized programme minutes that are to be simply exchanged, journalists become nothing more than 'image gazers' and that the plethora of information is utilized without context-related examination of its relevance (Mathieu 2002). In October 2001 a not untypical reaction of journalists faced with new technological developments occurred: a protest strike was called at the France 3 editorial office in Champagne-Ardenne.

The project *Télévisions Numériques Régionales* (TNR) can indeed be understood as an opportunity for public service television to accentuate its function – in the case of France 3, its *regional* function.

In addition to the project TNR, the project *Télévision Numérique Terrestre* (TNT) will be a further challenge to public service television. Nationwide the government has earmarked 22 frequencies for terrestrial digital television. A further 8 frequencies are reserved for public service television (the specialist channels that have already been mentioned shall broadcast here), the other 22 frequencies will be assigned to commercial operators. Earmarking frequencies for the public service is indeed a strong political statement in favour of public TV.

Thesis 3: the financing of public service television remains a potential means of State string-pulling. However, for the first time, France Télévision has relative planning certainty over a period of five years

In France, the financing of public service television is a controversially discussed topic and a sensitive instrument for controlling television. Put simply, neo-Gaullist-centrist governments grant public service television more limited public funds than socialist governments. This culminated in 1987 in the sale of the first French Channel, TF1. Again and again, the central issue in this debate is the question of the share of financial aid that shall be met by advertising revenue. For example, at the end of 1996, parliament, with a Gaullist majority, decided to extend the permitted advertising time for public service television. This was accompanied by an 'extreme commercialisation of the French channels' and the orientation of France 2 to the 'taste of the masses' (Bourgeois 1998). At the end of 1997 withering criticism of the political decision-makers appeared in the so-called Missika Report.[15] 'Chaotic decisions' had forced France 2 in particular into a 'schizophrenic situation' (quoted from Labé and Vulser 1997). By this is meant the constantly expressed, noble desire for a full-mix public service channel and the simultaneously practiced policy of advertising-time expansion and scarce public financing which forced France 2 into direct competition with the commercial TF1. According to the Missika report, the function of public service television had been 'neglected' by Gaullists and socialists alike. The report continues by stating that the State dealt with minor problems but was absent when there was a need for strategic decision-making. The crisis in which France 2 and France 3 found themselves could also be seen from their declining market shares from 1996 to 2000.

From 1997 the socialist government essentially decided on four media-policy measures to help public service television break out of this vicious circle:

- ■ Limitation of the advertising time for public service television
- ■ Increased public funding accompanied by longer-term financial planning
- ■ Conclusion of agreements on objectives with public service television accompanied by an examination of acceptance that is *independent* of the viewing figures (cf. in this regard thesis 4)

■ Creation of a joint holding for public service stations with the aim of improved strategic programme planning in the entire public service sector.

The limitation placed on advertising for France 2 and France 3 provides for the broadcasting of a maximum of eight minutes of advertising per hour of transmission. Whereas critics point to the associated 'undeserved' increase in the advertising revenues going to the commercial providers, defendants of the measure emphasize the need to decouple – at least in part – public service television from the battle for the advertising market. Overall, between 1997 and 2000 the share of public funds had settled down to a level of just under 50% in the case of France 2 and over 60% in the case of France 3 (cf. European Audiovisual Observatory 2001: 140; 2002: 82f.). Consequently, by European standards, France still allows advertising to have a relatively high share of the total financing of public service television.[16] Following the declared 'volonté du Gouvernement de renforcer la part des ressources publiques dans le financement du secteur public de l'audiovisuel' (MCC 2001: 5), in 2001 the percentage of public funds for public service television in France has increased further. According to France Télévision (2002), in 2001 it now amounts to 59.8% for France 2 and 69.8% for France 3.[17]

Besides the still relatively high share accounted for by advertising revenue, there was a further particularity in the financing of French public service television. The budget was decided on annually by parliament within the framework of the Loi de Finances, i.e. the general state expenditure. This rendered even medium-term planning by the television stations impossible. Instead, the stations were at the mercy of short-term developments and media-policy interests. Clément (2001: 18) calls these finance debates a 'ritual' in which again and again 'polemics about the channels belonging to public service television' are disseminated. Brun-Buisson (2001: 21) points out that, as a result of this procedure of finance allocation, the public service stations are treated de facto if not even, due to the vote in parliament, de jure 'like an administrative unit'.

A decoupling occurred for the first time at the end of 2001: first, a total of 500 million euro was made available to public service television for the years 2002 and 2003 for the purpose of developing terrestrially broadcast digital television. Second, the State committed itself to increasing public funding between 2001 and 2005 by an annual 3.1%. To this is added a variable share of 0.4% to 0.6% dependent on the extent to which the agreed targets are met (cf. thesis 4). At the same time public service television is obliged to reduce its expenditure. Clear targets have also been set here up to 2005.

Thesis 4: The certainty with regard to financial planning is supported by the first long-term agreements on targets in the history of public service television.

On the 12th of November 2001, the first long-term agreements on objectives and funding (contrat d'objectifs et de moyens) were concluded between France Télévision, the holding for the stations France 2, France 3, the educational channel La Cinquième (today: France 5) and the State. The basis for this is the skeleton media law of 1st of August 2000. In addition to the *cahiers des charges* that have already been mentioned, these agreements on objectives correspond to a mission statement for public service television. Since the agreements run until the end of 2005, they enable, for the first time, medium- to long-term strategic planning. For example, a complementary programme strategy for the stations or the above-mentioned development of terrestrially broadcast, digital regional stations and specialist channels are laid down in these agreements on objectives. There is, likewise, agreement on a 'savings plan' that enables, inter alia, the new limitation on the advertising times to be financed. Of particular note, though, is the following statement in the agreement on objectives: '*La télévision publique ne recherche pas une audience économique utile mais socialement légitime. France Télévision doit fédérer toutes les catégories de population*' (Mathieu 2001). For the first time, public service television is removed from the battle for viewing figures; the aim is not/no longer to target an 'economically useful number of viewers'. This said, television may not, of course, operate in a manner that is totally removed from the interest of the public because the objective is to serve a 'socially legitimate viewing public'. After the introduction of commercial television, fixation on the viewing figures frequently led – and not only in France – to a dulling of the profile of public service television. In the battle for viewing figures public service television in part saw itself forced to avail itself of channel formats similar to those of the commercial stations or to acquire particularly expensive rights for the transmission of mass sports events.[18] At the same time, the battle for high viewing figures was often employed as an argument for the receipt of public funding. Trautmann (2001: 16) calls this connection a 'contradiction flagrante'. This 'line of argumentation' was now broken in France. In order to be able to nevertheless evaluate the attractiveness, quality and balance – i.e. the performance – of public service television, once a year the French State will undertake a broad-based study as a 'barometer of satisfaction'. In addition, *an indicateur d'affinités* – a pluralistic panel – shall examine whether the stations orient their offering to all sub-groups of viewers in a balanced manner.

At the time of the copy deadline for this publication, it is not possible to determine whether these evaluation measures can be implemented effectively. They do, however, represent a brave step in the direction of public examination of the performance of public service television that looks beyond mere viewing figures.

Thesis 5: Online presence with a public service mission could be a new and further way of underlining French TV's general public service mission. However, France does not seem to be ready for this new field of public service media activities.

This last thesis will be examined in more detail below.

Public service and Internet[19]

France Télévision Interactive (FTVI)

In order to fulfil their official task, the French public television broadcasters do not simply rely on terrestrial aerial broadcasting, but deploy other means of communication like mobile telephones, videotext, Internet and also shortly – as has already been mentioned – digital terrestrial television.[20] Technological convergence is becoming more and more within reach; what effects does this have on the media-policy approach for determining television's public service mission? Is there a corresponding convergence of television and Internet policies, i.e. between TV policy and Internet regulation?

The coordination and development of the interactive services and programmes within public television broadcasting comes under the commercial unit France Télévision Interactive (FTVI).[21] One of its tasks is the maintenance and design of the webpages of the broadcasting stations France 2 and France 3 (France 5 has its own webpages and editorial department), but also of their minitel services, the mobile telephone service facilities and the implementation of digital terrestrial TV. FTVI does not confine itself to the sole development of online services but also deals with many other means of communication, in particular with their potential synergy effects. The Internet thus represents just one area of FTVI's competencies.[22] For Laurent Souloumiac, the director of FTVI since 2001, the aim is to extend the interactive opportunities for Audiotel and the development of SMS services, in order to strengthen the loyalty of viewers to the broadcasting station. The average number of hits on the webpages of FTV (France Télévision) was around 1.9 million per month in 2002.[23] Souloumiac is seeking to achieve a higher hit-rate by improving the quality of the online services, for example by developing the interactive facilities, by changing the graphic presentation of the website and by extending the synergies with terrestrial programmes, so that thematic content and actual broadcasts can be used in the Internet (cross media). This kind of statement from FTVI's director can certainly be interpreted as an unequivocal declaration of intent to expand online activities; however, this does not necessarily correspond to the views of other (higher ranking) decision-makers. Rather, as Thomass (2003) points out, France is pursuing a defensive strategy in relation to the implementation of public service online activities, aimed at defending the status quo in public television without envisaging any change of function in a digital media landscape. This situation is, according to Thomass, codetermined by the lack of support from political actors.

The online services are consciously orientated to current affairs, single television programmes and television series for the purpose of constructing cross-media links. Dedicated websites with additional information, discussion forums and archive footage of old broadcasts are placed at the users' disposal. For Souloumiac, FTVI fulfils the function of '*entité complémentaire à l'antenne en matière d'interactivité*'.[24]

In 2000 the investment budget for the following three years stood at 200 million francs.[25] There were just eight members of the team in 2000. Since then the team has grown to 60.[26] The online service is still in the development stage and is dependent on the financial support of FTV. Additional sources of finance include advertising revenues through Internet pages, since all interactive services and corresponding video footage are accessible free of charge. The websites of the three TV stations have introduced animated and static advertising banners. Other micro-sites are financed by sponsors. For example, the interactive weather service of France 2 is sponsored by Darty. The commercial department, France Télévisions Publicité markets and sells advertising slots and spaces, the webpages of the TV stations, of the nine thematic pages (e.g. the stock exchange link) and the thirteen regional pages.

The online platforms of France 2 and France 3: Predominantly supportive functions for existing TV contents

There follows a description of the structure of the online services of France 2 and France 3, in order to place them in the context of their public task. In their List of Duties, the deployment of new media is addressed in a separate chapter:

> France 2 (3 et 5) développe, dans le cadre de ses missions, les nouveaux programmes et services permettant, sur les différents supports de la communication audiovisuelle, de prolonger, de compléter et d'enrichir son offre de programmes. A cette fin, elle s'attache à faire bénéficier le public des nouvelles techniques de production et de diffusion des programmes et services de communication audiovisuelle. Elle favorise la relation avec le public par l'utilisation de toutes les techniques de l'interactivité. Elle exploite notamment à ce titre tout service télématique, interactif ou de communication en ligne complétant et prolongeant les émissions qu'elle programme. Elle assure la promotion de ces services. Elle participe au développement technologique de la communication audiovisuelle.[27]

The cited section from the List of Duties makes it clear that the new means of communication are supposed to be deployed in order to fulfil television's public mission, but that the medium of television remains dominant.

An editorial line which is independent of the TV products is accordingly still unthinkable, nor is there any sign of this emerging, either within France 2 or France 3. The main point of orientation and the main objective remains the strengthening of the product range and the brand of the television station. The online service of the television stations can thus be seen as an extension of terrestrial aerial programming. Hitherto the Internet has been above all an additional means of popularizing television programmes and not an explicit location for new experimental multimedia formats. Accordingly the Internet does not have its 'own programme'.

The online services of France 2 and France 3 are distinguished by three characteristics: dissemination of information, extension of the programme and interactive services.

There is a common information portal for the two channels (www.infos.francetv.fr). This portal contains links to thematic fields. All news broadcasts *('journaux télévisés')* are archived for a week in the network and can be consulted in this period in their entirety via videostreaming. Some current affairs are treated more thoroughly in 'dossiers' and supplemented in part by videos and photographs. Since 2001, France 2 and France 3 have been providing four further common portals: Youth, Games, Finance/Stock Exchange and Sport.

www.france2.fr

The provision of discussion forums on current affairs, broadcasts or virtual fan clubs is clearly presented.

Other foreign language media (including links to foreign newspapers, a review of the international press, radio stations) are not included in the website. Special services for minorities or immigrants still do not exist either. The cultural diversity demanded, which is supposed to reflect the broadcasters' television programming, has still to be added to the Net.

The interactive service in the fields of Finance, Weather and Traffic provides up-to-date information, search engines and a webcam for shots of the traffic situation in Paris.

The editorial management of and responsibility for what goes on the Internet is the responsibility of the interactive editorial board of FTVI which derives its information and contents from France 2 and France 3, as well as from Reuters (texts) and Agence France Presse (texts, photos, computer graphics). The pictures published on the websites are in part provided by the Reuters and APTN agencies and by the television company CNN.[28]

The visual presentation of the online service for the target group Youth is also very much orientated towards this group. The colourful icons direct the user towards webpages for popular broadcasts (e.g. the youth news programme *Mon Kanard*), the games portal, cellphone ring-tones, etc. The service would seem to be directed towards young people between the ages of 13 and 14; both the presentation and the contents are only slightly interesting for older age groups. Youth provision is not sufficiently diversified, as not all age groups are catered for. The quality and quantity of the content would indicate that this target group is not yet a strong thematic focus.

The sports pages provide ongoing information on current sporting events in a thorough fashion, including items on less popular sports. The Roland Garros tennis tournament was a landmark: for the first time the Internet accompanied a sporting event in real time. All the games are transmitted directly via the Internet. This service involves a cost, however, of €1.69 per hour. Souloumiac justifies this charge by pointing out that the costs of videostreaming already swallow up 80% of the website's total budget (Fraissard and Séry 2003). In addition viewers are offered articles, pictures, results, betting odds and discussion forums on the webpages. This kind of cooperation between terrestrial TV and Internet is, however, still rare, but is supposed to become the standard arrangement in the future, so that all target groups can be addressed.

The opportunities for website visitors to contact the broadcaster consist in writing to the producers by e-mail or by contacting the station's mediator by e-mail or post. The mediator is supposed to act as a link between the viewer and the television station. The three stations, France 2, France 3 and France 5, have one mediator, Geneviève Guicheney, who receives questions, suggestions and criticisms about programmes – apart from news broadcasts. France 2 and France 3 each have their own mediator for news and information-based broadcasts, Marc Francioli for France 3 and Jean Claude Allanic for France 2. The interaction between viewers and the mediator also contributes to television programmes directly. In the weekly broadcast 'L'hebdo du médiateur' the mediator Jean Claude Allanci meets journalists and viewers together to discuss criticisms of the week. The individual broadcasts have been archived in the network since September 2002 and are retrievable from there.

The medium of the Internet is not simply employed by the broadcasters as an additional medium of dissemination, but also as a medium for promoting their own broadcasts. The interactivity between the broadcaster and the viewer has been developing to the extent that the surfers are encouraged to express opinions, to make suggestions and pass judgment. The programme 'Ça se discute' is an appropriate example: its editorial board uses the Internet to recruit guests for the broadcast ('appel à témoin') and, in the shaping of the programme, takes account of the thematic wishes of the viewers.

The webpages of France 2 and France 3 are constructed according to the same model. The bulk of the information and the links on offer are identical, apart from the promotion of their own programmes and the broadcasting schedules of the two stations. They differ in terms of the regional accentuation of France 3. France 2 offers more national news, whereas France 3 on the Net as well as on the television has a regional focus with thirteen websites, providing information exclusively about a region and regional news programmes.

The third public broadcasting station, France 5, follows another model for its online service.

The online platform of France 5: Comprehensive and more independent contents

France 5 distinguishes itself from the two other stations in its online self-presentation both in terms of its layout and also in terms of the shaping of its editorial content. It offers a magazine-like online service; its strategy matches the global objective of the station to transmit knowledge and experience. The material offered on the Internet is viewed as a separate part of the station and is developed within the company. The online service is accordingly shaped by its own *independent* Internet editorial board. The Internet serves as a means for disseminating the television programmes (cross media), which are supplemented by additional information. However, the synergies of terrestrial television and the Internet within France 5 are not limited to a quantitative structuring of the content by another medium of communication. The online service has developed from the showcase vision of the Internet to a service in its own right alongside the activities of the television station. France 5 has a very large and varied range of pedagogical materials, which is directed towards the target group of teachers, trainers and schoolchildren from various fields of education.

France 5's online editorial board is not integrated into the FTVI group. However, it cooperates with FTVI in areas like the development of marketing strategies, the procurement of new technologies and the production of content.

Content is predominantly produced by external multimedia enterprises. Since October 2001, France 5 has been working with around 30 such service providers. France 5 maintains cooperative relations with large-scale portals like Wanadoo in the form of the production and dissemination of thematic webpages.

France 5's Internet budget stood at 1.5% of the overall budget of €146.8 million. Up until now, France 5 has funded its operations largely out of user charges. Revenue from advertising is still insignificant at around 5%.[29] All online services are provided free of charge.

These free services can be accessed according to the visitor's interest. At the visitor's disposal are teaching materials with exercises that can be downloaded, educational games for children, a platform on the theme of work, discussion forums and information providing greater depth on themes in the areas of education, culture and child-rearing. A search engine allows for key words and references to be sought in archived programmes. There is a data bank with 5,000 broadcast programmes at the disposal of teachers and educationalists (Agnola/ Le Champion 2003: 73). There are links to virtual universities, lectures and discussion forums. The educational mission of the television is thereby acquiring a new dimension, enhancing the range of services both qualitatively and quantitatively.

France 5 offers a personalized newsletter as a programme service, which informs viewers about the schedule. The visitor is invited to assess the articles and broadcasts on offer. The viewer can contact the TV station indirectly via the mediator or directly via e-mail to the producers.

The debate about the judicial framework for public online communication

The nature of the Internet raises questions about many of the existing regulations and legal statutes, since the boundaries between the areas of responsibility relating to the audio-visual field, telecommunications and e-commerce are becoming increasingly fluid. This development demands new regulations that take account of these convergence tendencies.

Hitherto there has been no foundation in law that sets out the legal position of online services, their product range or their operators. The 2000 modification of the 1986 Law governing Freedom of Communication contained no explicit statements concerning the tasks, the legal position and the monitoring of interactive services. A supervisory body, responsible for the production of multimedia products and their dissemination via the Internet, still does not exist. The CSA's area of responsibility is limited to the audio-visual sphere, to which online services and web-based television are not yet assigned. For this reason, the online services of the television stations have until now been operating in a kind extra-legal zone without explicit judicial or substantive regulations.

The CSA reacted to this state of affairs by demanding an extension of its area of competence relating to television on the Internet (AFP 17.12.2002). It establishes the need to create a body which monitors the maintenance of human dignity, the freedom of others, the protection of children, cultural diversity, the rules of advertising and marketing and the question of value added tax being applied to Internet activities (Agnola and Le Champion 2003: 17).

In January 2003 the CSA published a snapshot account of the position of television on the Internet (*La télévision sur Internet: état des lieux*). In this report the CSA defines Web-TV as 'television that is broadcast on the Internet', and more precisely as a portal whose main business consists in processing the audio-visual programme in a thematically structured form.[30] Within this report, however, the online service of public television is only mentioned in a few lines.

At European level a comprehensive reform in the field of telecommunication was introduced in 1999 that has led to the adoption of the so-called Telecom Package. This consists of six directives and one ruling. The French government has adopted these guidelines in 2003 in national law with two complementary bills under the title *'Projet de loi pour la confiance dans l'économie numérique'* (Law concerning Trust in the Digital Economy) and the *'Projet de loi sur les communications électroniques'* (Law concerning Electronic Communication). In the process it is reacting to the long-standing demand to create a legal basis for Internet services and Internet providers.[31]

The draft bill concerning Trust in the Digital Economy defines public online communication, the responsibilities of the technical providers and in particular the legal position of the providers as well as the question of filtering illegal material. The definition of public online communication as a 'sub-group of audiovisual communication' is of particular interest for the online services of broadcasting stations. The definition would mean an essential extension of the competencies of the CSA that would accordingly become responsible for all the services of radio and television. The bill was debated in parliament in February 2003. A majority of MPs judged the given definition to be inapplicable.[32]

The ensuing discussion about whether it was more appropriate to adapt existing laws to the technical developments in the broadcasting sector or to create new laws, is still in progress. The question of whether it makes sense to fall back on existing institutions and instruments or whether new organizational forms are necessary cannot yet be answered conclusively or in global terms.

According to statements from the French Internet Forum (http://www.foruminternet.org)[33] most of those affected are critical of this conceptual definition and its implications. They fear that the separation between the broadcasting sphere and the Internet services contained in the draft bill will become even vaguer, with the consequence that the laws and instruments relating to the broadcasting sector will be simply transferred to the Internet services, without considering the particularities of the Internet as a medium.

The Forum has produced an official position. It declares the definition of 'public online communication as a sub-group of broadcasting communication' to be too imprecise and insubstantial. It recommends that the service products of television and radio be defined independently of their means of communication.

> *[...] le Forum estime opportun de définir de manière légale ou réglementaire les services de radio et de télévision indépendamment de leur support afin de permettre au régulateur d'exercer ses missions en toute sécurité juridique et aux différents acteurs de connaître les règles qui leur sont applicables.*[34]

Furthermore they demand a specific regulatory framework dedicated to Internet services.

En outre, il apparaît essentiel au Forum des droits sur Internet (FDI) de mettre en œuvre une régulation originale de ses services sans pour autant que celle-ci conduise à la reconnaissance d'une nouvelle branche du droit.[35]

On 26th June 2003 the French Senate debated the draft bill and in part took on board the criticism expressed by Forum Internet and by the CSA and the ART. Accordingly the Senate made additions to Articles 2 and 4 of the Law of September 30 1986, determining the role of the CSA more precisely by employing the definition of public online communication (*communication publique en ligne*).

The adoption of the Telecom Package in national law as well as the implementation of terrestrial digital television will thus remain a topic of public debate in France for some time to come. New models of regulation are being sought which take account of the convergence tendencies between the broadcasting and the telecommunications sector. Within this technical-legal discussion the question of new contents and the future of public service television plays only a marginal role. The deployment of the Internet for the fulfillment of television's public mission has hitherto hardly been discussed or at most superficially. A process of development, the aim of which would be to accord the Internet services a key role in the activities of FTV, does not therefore appear to be on the agenda in the immediate future. Apart from this it is noticeable that many questions relating to the position of the FTVI Directorate towards the future role of the Internet in FTV's development projects have remained unanswered. France 5's internet service range shows how the functional task of public television can be adequately fulfilled with its own editorial team and its own editorial content. Extending this concept to encompass all of French television does not seem to be in the interest of media policy, however.

Conclusion

Against the background of the knowledge accumulated in the course of numerous media-policy inconsistencies in the 1980s and 1990s which contributed to a fuzzy image of the function of public service television, on the threshold of the twenty-first century the French government has taken groundbreaking decisions which provide public service television with a clear opportunity for development – in the digital age, too – and serve to specify its mission. Apart from the culture-protectionist impetus that continues to exert considerable influence on French television policy, these decisions are above all shaped by the use of technological developments for the construction of public service regional stations and specialist channels, by the conclusion of agreements on objectives, by the limitations imposed on advertising times and the increase in public funding, by the decoupling of public service television from the viewing figures as a dominant measurement instrument for determining the success of a channel and by medium-term financial planning instead of a broadcasting tax that must be decided anew every year.

The function of public service television in France is defined by agreements on objectives made by France Télévision and the State (agreements concluded for the first time in November 2001), the specification booklets unilaterally laid down by the legislator (*cahiers des charges*) and numerous decrees which oblige public service (and to a certain extent also commercial) television to pursue higher order media-policy goals such as support for French and European film and television production or protection of the French language. From the point of view of media-policy research, the development of the new instruments for contouring public service television is a welcome sight. The results and recommendations of research and reports such as, for example, the Missika Report of 1997 or the analyses performed by the sociologist Monique Dagnaud (2000), who in the 1990s was herself a member of the CSA, have found their way into media-policy practice.

A certain risk remains: the clear strengthening of public service television associated with medium-term (financial) perspectives occurred during the cohabitation of the socialist government with the Gaullist State President Jacques Chirac, a phenomenon that was particularly hated by the Gaullists. Now, since 2003, the Gaullists enjoy the absolute majority in the National Assembly and in the Senate and the State president is also drawn from their ranks. On the other hand, the ideological edge is missing from the media-policy argument at a time when numerous foreign channels can already be received in France via cable and satellite and more than 30 French channels stand *ante portas* to implement terrestrially broadcast digital television. Thanks to technological progress, strengthening public service television is not necessarily associated with a weakening of commercial television. Consequently, there are grounds for assuming that the accentuation of the mission for public service television will be a permanent feature and can be developed further.

However, when it comes to online activities, French media policy does not seem to be ready to allow public television to play a vital role. The question whether online content should exclusively have a supportive function for existing TV programmes or whether more independent online 'programmes' should be developed has not been answered.

Notes

1. Some parts of this contribution have been published in German language in the article *Die Funktion des öffentlichen Fernsehens in Frankreich. Medienpolitische Instrumente zur Sicherung des Funktionsauftrages*. In: P. Donges and M. Puppis (eds.): Die Zukunft des öffentlichen Rundfunks. Internationale Beiträge aus Wissenschaft und Praxis. Köln: Halem 2003.
2. Decree 2001–142 of the 14th of February 2001, published in the *Journal Officiel de la République Française* of the 16th of February 2001, p. 2584f.
3. Even though different in large areas, detailed requirements are placed on the commercial stations, too. However, in this contribution I concentrate on the public service stations. The specification booklet for France 3 is only marginally different. For a full overview, see Machet, Pertzinidou and Wird (2002: 35ff.).
4. The specification booklet for France 3 is only marginally different. For example, there is the specific demand for 30 minutes of broadcasting for foreigners (whereas France 2 only has the general duty to provide such programmes). The main difference lies in France 3's duty to offer regional and local programmes.

5. Article 13 of the *Loi Touban* supplements the 1986 skeleton media law (cf. Loi 86–1067) and incorporates the above-mentioned obligation into the Articles 24, 28 and 33 of the skeleton media law.

6. In addition to being French-speaking (i.e. francophone), francophony is, above all, understood to refer to the special relationships that exist among French-speaking countries. The institutionalized form took shape in 1969 under the Minister of Culture André Malraux whose area of responsibility also included the media (cf. for details Deniau 1992).

7. I have analyzed the implementation of the broadcasting and production quotas in detail elsewhere (Machill 1997: 124–176).

8. During this period the legislator operated on the 'living object': after the first mandatory quotas the television operators switched the quota programs that were felt to be unattractive to the night hours, with the result that the quotas were fulfilled *de jure*. The legislator then fine-tuned the provisions and laid down quotas specifically for prime time.

9. An overview of relevant studies can be found in Machill (1997: 118–122).

10. *Haute Autorité de la Communication Audiovisuelle*, created by the law of the 29th July 1982 under the new socialist government.

11. *Commission Nationale de la Communication et des Libertés*, created by the law of the 30th of September 1986 under the new neo-Gaullist-centrist government.

12. 'I for my part consider public service television as the *response of the State* to cultural and social demands which have been explicitly identified *by the State itself* [...]' (emphases by the author).

13. Cf. for more details IRIS, legal bulletin of the European Audiovisual Observatory, February 2002, pp. 8–9.

14. Paris, l'Ouest, le Nord-Pas-de-Calais, le grand Est, Rhône Alpes, la Méditerranée, le grand Sud-Ouest, le Centre.

15. Jean-Louis Missika's report on public service television was handed to the Minister of Culture Cathérine Trautmann on the 15th of December 1997.

16. Numerous EU countries as well as Norway and Switzerland finance their public service stations by over 70% using public funding. Norway (NRK): 100%; Sweden (SVT): 97.6%; UK (BBC): 83.0%; Germany (ZDF): 78.1%; Germany (ARD): 76.0%; Belgium (BNT): 72.7%; Switzerland (SRG): 72.2%; the Netherlands (NOS): 66.9%; Belgium (RTBF): 63.7%. Exceptions here are Italy (RAI): 50.3% and Spain (RTVE): 10.6%.

17. Unfortunately, the data from the year 2001 and the years 1997–2000 are not directly comparable because the data from 2001 from France Télévision are calculated differently from those provided by the European Audiovisual Observatory. However, the trend is clear.

18. The 2002 World Cup which France started as holders was not shown on public service television but broadcast exclusively by commercial television.

19. For her support in preparing chapter 3, I would like to thank Ms Verena Wuthnow.

20. Cf. http://www.culture.fr/culture/actualities/politique/audiovisuel/audiovisuel1/htm (accessed 22.04.03).

21. Law Nr. 2000–719 from 01.08.2000, which modified Law Nr 86–1067 from 30.09.1986 concerning the freedom of communication, published in the *Journal Officiel de la République Française* from 02.08.2000, p. 11903.

22. Cf. http://francetelevisons.fr/data/doc/resultats_2002.pdf [as of May 2003].

23. Cf. http://francetelevisons.fr (as of May 2003).

24. 'An entity complementing terrestrial broadcasting with interactive material'; Interview with Laurent Souloumiac from 21.06.2002, in: http: //www.journaldunet.com/printer/it_souloumiac2.shtml (as of 28.04.2003).

25. Cf. Ecran Total: 'France Télévision Interactive: 200 Millions de France d'investissement sur 3 ans', of 23–29.02.00, Nr. 310, p.7, in: http: //www.europresse.com [as of 14.05.03].
26. Cf. Sud Oest: 'La TV publique pousse ses sites Internet', 27.09.02, in: http: //www.europresse.com (as of 14.05.03).
27. 'France 2 (3 and 5) is developing, within the framework of its mission, new programmes and services which, with the help of different dimensions of audiovisual communication, allow the extension, supplementation and enhancement of its range of programmes. To this end, it is committed to provide the viewing public with the benefits of new production and broadcasting technologies in relation to its programmes and services. It seeks to enhance the relationship with the viewing public by using all interactive technologies. In this regard it makes particular use of all telematic, interactive or online communication services, supplementing and extending the broadcasts in its conventional programme. It promotes these services and participates in the technological development of audiovisual communication.'
28. Cf. Decree 94–813 of 16 Septembre 1994 modified with the decree n°2002–750 of 02 May 2002.
29. Cf. http: //www.francetv.fr/commun/datas/infoslegales.htm (as of 30.05.2003).
30. Ibid.
31. Cf. Letter from the CSA, nr. 158, January 2003.
32. Cf. http: //www.telecom.gouv.fre (as of June 2003).
33. Cf. http: //www.forumInternet.org: summary of the reactions to the first reading of the bill in the Assemblé Nationale (as of June 2003).
34. Forum Internet is an independent organization with members from the business sector, from public bodies and associations. It is financed out of public funds and has the task of providing information on legal and social questions relating to the Internet. The chairperson is Isabelle Falque-Pierrotin (Conseiller d'État or state councillor).
35. Cf. ForumInternet (2003), 'La recommandation de projet de loi pour la confiance dans l'économie numérique', p.3, in: http: //www.forumInternet.org. [Translation: The Forum considers it opportune to produce a legal or regulatory definition of radio and television services independently from their technological platform in order to allow firstly the regulator to fulfil his/her tasks on a completely sound judicial basis and secondly to give the different actors a clear view of the rules which apply to them.]
36. Ibid., p.4, [translation: In addition, it would seem essential to the Forum for Internet Law to implement an original ruling concerning its services without this leading in any way to the recognition of a new branch of law.]

References

Agnola, M. & Le Champion, R. (2003), La Télévision sur Internet. Paris: Presses Universitaires de France.

Baris, M. (1978), Langue d'oil contre la langue d'oc. Lyon: Fédérop.

Bell, D.A. (1995), Lingua Populi, Lingua Dei: Language, Religion and the Origins of French Revolutionary Nationalism. In: American Historical Review, 5, 1995, p. 1403–1437.

Bezat, J-M. & C. Chombeau (2001), Droite et gauche s'opposent à Jean-Marie Messier sur l'exception culturelle. In: Le Monde, 29th of December 2001.

Bourgeois, I. (1998), Mehr Beihilfen, aber weniger Werbung für das Staatsfernsehen. In: Frankfurter Rundschau, 5th of October 1998.

Brun-Buisson, F. (2001), Le reflet d'une culture étatique. In: Dossier de l'Audiovisuel, 100, 2001, p. 20–23.

Chirot, F. (2001), La dernière chance de la télévision publique. In: Le Monde, 20th of April 2001.

Clément, J. (2001), Place aux contenus. In: Dossier de l'Audiovisuel, 100, 2001, p. 18–19.

CNC [Centre National de la Cinématographie] (1991), La politique culturelle. Le cinéma 1981–1991. Paris. CNC/Ministère de la Culture.

CSA/CNC [Conseil Supérieur de l'Audiovisuel/Centre National de la Cinématographie] (1994), Le cinéma à la télévision en 1992–1993. Paris: Conseil Supérieur de l'Audiovisuel/CNC.

CSA, letter nr. 158, January 2003.

Dagnaud, M. (2000), L'Etat et les médias, fin de partie. Paris: Editions Odile Jacob.

De Broglie, G. (2001), L'esprit du service public. In: Dossier de l'Audiovisuel, 100, 2001, p. 23.

De Certeau, M. & D. Julia/Jacques Revel (1975), Une politique de la langue. La Révolution Française et les patois. Paris: Gallimard.

Décision 94–345 DC du 29 juillet 1994, Loi relative à l'emploi de la langue française.

Décret 2001–1329 du 28 décembre 2001 modifiant le décret 2001–609 du 9 juillet 2001 pris pour l'application du 3o de l'article 27 et de l'article 71 de la Loi 86–1067 du 30 septembre 1986 et relatif à la contribution des éditeurs de services de télévision diffusés en clair par voie hertzienne terrestre en mode analogique au développement de la production d'oeuvres cinématographiques et audiovisuelles.

Décret 2001–1330 du 28 décembre 2001 modifiant le décret 90–66 du 17 janvier 1990 pris pour l'application du 2o de l'article 27 et du 2o de l'article 70 de la Loi 86–1067 du 30 septembre 1986 relative à la liberté de communication et fixant les principes généraux concernant la diffusion des oeuvres cinématographiques et audiovisuelles.

Décret 2001–1333 du 28 décembre 2001 pris pour l'application des articles 27, 70 et 71 de la Loi 86–1067 du 30 septembre 1986 et fixant les principes généraux concernant la diffusion des services autres que radiophoniques par voie hertzienne terrestre en mode numérique.

Décret 90–66 du 17 janvier 1990 pris pour l'application des articles 27, 33 et 70 de la Loi 86–1067 du 30 septembre 1986 et fixant les principes généraux concernant la diffusion des oeuvres cinématographiques et audiovisuelles par les éditeurs de services de télévision.

Décret 90–67 du 17 janvier 1990 modifié pris pour l'application du 3o de l'article 27 de la Loi 86–1067 du 30 septembre 1986 modifiée relative à la liberté de communication.

Décret 94–813 du 16 septembre 1994 portant approbation des cahiers des missions et des charges des sociétés France 2 et France 3.

Décret n°2002–750 du 2 mai 2002.

Deniau, X. (1992), La Francophonie. Paris: PUF.

European Audiovisual Observatory (2001), Statistisches Jahrbuch 2001. Filmindustrie, Fernsehen, Video und Neue Medien in Europa. Strasbourg: OEA.

European Audiovisual Observatory (2002), Jahrbuch 2002. Film, Fernsehen, Video und Multimedia in Europa. Strasbourg: OEA.

European Council: Richtlinie 89/552/EWG des Rates vom 3. Oktober 1989 zur Koordinierung bestimmter Rechts- und Verwaltungsvorschriften der Mitgliedstaaten über die Ausübung der Fernsehtätigkeit (Fernsehrichtlinie).

Fraissard, G. & M. Séry (2003), Les chaînes tissent leur Toile. In : Le Monde, 24th of May 2003.

France Télévision (2002), Résultats financiers du groupe en 2001. Available online: http://www.francetv.fr/groupe/resultats2001_CA_11042002_bis_files/frame.htm (27.02.2003).

Garrigos, R. & I. Roberts (2002), La TNR va faire de France 3 un bouquet de chaînes. In: Libération, 18th of February 2002.

Guillon, M. (1993), La francophonie. Nouvel enjeu mondial. Paris: Hatier.

Hagège, C. (1987), Le Français et les siècles. Paris: Odile Jacob.

Hoffmann-Riem, W. (1996), Regulating Media. The Licensing and Supervision of Broadcasting in Six Countries. New York/London: Guilford Press.

Hugot, J-P. (2001), La mission du secteur public. In: Dossier de l'Audiovisuel, 100, 2001, p. 25–26.

INA [Institut National de l'Audiovisuel] (1995), Le cinéma à la télévision. In: Dossiers de l'Audiovisuel, 62.

Labé, Y-M. & N. Vulser (1997), Le rapport Missika sur l'audiovisuel public critique sévèrement l'Etat. In: Le Monde, 11th of December 1997.

Loi 74–696 du 7 août 1974 relative à la radiodiffusion et à la télévision.

Loi 86–1067 du 30 septembre 1986 relative à la liberté de communication.

Loi 94–665 du 4 août 1994 relative à l'emploi de la langue française.

Machet, E/Eleftheria Pertzinidou/David Ward (2002): A Comparative Analysis of Television Programming Regulation in Seven European Countries. A Report by the European Institute for the Media Commissioned by the NOS. Düsseldorf: European Institute for the Media.

Machill, M. (1997), Frankreich Quotenreich. Nationale Medienpolitik und Europäische Kommunikationspolitik im Kontext nationaler Identität. Berlin: Vistas.

Mathieu, B. (2001), France Télévision doit investir mais économiser, sans contrainte d'audience. In: Le Monde, 13th of November 2001.

Mathieu, B. (2002), 2001, année numérique et politique pour francetélévisions. In: Le Monde, 15th of January 2002.

MCC [Ministère de la Culture et de la Communication]: Une année stratégique pour l'audiovisuel public. Budget 2001. Available online: http: //www.culture.fr/culture/min/budget2001/audiovisuel.pdf (27.02.2003).

Minc, A. (1993), Le média choc. Paris: Grasset et Fasquelle.

Thomass, Barbara (2003), Public Service Broadcasting und Digitalisierung: Erfahrungen in Frankreich und Großbritannien, In: Donges, Patrick/ Puppis, Manuel (Hrsg.): Die Zukunft des öffentlichen Rundfunks, Internationale Beiträge aus Wissenschaft und Praxis. Köln: Halem, p. 223–238.

Trautmann, C. (2001), Le service public de l'audiovisuel: un pôle d'équilibre. In: Dossiers de l'Audiovisuel, 100, 2001, p. 16–17.

Weber, H. (2002), Faire vivre l'exception culturelle. In: Le Monde, 8th of January 2002.

Websites of interest to this research

http: //www.lemonde.fr
http: //www.francetelevisions.fr
http: //www.france3.fr
http: //www.france2.fr
http: //www.france5.fr
http: //www.foruminternet.org
http: //www.ddm.gouv.fr
http: //www.telecom.gouv.fr
http: //www.acrimed.samizdat.net
http: //www.csa.fr
http: //www.obs.coe.int
http: //www.webinfocom.msh-paris.fr
http: //www.ina.fr
http: //www.assemblee-nationale.fr
http: //www.culture.fr

http: //www.idate.fr
http: //www.crepac.com
http: //www.journaldunet.com
http: //www.qualisteam.fr
http: //www.europresse.com
http: //www.cfjp.fr
http: //www.industrie.gouv.fr
http: //www.pressed.com
http: //www.francofil.net
http: //www.packline-france.com

About the Contributors

Cristina, M. Chisalita Ph.D. is Assistant Professor at the Department of Organizational Psychology and Human Resource Development, the Faculty of Behavioural Sciences, Twente University, The Netherlands. She has several publications including journal papers and book chapters on topics related to communities of practice, contextual aspects of technology use in organizations and cultural aspects in designing technology. One recent publication is Veenswijk, M. and Chisalita, C. (2007), The Importance of Power and Ideology in Communities of Practice. The case of a de-marginalized user interface design team in a failing multi-national design company published in *Information, technology and people.*

Dr Päivi Hovi-Wasastjerna is Research Director at the University of Art and Design Helsinki, Finland. Her research focus is on visual communication and media culture.

Maria Heller is Director of the Institute of Sociology at Eötvös Loránd University, Budapest. She is the programme director of the Sociology major, BA and MA and of a special three-year study programme: Communication and Media Sociology. Coordinator of several large international research and exchange programmes, she is also Vice-Dean for International Relations. Research and teaching areas: the public sphere, public and private, public debates, speakers' discursive strategies, national identity, information society, globalization, discourse analysis, market communication, sociolinguistics, communication theory, the sociology of advertising, the sociology of games. She has more than one hundred publications in Hungarian, English and French. Member of several international associations and editorial boards, she has participated in several international educational and research programmes. Some recent publications: "The blurring dividing line between public and private and the redefinition of the public sphere", in: Karvonen, E. (ed.): Informational Societies. Tampere: Tampere University Press, 2001. "Social and political effects of new ICTs and their penetration in Hungary". In: Nyíri, K. (ed.): Mobile Democracy. Essays on Society, Self and Politics.

Vienna: Passagen Verlag, 2003, pp. 147–164. "Le service public en Europe de l'Est", in: Bourdon, Jérome (ed.) Médiamorphoses, janvier 2005, Paris: INA, pp. 103–114. "New ICTs and the problem of 'publicness'". In: *European Journal of Communication*. Volume 21/3. 2006, pp. 311–329.

Rune Klevjer is Research Fellow at the Department of Information Science and Media Studies, University of Bergen. He teaches New Media and computer games while finishing his doctoral dissertation, 'Gunplay: The aesthetic of the single-player First Person Shooter'. He has published various papers and articles on rhetorics and computer game aesthetics and contributes regularly on the game research blog Power Up. More information about his work is available on http://www.uib.no/people/smkrk/.

Peter Ludes is Professor of Mass Communication, Integrated Social Sciences, at Jacobs University Bremen. He was the Speaker of Team 3 'Convergence - Fragmentation: Media Technology and the Information Society' (from 2001 to 2004) and has been the Vice Head of the Research Network *'Mass Media and Communication'* of the European Sociological Association since 1997. Since 2003, he coordinates an international group of researchers from the humanities, social and computer sciences, which focuses on visual hegemonies: the modeling and decoding of key visuals in intercultural comparisons (Brazil, China, Germany and the United States; see www.keyvisuals.org). More than one hundred publications, recently on Multimedia and Many Modernities: Key Visuals (with a CD-ROM), Wiesbaden, 2001, the DVD-ROM 'Medien und Symbole: €uropäische MedienBILDung', Siegen 2002, and (ed.) Visual Hegemonies: An Outline, Munster, 2005 – in 2007 published as well in Brazil and China. Studies, research and teaching at Brandeis, USA; Newfoundland, Canada; Siegen, Germany; Harvard, USA; Mannheim, Germany. Primary research areas: mass and multimedia communication, global visual communication, inter- and transcultural comparisons, sociology of knowledge and culture, of multiple civilizing and globalizing processes.

Knut Lundby is Professor of Media Studies at the Department of Media and Communication, University of Oslo. He was the founding director of InterMedia at the same university, an interdisciplinary center researching design, communication and learning in digital environments. He also coordinated a strategic programme on Competence and Media Convergence at the University of Oslo. He has been a member of several programmes on new media and applied ICT at the Research Council of Norway. He has published on Net-based learning and on the relationship between media, religion and culture. Recent publications include *Implications of the Sacred in (Post)Modern Media* (ed. with Johanna Sumiala Seppänen and Raimo Salokangas), Göteborg: NORDICOM, 2006, and "The global mover", in: A. Fjuk, A. Karahasanovic and J. Kaasbøll (eds.): *Comprehensive Object-Oriented Learning: The Learner's Perspective*. Santa Rosa, CA: Informing Science Press, 2006.

Dr Ursula Maier-Rabler is the academic director of the ICT&S Center at the University of Salzburg, a recently established interdisciplinary and international Center for Advanced Research and Studies in Information and Communication Technologies & Society. From 1989 on, she is Assistant Professor at the Department of Communication at the University of Salzburg. In 1993/94 she was a visiting researcher at CAST (Center for Advanced Study in Telecommunication) at the Ohio State University in Columbus, Ohio. She was Vice-Chair and Chair of the CTP Section (Communication Technology Policy) of the IAMCR (1994–2000) and President of the Austrian Association of Communication (1994–2000). Her main research areas are Internet & Society (ePolicy; eDemocracy/eGovernment/ eParticipation), Culture and ICTs and Online Communication.

Marcel Machill is a tenured professor of journalism, with an emphasis on international media systems, at the University of Leipzig in Germany. From 1997 to 1999, Dr Machill was a McCloy Scholar at Harvard University in Cambridge, USA. He holds academic degrees from three countries: Before going to Harvard's John F. Kennedy School of Government (1997–99), he studied journalism and psychology in both Paris, France and Dortmund, Germany. He holds an MA (1993) from the French journalism institute Centre des Formation des Journalistes (CFJ) and a diploma (1994 – 'with honors') from the University of Dortmund. In 1997 he graduated ('summa cum laude') with a Ph.D. from the chair of media policy and media economy.

Werner A. Meier is a senior lecturer and researcher at the Institute in Mass Communication and Media Research at the University of Zurich, Switzerland. He is the co-director of SwissGIS – Swiss Centre for Studies on the Global Information Society and co-chairman of the Euromedia Research Group (EMRG). His research focus is on media policy, international communication, political economy of media and information society on which he regularly teaches and publishes.

Bernard Miège, Professor in Communication Studies at the University Stendhal Grenoble 3, Unesco Chair in International Communication (since 1997). Orientations: The cultural and Informational Industries; ICTs in the societies and in the different social fields. Sciences of the Information and Communication Sciences (epistemology, methodology). Selected recent work: Capitalism and Communication: a New Era of Society or an Accentuation of Long-Term Tendencies, in 'Toward a Political Economy of Culture: Capitalism and Communication in the Twenty-First Century', edited by Andrew Calabrese and Colin Sparks, Boulder CO: Roman and Littlefeld Publishers, Boulder CO, 2004.

Katri Oinonen worked as a junior researcher in the Amsterdam School of Communications Research during the SCALEX project.

Lars Qvortrup is rector (vice chancellor) for the Royal School of Library and Information Science, Copenhagen. From 1996 to 2000 he was professor at the University of Aalborg, between 2000 and 2007 professor at the University of Southern Denmark and director of Knowledge Lab. Since 1977 Lars Qvortrup has written and/or edited approximately 35 books in Danish or English and more than 200 articles in Danish and international readers and journals. Recent books include: *The Hypercomplex Society*, New York 2003. *Knowledge, Education and Learning – E-learning in the Knowledge Society*, Copenhagen 2006. Together with Niels Lehmann and Bo Kampmann Walther (eds.): *The Concept of the Network Society: Post-Ontological Reflections*, Copenhagen 2007. Together with Heidi Philipsen (eds.): *Remediation Revisited. Moving Media Studies*, Samfundslitteratur Press, Copenhagen 2007.

Bas Raijmakers graduated in 2007 with a Ph.D. in Design Interactions at the Royal College of Art in London. He currently runs his own Anglo-Dutch user research company, STBY (www.stby.eu), with Geke van Dijk. After his academic training in Cultural Studies, focusing on how people use media and technology, he co-founded Internet company ACS-i that was later acquired by LB Icon. His work in the industry showed him that the erratic, elusive aspects of everyday life that make everyone a different individual have a strong influence on how people use technology but are hardly taken up in the research done to inform design processes. Nevertheless, these idiosyncratic details of everyday life are very inspiring to designers. These observations led him to developing a new research method that informs and inspires design processes by looking at the rich fabric of everyday life: Design documentaries.

In recent years, he co-operated with industry and academia, for instance, IRC Equator (UK), HP labs (UK), France Telecom/Orange (F), Goldsmiths College (UK), Intel (US), Intelligent Textiles (UK), The Open University (UK) and Philips Medical Systems (US). Contact: bas@stby.eu.

Tanja Storsul is Associate Professor at the Department of Media and Communication, University of Oslo. Her research interests and publications are within the areas of digital media and telecommunications. She focuses especially on political and economic developments within new media markets. Her current research project investigates the impact digital television may have on television policy and market structures. Among her recent publications is the article from 2007 co-authored with Trine Syvertsen on 'The Impact of Convergence on European Television Policy. Pressure for Change – Forces of Stability' in *Convergence*, vol 13 (3), and the book *The Ambivalence of Convergence* co-edited with Dagny Stuedahl, which is to be published by Nordicom, Gothenborg in 2007. Storsul participates in several national and international research networks, and she is coordinator of the research group *Participation and play in converging media*. http://imweb.uio.no/pap/.

Ed Tan is Professor of Media Entertainment at the Department of Communication at the University of Amsterdam. He has studied experiences provoked by media and arts for 30 years. Trained as a psychologist, he taught at various humanities departments in the Netherlands, including theatre and film studies and comparative arts. His current research specializations include emotion and film and visual communication. He is interested in the use of new media in the areas of entertainment, culture and the arts, and the competences that users acquire in dealing with new media. He has participated in interdisciplinary teams developing information systems for culture and the arts. Recent publications include 'Three views of facial expression and its understanding'. In J. D. Anderson & B. Fisher Anderson (eds.), *Moving Image Theory*, 128–148. Carbondale: Southern Illinois University Press, 2005. See also the web page http: //home.medewerker.uva.nl/e.s.h.tan.

INDEX

Page numbers in italics denote information in Tables not already referred to in the text.

A list of authors cited in the text